TARGET 9

IELTS

SPEAKING

Your ultimate guide to IELTS Success

FREEDOM PUBLISHING HOUSE

IELTS SPEAKING

Author: Darshan Singh

Published By:

FREEDOM PRESS
SCF-32, 2ND FLOOR, PHASE–5, Mohali, Pin-160059

For any suggestions, you can reach us at freedompressteam@gmail.com

or visit – https://g.page/FreedomPublishingHouse?gm

© All rights reserved with the Publisher
Copying of this book and its contents is prohibited.

No part of this book should be reproduced in any form, Electronic, Mechanical, Photocopy or any information storage and retrieval system without prior permission in writing, from FREEDOM PRESS, SCF-32, 2ND FLOOR, PHASE–5, Mohali, PH: 8968285246

ISBN –

EDITION – 2022

Printed by – Freedom Publishing House

Author's Word

I have been in the field of education for the past 10 years. I have the experience of training more than 10,000 students over a decade for the IELTS exam.

I have collected the latest data by interacting with the candidates that have taken the IELTS exam from all over India. With extensive research and foresight, this book has been amassed for your help in the speaking module of IELTS.

Don't try to memorize the content instead read it, take out ideas from it and use these ideas while speaking practice.

I have compiled my experience of training from all these years and have locked in this book.

So, what are you waiting for? You have the key to this lock now. Open this book and be successful.

I hope this book helps you in achieving your goals.

- **Darshan Singh**
Author | Speaker | Trainer

About the Book

This book is written after thorough research in the field of IELTS. This book will offer you a comprehensive variety of topics that are asked by the examiners in the IELTS Speaking Test.

This book contains more than 1000 solved questions and answers for the follow-up round as well as 200 + solved Cue-card topics from the past and current exams.

This book includes four parts in which the solutions are given for all the questions. This book should be read systematically to gain a high band score in your IELTS exam.

This book contains 2000 + useful vocabulary words along with speaking tips for the candidates. Read all those tips before you go to the exams.

This book is a compilation of the most common and frequent questions and topics asked in the IELTS speaking test. This is entirely guesswork and shouldn't be considered as the final syllabus of the exam.

Table of Contents

PART – ONE

Sr. No.	Cue-Card Topics	Page no.
1	Describe a difficult decision that you might take in future	12
2	Describe a journey that took longer than expected	13
3	Something you have learned recently from the internet	14
4	Describe a happy family event from your childhood	15
5	Talk about a time when you had to wake up extremely early	16
6	Describe the greatest success of your friend that made you feel proud	17
7	Describe about a time when you were nice to someone you do not like	18
8	Describe a time when you received a good service	19
9	Describe a personal goal which you have not been able to achieve	20
10	Job you think you would be good at	21
11	A movie you would recommend a friend to watch	22
12	Describe a difficult thing you did	23
13	A software that you often use OR	24
14	Speak about an aquatic animal	25
15	Describe a historical event that you find interesting	26
16	Describe a water sport	27
17	Special date in your country's history	28
18	Describe a skill that takes long time to learn	29
19	A video game / computer game / puzzle you played in your childhood	30
20	Speak about any recent change or development in your hometown	31
21	An English lesson	32
22	A live match you have watched	33
23	Describe a scary activity you did	34
24	An international leader or politician you like	35
25	A book you have read that made you think a lot	36
26	Talk about a time when you visited somewhere and lost your important thing there	37
27	Describe a person who apologized to you	38
28	Talk about a time when you unexpectedly met someone	39
29	Talk about a performance you gave at school or college	40
30	Describe an important journey that was delayed	41
31	Describe your dream workplace	42
32	Describe a company which employs many people in your hometown	43
33	Describe a bicycle tour you took	44
34	Describe a night when you could not sleep at all	45
35	Describe a person who likes to travel by plane	46
36	Describe some advice you received on your subjects or work.	47
37	Describe an experience when you were with people and got bored	48
38	Describe a time when you first met someone OR A famous personality you have met.	49
39	Describe a time you were sleepy but had to stay awake	50
40	Talk about a person in news whom you would like to meet	51
41	Talk about a meeting you attended at your school or workplace	52
42	Talk about a time when you used a foreign language to communicate	53
43	Describe a wrong decision you once made	54
44	Describe something that helps you in concentration (yoga/meditation)	55

45	What makes you angry	56
46	A female leader you would like to meet	57
47	A piece of clothing you received as a gift	58
48	Speak about a time when you felt anxious	59
49	Describe a good law for women	60
50	Describe a village near your hometown	60
51	A foreign personality who motivates you to do well	61
52	A quality or skill your friend has that you want to adopt	61
53	Describe a creative person whose work you admire	62
54	Describe a time when you were waiting for something special to happen	62
55	Describe a time you bought something from a street or outdoor market	63
56	Describe a café you like to visit	63
57	Describe an article which you have read about health	64
58	Describe a time when you felt proud of a family member	64
59	Describe a person who impressed you the most when you were in primary school / childhood	65
60	Describe an activity that you usually do that wastes your time.	65
61	Describe an occasion when many people were smiling	66
62	A house you visited but you would not want to live in.	66
63	Describe your favourite curtain	67
64	A time you had to wait in a queue / long line	67
65	Your favourite wild animal	68
66	Describe a job you would never do	68
67	A poisonous plant you know	69
68	Describe an environmental law in your country	69
69	A bag you want to own	70
70	Describe an item on which you spent more than you expected	70
71	Your favorite item of clothing	71
72	An occasion when you helped someone	71
73	Something you planned to do but have not done yet	72
74	A car journey you remember	73
75	An important letter you received	73
76	A time when you teamed up with an old person	74
77	Speak about a time when you participated in a competition	75
78	Your ideal home	75
79	Your favorite sports	76
80	A product of your country	76
81	A big company/organization near you	77
82	A businessperson you admire	78
83	A holiday you enjoyed	78
84	An interesting place in your country that tourists do not know about	79
85	Describe a piece of art (statue or painting)	80
86	Describe a time when you went to a crowded place	80
87	Favourite author	81
88	Something that you bought online	82
89	You were going on a tour and your vehicle broke down	82
90	A national building in your country	83
91	Favourite weather	83
92	A tranquil place you enjoy going to	84
93	A foreign dish you want to eat	85
94	A musical instrument you like to play	85
95	A historical building you have visited	86
96	A speech you heard recently	86

97	What kind of job you would like to do in future?	87
98	A prize/award you want to win	87
99	An occasion where you arrived late	88
100	Speak about a time when you participated in a competition	89
101	An animal you like most	89
102	A bird you like	90
103	A language you would like to learn (apart from English)	90
104	Exercises people do in your locality	91
105	Anything you would like to buy from foreign country	91
106	A season you like the most	92
107	A time when someone helped you	92
108	A quality that you appreciate about your friend	93
109	Describe a time when you complained about something	94
110	Remote place you wish to visit in the future	94
111	Describe a shop that recently opened in your locality/city	95
112	Describe an invention that has changed the life of people	95
113	Describe a nation (not your own) that you know well	96
114	Describe an outdoor activity that you did for the first time	97
115	A time you had to search for information	97
116	Describe a building in your city	98
117	An advertisement you watched on TV recently	99
118	Describe a thing that has become a fashion or a matter of status nowadays	99
119	Describe certain laws of your country	100
120	An intelligent person you know	101
121	Describe a hotel you stayed at	101
122	Describe a pet that you have or once had	102
123	A part of your rituals or customs that you do not like	102
124	Any souvenir that you bought during your holidays	103
125	Describe a thing for which you saved money from a long time	104
126	Speak about an interesting tour guide	104
127	Speak about a family that resemble yours	105
128	Speak about a time when you admired the sky	105
129	Describe a handcrafted item which you made yourself.	106
130	Describe a dish you like the most which is served during the festivals.	106
131	Describe a place full of colors	107
132	Describe a product or application which is based on Artificial Intelligence	107
133	Something kind that someone did for you	108
134	Describe a time when you taught something new to an older person	109
135	Describe an instance when you solved a problem using the internet	109
136	A happily married couple	110
137	Something you got for free	110
138	An occasion when you received a lot of guests at your home	111
139	A conversation with stranger	111
140	A city or town you visited	112
141	A website that is useful	112
142	A place where you like to listen to music	113
143	A happy memory from childhood	114
144	A time you moved home	114
145	A time you moved school	115
146	Your favorite TV program you watch	115
147	A time when you felt embarrassed	116
148	A time when you felt nervous / anxious / frightened	116
149	Describe a person you think is a good parent	117

150	Describe a piece of furniture at your home	118
151	Describe a way to stay healthy	118
152	An expensive thing you want to buy in future	119
153	A time when you gave suggestion in a survey	119
154	Your favourite singer	120
155	Visit to a strange place	121
156	Describe a piece of good news that you heard from someone	121
157	A club that you have joined	122
158	Tell about a subject you disliked in school	122
159	An interesting old person you know well	123
160	A time when you felt angry	123
161	Talk about an important photograph	124
162	Describe an old thing	125
163	First day at school/college/university	125
164	An activity you do to maintain good health	126
165	Speak about a room in which you spent a lot of time	126
166	Speak about an adventurous person you know	127
167	A meal you enjoyed at a restaurant	128
168	Describe an important decision you made	128
169	Speak about someone who is a good cook	129
170	Describe a stressful day at school/college/university	130
171	A place where you like to read books	130
172	A movie or TV show that made you laugh	131
173	Talk about a dish you know how to cook	131
174	A time when someone did not tell you the whole truth	132
175	Talk about something you taught to a teenager	133
176	When you found something that someone lost	133
177	Describe a beautiful home you have seen	134
178	A subject you did not like but now you find interesting	135
179	Something you bought but did not use	135
180	Time when you had to change your plan	136
181	A sportsperson you admire the most	137
182	An occasion when you bought/made a special cake	138
183	An aspect of modern society that you dislike	138
184	Describe a famous scientist/inventor you know about	139
185	Describe a school you have studied in	140
186	Expensive clothing you have bought lately	140
187	Time when you had to take care of a baby	141
188	Something that you borrowed from your friend or family	142
189	Describe a noisy place you have been to	142
190	Describe a social networking website/platform you use	143
191	Describe the politest person you have come across in your life	144
192	Describe a place you visited that has been affected by pollution	144
193	A talkative person	145
194	Interesting news you read in a newspaper	145
195	Talk about an instance when you invited a friend for a meal in a restaurant or at home	146
196	Describe a meeting or discussion about fake news	146
197	Talk about a job one of your grandparents did	147
198	Describe a family business you know	147
199	Talk about your favorite movie star	148
200	A person who has encouraged you recently	148
201	Talk about a practical skill you have	149
202	Describe an unusual vacation you had	150

203	Describe a surprise party you organized for your friend	150
204	Describe people who raise awareness about the environment	151
205	Describe an experience when children made you laugh	151
206	Talk about a situation when you complained about something and got good results	152
207	Talk about a job that helps make the world a better place	153
208	Describe a person you know who likes to help people in free time	153
209	Describe a person who speaks foreign language very well	154
210	A time when you had to wait in a traffic jam	154
211	Describe an important year in your life	155
212	Describe your favorite way to relax	155
213	Your favorite means of transport	156

PART – TWO

Sr. No.	Follow Up Question and Answers Topics	Page no.
1	Sports	157
2	Plant	157
3	Food	158
4	Education	158
5	Leisure activities	159
6	Wealth	159
7	Weather	159
8	Travelling	160
9	Animals	160
10	Happiness	161
11	Laws	161
12	Schools	161
13	Dance	162
14	Wedding	162
15	Sleep	163
16	Family	163
17	Friends	163
18	Hometown	164
19	Colours	164
20	T.V.	165
21	Cultures	165
22	Business and Jobs	165
23	Globalization	166
24	Magazines	166
25	Newspapers	167
26	Library	167
27	Zoos	168
28	Museums	168
29	Vegetarianism	169
30	Computer	169
31	Internet	169
32	Sky	170
33	Cars	170
34	Tourism	171
35	Crime	171
36	Health	172

37	Exercise	172
38	Foreign language	172
39	Space exploration	173
40	Future	173
41	Hotel	174
42	City/village	174
43	Childhood	174
44	Jewellery	175
45	Songs/music	175
46	Art and craft	176
47	Parks	176
48	Books	176
49	Festivals	177
50	Politics	177
51	Superstitions	178
52	Fashion	178
53	Gifts	178
54	Name	179
55	Bar-b-que	179
56	Shoes	180
57	Web series	180
58	Decorating	180
59	New Year	181
60	Nature	181
61	Shopping	181
62	Technology	182
63	Bicycle	182
64	Work	182
65	Studies	183
66	Email	183
67	Smoking	184
68	Your country	184
69	Going out	185
70	Clothes	185
71	Trains	185
72	Time	186
73	Reading	186
74	Restaurant	187
75	Pollution	187
76	Population	187
77	Home	188
78	Mobile phones	188
79	Drink	189
80	Malls	189
81	Swimming pool	189
82	Fruits	190
83	Photography	190
84	Role model	190
85	Women	191
86	History	191
87	Media	192
88	Boats / ships	192
89	Online shopping	193

90	Tea / coffee	193
91	Smile	194
92	Mathematics	194
93	Garbage / rubbish	194
94	Perfume	195
95	Borrowing / sharing	195
96	Bottled water	195
97	Copyright	196
98	Life experiences	196
99	Retirement and old age	197
100	Eating habits	197
101	Universities	197
102	Work and life balance	198
103	Island	198
104	Makeup	198
105	Tiredness	199
106	Beach	199
107	Street market	199
108	Visiting family and friends	200
109	Places to play	200
110	Sun	200
111	Sunglasses	201
112	Cakes and desserts	201
113	Numbers	202
114	Breaks	202
115	Wild animals	203
116	Scenery	203
117	Voice	203
118	Haircut	204
119	Plan	204
120	Spending time alone	205
121	Jeans	205
122	Science	205
123	Laughter	206
124	Water sports	206

PART – THREE

Sr. No.	Topic	Page no.
1	**Important Vocabulary for IELTS Speaking**	**207**

PART – FOUR

Sr. No.	Topic	Page no.
1	**8 BAND Tips for IELTS Speaking Test**	**218**

PART – 1

SOLVED CUE-CARD TOPICS

Describe a difficult decision that you might take in future

What the decision is about?
Why you want to take it?
How will it affect your prospects?

As I am on a crucial juncture of my life, I often make important decisions that not only affects my future but also my present. Right now, I am pursuing my (education / job in own country) and planning to go abroad, so unquestionably I will have to make some decisions that will decide my fate. There are going to be a lot of decisions regarding my education / job, but the one that I will have to make is choosing between my passion and money. I am the kind of person who always prefer passion of doing something over money. There could be a time when I might have to make this difficult choice between choosing money or passion because money is as important as anything in life. On the other hand, I am someone who values passion the most. All the hard work that I am doing right now and all the money that I have spent on my education will force me to choose a better paying job. But my instincts will force me to choose a passionate job and keeping the aspect of money aside. This is the decision that most people make at this stage of life. So, I expect to face such situation and if this situation arises, I think I will be really confused and will have to consult my parents or sibling to conclude. This decision will be confusing because doing something that gives me satisfaction is my priority, but one cannot deny that money is one of the most crucial aspects of life. This decision will surely affect my chances because choosing money will provide me materialistic possession while choosing passion and a job that makes me happy will give me job satisfaction. I guess this is the difficult decision that I might have to take in future.

Follow-up questions for practice

- Do you take decisions on your own?
- Do you consult someone before taking important decisions?
- Is it crucial to ask your parents before doing anything?
- How do you generally take important decisions?
- Do you consult your parents for any decision?
- Why do people take wrong decisions?
- Have you taken any decision that has proved to be bad?
- What sort of people take decisions on their own?

IMPORTANT VOCAB FOR THIS TOPIC
- **Juncture** – stage / moment
- **Unquestionably** – undeniably
- **Instincts** – senses / reflexes
- **Sibling** – brother / sister
- **Priority** – importance / main concern
- **Aspect** – part / facet
- **Materialistic** – worldly
- **Possessions** – belongings

Describe a journey that took longer than expected

Where were you going?
What happened that delayed your journey?
What did you do during the journey?

I love travelling to new places and there have been times when our journeys were delayed. But the incident that I am going to share with you today was highly unexpected.

A couple of years back, my family planned to visit Dubai for our Christmas holidays. We booked a one-stop flight from New Delhi. The flight was scheduled to take off from Delhi and after spending a lay over time of one hour in Mumbai, it would reach Dubai. Total time of the journey was about five hours.

We safely boarded the plane from Delhi and reached Mumbai on scheduled time, however our journey was about to get delayed due to a technical error in flight. When the flight was about to take off from Mumbai, we were suddenly told by the flight crew that all of us need to get off the plane as there is a technical error in the plane which will not take long to resolve.

We were escorted to the waiting area and were told to wait for the next update. We were all worried at that time and could hardly wait patiently as we were extremely excited for the trip. It was frustrating that no update about the situation was provided by the flight crew or at the information desk. Everyone in the waiting room was feeling annoyed and complained about the situation online as it was nearly 3 hours of waiting.

After a few minutes, there was an announcement that the delay would be too long if we waited for the problem to get resolved, so the company decided to shift the passengers to another plane / flight. One by one we were allotted the designated flight numbers and boarding passes, but the process took a long time as the luggage had to be reclaimed and send to the other plane.

This was a disappointing moment for all the passengers and the journey was deferred by more than 10 hours. This was something that we never expected.

Follow-up questions for practice

- Do you like long journeys?
- How often do you go on a journey?
- With whom do you like to go on journeys?
- What are the benefits of travelling?
- Do you like travelling?
- What things you keep in mind before travelling?
- Why do you think people get late in journeys?
- Do you complete your journeys on time?
- How do you feel during journeys?

IMPORTANT VOCAB FOR THIS TOPIC
- Unexpected – surprising
- Scheduled - planned
- Boarded – embarked
- Crew – team
- Resolved – fixed
- Escorted – accompanied
- Designated - selected
- Deferred – delayed

Something you have learned recently from the internet

Do you use internet every day?
What have you learnt and is it useful to you?
Can we learn skills from the internet efficiently?

We can learn myriad skills from the internet efficiently. Most of the people these days find internet the best place to learn anything. People are more dependent on internet to learn anything more than ever before.

I have learnt many things from the internet but one thing that I would like to share with you is the art of playing guitar. From my childhood I was very keen on learning guitar. I tried many times but could not get enough time to learn this musical instrument. I love listening to the sound of a guitar.

I made up my mind to learn guitar one day. But the main issue was that I did not have much time back then. I was busy in my studies and only got free at night. I bought a guitar and downloaded few lessons for practice. I used to see the downloaded videos everyday but could not grasp much of it.

One day I came to know about a YouTube channel in which a person named Jack teaches people how to play guitar free of cost. He has uploaded hundreds of videos related to the basic lessons of guitar. There are numerous videos that are tailor made for the beginners. I used to open the videos and would hold guitar in my hands.

He thoroughly explained in the videos about holding the guitar and which string should be pressed to play a certain note. I followed all his lessons carefully and learned the techniques of playing guitar. I made notes of the things he told in the videos. He taught everything patiently and creatively. I am not an expert in playing guitar, but I can play few basic notes that I learned from the internet. I am very thankful to the internet for teaching me so many things, including guitar.

Follow-up questions for practice

- Do you feel we have become slaves of internet?
- Is internet good or bad?
- How often do you use internet?
- Are kids addicted to using internet these days?
- How has internet helped you in life?
- Have you ever learned anything from the internet?
- Do you feel internet is a reliable source for information?
- Do you read news from the internet?
- Do you feel rumors spread fast these days due to internet?
- Do you feel there should be censorship on the internet?

IMPORTANT VOCAB FOR THIS TOPIC
- Myriad – many
- Efficiently – resourcefully
- Grasp – hold
- Patiently – tolerantly
- Addicted – dependent
- Reliable – dependable
- Censorship – control

Describe an exciting experience in your life

OR

Describe a happy family event from your childhood

Do you remember events that happened in your childhood?
What was the event about?
Is it important to celebrate events in life?

I remember most of the events that occurred in my childhood. There were many events that happened during my childhood, but I would like to tell you about an event that I remember well.

I am talking about my aunt's wedding. My mother's sister got married when I was eight. I had a fantastic relation with my aunt. Her name is Nisha, and she is a great person who always smiles in every situation. She is the youngest of the siblings, so her wedding was celebrated in a grand fashion.

I remember that many arrangements were made for the wedding. There were three functions in total. The first one was held at the residence of the bride. The name of the function was Sangeet. In that function all the friends and family members gathered to sing traditional songs and performed old style dance as a ritual.

The second function was held at a hotel. All the relatives and friends from both bride and groom's side congregated there for the Ring ceremony. The couple exchanged the rings, and everyone applauded with joy. That was a great memory as we danced all night and had great food there. In the last function all the rituals and ceremonies were held. We all assembled at a temple where the proceedings took place. After the ceremony got over, all were served with traditional meals in the temple. After that it was time to bid goodbye to the bride. I recall I was very emotional at that moment and could not stop crying. It is crucial to celebrate events in our life. It creates a chance to meet relatives and friends. Also, it provides a break from the monotony. People can relax and enjoy the moment.

Follow-up questions for practice

- Did you enjoy your childhood?
- How was your childhood like?
- Do you remember all events from your childhood?
- Tell me about an interesting memory from your childhood?
- Is there any bitter memory from your childhood?
- Did you enjoy studies as a kid?
- Do you feel childhood of past was different from that of today?
- How do children enjoy in events such as marriages in your country?
- Do kids play a lot of video games in your country?
- What are the famous sports among kids in your country?

IMPORTANT VOCAB FOR THIS TOPIC
- **Grand** – majestic / huge
- **Congregated** – assembled
- **Applauded** – clapped
- **Assembled** – gathered
- **Recall** – memory
- **Monotony** – boredom
- **Bitter** – unpleasant

Describe a time you got up early

OR

Talk about a time when you had to wake up extremely early

At what time you had to wake up?
What was the case?
Were you able to wake up and complete the task?

There have been many instances in my life when I had to wake up early in the morning. But on one occasion, I had to wake up extremely early because I had to catch a flight to Dubai with my family. Our flight was scheduled to fly at 7 in the morning from the Indira Gandhi International Airport, New Delhi.

I live in Chandigarh which is a five-hour journey from Delhi. Our flight's departure date was 24th December at 7 AM and we reached Delhi on the 23rd. We stayed at a hotel and slept early to make sure everyone wakes up on time in the morning. We had to reach the airport by 4 AM. So that meant we must wake up at 3 and leave the hotel by 3:30 AM.

We were extremely anxious as getting late would prove to be detrimental for us. We all made sure that everyone set the alarm on their phones, and we also informed the hotel staff to give us a wakeup call between 2:30 and 3:30 AM.

I was so excited for the trip that I could hardly sleep. But somehow, I managed to sleep at 1 AM. That meant that I had only 2 hours of sleep. When my alarm sounded, I got up with swollen eyes and severe headache. The reason of my condition was the lack of sleep. I quickly got up and took bath to get ready. After some time, I sipped some coffee to come to my full senses.

Generally, I wake up at 6 or 7 in the morning, but this was the time when I had to wake up extremely early.

Follow-up questions for practice

- What are the benefits of getting up early?
- Do you enjoy getting up early?
- How do you feel when you get up early?
- Why do people get up early?
- Are there any negatives of getting up early?
- Do you feel a person can manage his/her day better by getting up early?
- Do you get up early on weekends?
- What do you do when you get up extremely early?

IMPORTANT VOCAB FOR THIS TOPIC
- **Instances** – examples
- **Anxious** – nervous
- **Detrimental** – harmful
- **Swollen** – puffy
- **Severe** – acute / very bad
- **Headache** – pain in head
- **Sipped** – tasted / drank
- **Senses** – awareness / consciousness

Describe the greatest success of your friend that made you feel proud

Speak about your friend
Tell about his/her achievement
How does the success of your friend make you proud?

I am going to speak about one of my best friend Amit. He lives near my house, and I share a tremendous relationship with him. He recently completed his 12th class and decided to join the Indian Army. Nature wise, he's a regimented person and speaks less. He is slim and handsome looking. He is tall and has fair colour.

I know Amit from my childhood, and I also know that he always dreamt of joining the Indian Army. From childhood, he was passionate about serving the country through Army. He always told me that he wants to wear that Army uniform and use those guns to annihilate the enemy.

After completing his 12th class, he joined the best coaching classes to clear the NDA (National Defense Academy) entrance exam. This exam is one of the most difficult exams to clear as millions of youngsters appear for this exam every year but very few of them crack it.

Every year there are a lot of vacancies that go vacant in the Army, but they never chose quantity over quality. They only select the deserving candidates. I remember he used to study day and night to crack the NDA exam. He studied for more than ten hours a day apart from the tuitions.

He was so indulged into studies that he never played with other kids, and he never showed up at any party from friends. He was always into his studies and never bothered about anything happening outside of it.

I feel proud of his success as he is serving our country and placing his life in danger for the citizens of our country. I have utmost respect for the Army men, and I feel proud that my friend is doing the duty that many people can only dream of.

Follow-up questions for practice

- Do you have one or two friends or many best friends?
- Do your friends help you in your tough times?
- Do you feel friends are the best people to go to in your tough times?
- Has any friend of yours achieved something commendable?
- How do you celebrate the success of your friends?
- Do you generally talk about your plans with your friends?
- Do you feel proud of your friends?

IMPORTANT VOCAB FOR THIS TOPIC
- **Tremendous** – wonderful
- **Regimented** – disciplined
- **Annihilate** – defeat
- **Deserving** – worthy
- **Utmost** – highest / greatest
- **Commendable** – admirable / worthy

Describe a time when you were nice to someone you do not like

OR

Describe an irritating person in your neighborhood

Who is that person?
Why does he/she irritate you?
Do you like his/her company?

Most of my neighbours are wonderful and I love spending time with them occasionally. They are welcoming and generous. But there is one guy whom I do not like as he is irritating in nature.
He works in a gym as a fitness trainer, and I had my first interaction with him last year. In the first meeting I thought him to be a decent guy but after a few meetings I found him to be mysterious, cunning, and over smart. He is always praising himself for what he has achieved. He always says that he is the best and he does not like other people in the neighbourhood. I do not usually meet him these days and other people in the neighbourhood do not like him either. He does some irritating things that annoy me and other people living nearby. He goes to gym early in the morning and comes back in the afternoon. After he comes back, he plays extremely loud music on the speakers. This bothers everyone in the locality and many neighbours have tried to explain him about that situation, but he has showed no courtesy towards them. Nowadays he plays it intentionally at night and early in the morning. Many elderly people and kids get disturbed by it. He also calls his friends late at night and parties by playing loud music. This habit of his annoys everyone and nobody likes him in the area. Last month everyone in the neighbourhood gathered and asked his landlord to tell him to vacate the house so that everyone could live in peace. Some of my neighbours even had altercations at that point of time but I took the charge and explained him calmly. I politely told him that we live in a society, and we must also abide by its rules. I told him that as good citizen, he should behave decently and not disturb others in the area. I think I was nice to him and was able to explain our concerns to him because from that day, there was a change in his behaviour.

Follow-up questions for practice

- Do you like your neighbourhood?
- What kind of people live in your neighbourhood?
- Who is you favourite neighbour?
- Do you invite your neighbours to your family functions?
- Do you celebrate festivals with your neighbours?
- Is there any person in your neighbourhood you don't like?
- Is there any person in your neighbourhood who doesn't talk to you?

IMPORTANT VOCAB FOR THIS TOPIC
- **Interaction** – communication
- **Decent** – reasonable
- **Mysterious** – strange
- **Cunning** – clever
- **Courtesy** – politeness
- **Intentionally** – deliberately / purposely
- **Altercations** – clashes / disagreements

Describe a time when you received a good service

OR

Describe a time when you received a good service from a hotel or a restaurant

What type of hotel/restaurant did you go to?
What did you most like about their service?
Would you again go to that restaurant?

I have been to many restaurants which have provided great services. The one I would like to explain is in a mall nearby my house. The name of the restaurant is Masters of Grill. This restaurant is located on the top floor of the mall and is opened newly in our area. The reason I visited there was to celebrate the birthday of my cousin. This was my first visit to this restaurant. It is a buffet style restaurant where both vegetarian and non-vegetarian food are served. We ordered vegetarian buffet and soon the service of the food began. The service was so slick that we could not believe. The waiters were well dressed and well mannered. They courteously explained the dish before serving it. I had never seen such trained waiters in any other restaurant. They served us steaming hot snacks along with drinks. The drinks were perfectly made to our requirements. Every now and then the waiters were confirming about the taste and presentation of the snacks. They also offered us to order any other dish apart from the menu. We ordered chilly cheese which was not in the original menu. During our meals, the manager personally came to our table and asked us about the experience of the restaurant. I was glad to see that the restaurant staff was so concerned about us. He also asked about the service of the waiters and quality of the food. At the end, they gave us a mobile tablet in which they asked us to fill the feedback form. I ticked all the boxes and gave 10 on 10 as the overall rating. I have never had such an experience of good service from a restaurant in my life. Now I am a regular customer of that restaurant and I also recommend it to other people.

Follow-up questions for practice

- How do you appreciate people who give you good service?
- Do you generally get good service when you visit restaurants or shops?
- Is it crucial to give good service to customers?
- What will happen if a customer doesn't receive good service?
- Do you like visiting hotels/restaurants?
- What do you generally order in your favourite restaurant?
- Do you like restaurant food?
- What type of restaurants are there in your hometown?

IMPORTANT VOCAB FOR THIS TOPIC
- **Slick** – smooth
- **courteously** – politely
- **Recommend** – suggest
- **Concerned** – worried

Something you were unsuccessful at

OR

Describe a personal goal which you have not been able to achieve

What is your goal?
Why have you not been able to achieve it in the past?
How do you plan to achieve it?

We cannot get everything in our life. There are certain goals in my life that I aspire to attain but I have not been able to achieve them yet. Some are professional while others are personal. One of my most desired goals of all time is to reduce my weight.

I need to reduce some weight and get a healthy and fit body. I have become a bit overweight in the past few years because of my sedentary lifestyle. I sit for several hours to study, and I rarely get any time for the physical activity. If I get some time in my daily life, I spent it on various indoor activities like watching TV and using mobile phone, which has made me quite dull and inactive in my daily life.

So, I am planning to start a regime where I can cut on my calories and start some modular workout on a regular basis. I think I need to spend at least an hour daily on exercise and other workout regimes. I know I can shed my weight easily, but initiation is required. Since I was having exams a few days back, I could not start it, but soon I will stick to this strict routine.

I have a sweet tooth, so the first thing I need to do is to cut on my sugar intake. Next thing, I will be doing is to join a gym in the evening and go for some intensive workout.

Sometimes, I feel ashamed of myself when I look into the mirror as I was never like this. Even my friends and relatives have started taunting me for my plight. I feel bad when people centralize me for the discussion of being overweight. But now I have become so determined that I will get back to my toned body very soon with a disciplined lifestyle.

I tried to pursue this goal in the past year but have not been able to make a routine. But this time I am quite sure of achieving it. Health is everything for a human being. If we do not maintain our health, it is not worth living

NOTE: You can also speak on reducing sleeping hours or not been able to learn a musical instrument or any skill

Follow-up questions for practice

- How do you plan to achieve your goals?
- Do you achieve all your goals?
- What do you do when you fail to achieve your goal?
- Do you keep on trying after unsuccessful attempts at your goals?
- Is there any target that you want to achieve in future?
- Tell me about a goal that you almost achieved but could not.
- How do failures make you feel?
- Do we learn from our failures?

Job you think you would be good at

OR

Describe something you would like to do in the future

Why do you think you will be good at this job?
Would you pursue your career in it?
How will you do your job?

I have not decided much about my future but there are some things that I like to do and one day may pursue career in that. The thing that I love doing is travelling and searching about new places across the world.

I have been to a couple of foreign countries and a lot of cities in India. So, I have deep knowledge of travel and know about the things to remember before travelling. I like to explore new places and I also like to tell people about them. I think I would be good at being a travel guide.

Not only I like to travel to new places, but I also want people to see those places and learn about them. I got this habit in my childhood when I was taken to Shimla by my father. He showed me the city and explained each and everything there. I fell in love with travel and discovering new places.

I think I would be able to guide people about the places according to their behaviour and choice. I can make itinerary according to the needs of travelers. I can be good at guiding them about the important cities and places to learn about culture and history.

I am extremely good at planning the holidays. Whenever our family decides to go on a holiday, they always put this responsibility on my shoulders. I always search about the flights and hotels at cheap price. I also seek important information about the places before I visit. I like to make notes of important information such as transport, weather, and local food of the city I am going to visit. Getting this information really helps at the time of travel.

Even if I am not travelling anywhere, I still like to collect useful information about the tourist destinations and educate people about them. I think I can be a good tour guide in the future.

Follow-up questions for practice

- What sort of jobs do you like?
- Would you trade job satisfaction for money?
- Do you consider jobs to be better than business?
- Have you planned anything regarding your career's future?
- Is it important to plan future?
- What are the benefits of planning future in advance?
- Would you choose a job or business in future?
- Speak about the benefits of doing job.

IMPORTANT VOCAB FOR THIS TOPIC
- **Pursue** – follow / chase
- **Itinerary** – tour / journey route

A movie you watched recently

OR

A movie you would recommend a friend to watch

What genre of movies do you watch?
How often do you watch movies?
How has this movie inspired you?

Watching movies is one of my favorite leisure time activities. It is a great source of entertainment. I like to watch movies on weekends as I have ample of free time. I like movies based on real events or people. One such movie that I watched recently was MS DHONI – The untold story. This movie is about my favorite sports star i.e., M.S Dhoni. He is one of the finest cricketers our country has ever produced. He is acknowledged worldwide for his playing skills and management too as a captain of the team. This movie captures various moments from his personal as well as professional life. I came to know about a lot of things from his personal life that I did not know earlier. The role of the lead character was played by one of the finest actors, Shashank Singh Rajput. His acting was praised by one and all. The movie depicts the struggles of MSD in his initial days. The movie shows all the aspects of his life, his career defining moments, his best playing days, his achievements, his marriage, his earlier jobs, friends, and family. This movie reveals a lot of things about the character of MSD. He has millions of fans all over the world who wanted to know everything about this champion. So, he decided to make a movie on him that was also a block buster. The movie also includes some of the shots captured from his real life. This movie has left a long and lasting impact on me as we can learn so much from it. I have seen this movie many times as every time I watch this movie, I get engulfed in the storyline and brilliant acting of all the actors. I learned a huge life lesson from this movie that anyone can make his dream come true if there is right intent and hard work. Lastly, the songs played in the movie are also composed by top musicians and singers. This is the movie that I saw recently, and it is one of my favourite movies as well. I highly recommend this movie for a friend to watch as this movie not only teaches life lessons but also has entertaining scenes and music.

Follow-up questions for practice

- Do you watch a lot of movies?
- What type of movies you like?
- Do you watch movies made in foreign language?
- What is the difference between Hollywood and movies made in your country?
- Do you feel the quality of movies has risen due to the advancements in technology?
- What is the future of cinema?
- Do you like watching movies in theatre?
- Do you feel movies are a waste of time?

IMPORTANT VOCAB FOR THIS TOPIC
- Acknowledged – recognized
- Lead – be in charge of
- Depict – portray / describe
- Defining – crucial
- Captured – trapped
- Engulfed – submerged
- Composed – made by / written by

Describe a difficult thing you did

OR

A task you completed on time

OR

Describe a task you did well

What was the task about?
How much time did you take to complete it?
Did you take help of someone to complete the project?

Completing tasks in time surely makes you a successful person. I am punctual, so I like to do all my tasks on time if everything goes right. The task that I remember the most is when I had to complete a huge project in a limited time. I not only did this within time but also did it well.

I remember in my college days when I was given a project regarding my field to be submitted within 15 days. All students were given different task in the class. The task that was given to me was very time consuming and difficult. So, finishing it in such a short span of time was backbreaking. There was some fieldwork involved in my project, so I used to travel quite frequently to different places to get the information and most of the days' time was consumed in travelling. So, I had to work till late night to complete my assignment on time.

This project involved a survey about an environment issue prevailing these days. In the assignment I had to collect all the information regarding the project from different parts of the city. Furthermore, I had to take survey of at least two hundred people. The survey involved questions regarding the issue and the answers were to be given in two to three lines.

No doubt, my project was a stimulating one, but if more days were permitted, it would have been a bit easy for me to complete. I took this project as a challenge to test my capability. So, I got motivation each day to complete it on time.

Finally, the day came when I had to submit my project. I was glad that I had completed my project on time. When I gave my paperwork to my professor, she was extremely happy and a bit shocked that I have completed such a complicated project on the official submission day without any discrepancy.

She told me that in her entire teaching experience, she has not seen a single student completing this project in the given time. She was proud of me and gave me extra marks for completing my task in such a short time.

Follow-up questions for practice

- Do you find any type of task difficult?
- Do you take help from others while performing difficult tasks?
- How do difficult tasks make us better?
- Do you like taking challenges?
- Have you ever failed in a difficult task?
- What do you do after a failure in difficult task?
- How can we make our tasks less complicated?

A software that you often use

OR

An application you commonly use

What is the software about?
Why do you use it?
Do you feel that the introduction of software use has eased our life?

I am not a person who use a lot of software on computer. But there is one software that is found everywhere, and a lot of people use it around the world. The name of the software is Microsoft office. It is one of the most common software that can be found in everyone's computer. Microsoft office includes many other subcategories of software that are used to make official work easy. Not only this, but Microsoft office is also used by students around the world to make presentations on computer. They also make a lot of projects that are given in the schools.

The most common type of software in Microsoft office is the Word. In this you can write whatever you want in different formats and languages. You can save the file on it, and you can edit that file whenever you want. The file can also be printed by giving a print command from the software. The word file can also be transferred to anyone through an email. Other software in Microsoft office is the Powerpoint. I had used this software extensively in the past for making presentations on our school projects. I have made a lot of animations and project slides in my school time. In Powerpoint one can add images and symbols to depict whatever they want. Then the slides can be run in the Powerpoint mode in which we can see the slides one after the other automatically. I also use Microsoft excel in which I can log important data such as phone numbers and addresses of my near and dear ones. I also used this software once to make a project report for the class attendance in my school.

In my opinion, using these types of software has made our lives better. In the past, people used to maintain a lot of written records but now computers have taken their place. One can store millions of soft copies of files in a single computer.

Follow-up questions for practice

- Do you feel information technology has come a long way?
- Do you use any software in your daily life?
- How does software help us in work?
- Which is your favourite mobile application?
- Do you use a lot of applications in your mobile?
- How much time do you spend on mobile applications?
- Do you feel privacy is a concern while using mobile applications?

IMPORTANT VOCAB FOR THIS TOPIC
- Extensively – widely / significantly

Speak about an aquatic animal

Have you seen that animal?
What are the characteristics of that sea animal?
How is it different from other sea mammals?

Our world is full of animals and birds. One cannot even count the number of different species that thrive on the earth. There are some aquatic mammals that are famous throughout the world like Dolphins but here I would like to talk about Walrus.

Walrus is a huge marine mammal which is mostly found in the regions near Arctic Ocean and North pole. It is one of the unique and rare species of mammals on Earth.

This species is further separated into two subspecies. One is Atlantic Walrus and the other one is Pacific Walrus. The Atlantic species is found in the Atlantic Ocean and the other one is common in the Pacific Ocean.

The striking feature of Walrus is the long elephant like tusks. They were hunted in the past by the indigenous arctic people for its meat and tusks. Male Walrus found in the Pacific can weigh more than two thousand kilos. Males are bulkier than the females.

They generally dwell in shallow waters. They are more social than other species found around them. Walrus mostly consumes fish and other small sea creatures.

There has been a rapid decline in the population of Walrus from the last few years. It is also believed that ancient Alaskans wore dress made of Walrus skin.

Some even say that these mammals were worshiped by the ancient people near the north pole as they believed this creature was a monster.

I have seen on the internet that there are a couple of conservation centers for Walrus in Canada. I think it is a good step towards the preservation of this unique species.

(You can also speak about Dolphin in this topic)

Follow-up questions for practice

- Have you seen a marine animal?
- What are the threats to marine life?
- How can we preserve aquatic animals?
- How are aquatic animals different from land mammals?
- Do you like aquatic animals?
- Should we keep small fish and creatures in aquarium?

IMPORTANT VOCAB FOR THIS TOPIC
- Mammals – animals
- Marine – naval / aquatic / sea
- Rare – unique
- Striking – unusual / stunning
- Indigenous – native
- Bulkier – larger
- Dwell – lie / live in / stay
- Rapid – quick / speedy
- Conservation – protection / preservation

Describe a historical event that you find interesting

OR

A world event you find interesting

There were many historical events in the past that shaped our society in a better way. They were so interesting that those events are taught worldwide in history books. One such event is Apollo 11 which I find most interesting.

I came to know about this when I was 8. We had a chapter in our school's history book regarding the first moon landing. This mission was named Apollo 11. In this mission, three astronauts, Neil Armstrong, Buzz Aldrin, and Michael Collins, achieved the feat of landing a manned aircraft on the moon.

Two of the three astronauts landed on the moon. First man in the history of world to land on moon was Neil Armstrong and after a few minutes, Buzz Aldrin landed. As soon as Neil landed on the moon, he quoted the famous lines 'It's one small step for man and giant leap for mankind.

The live telecast was aired to over 150 countries across the globe and estimated two billion people watched it live on their TV sets. I have seen some of the videos of this mission on the internet, I find it interesting and unbelievable as it happened in 1969. It is hard to believe that scientists had this kind of technology, and they could accomplish such a complicated task back then.

This mission was achieved by NASA, an American space research organization. The whole world was in awe of this fantastic event. When the astronauts returned to the Earth safely, they were honored in every corner of the world.

They were welcomed as heroes and their names were written in golden letters in history. Neil Armstrong continued as a university professor after the mission and lead a low-profile life. He never liked to give TV interviews.

Neil Armstrong died in 2012 but other astronauts, Buzz Aldrin and Michael Collins are still alive. All three astronauts have written several books about their unique experience and shared the untold details about their life and Apollo 11 mission. I believe that till date, this is the most interesting event that has taken place.

Follow-up questions for practice

- Is it crucial to read history?
- How has reading about history helped you?
- Do we learn from history?
- Which country has rich history?
- Do you like watching events?
- Which is the most important event in the history of your country?
- Do we learn something from historical events?

IMPORTANT VOCAB FOR THIS TOPIC
- Shaped – moulded / sculpted
- Manned – staffed / crewed
- Giant leap – big step towards something (especially a goal)
- Accomplish – achieve / complete
- Complicated – complex / difficult

Describe a water sport

OR

Describe a water activity that you want to try

OR

An activity in sea you want to do

There are many activities that I have still not tried in life. One of them is Scuba diving. It is a water sport that I want to try at least once in my lifetime. Scuba diving is an activity that is not common in the place where I live. This kind of activity is most famous in the coastal area as it is done in the sea. This activity includes going deep in the sea waters and exploring the marine world. Generally, people discover the corals on the seabed. This sport gives a lot of adrenaline rush and is performed under the guidance of experts.

A huge number of equipment is put up and some lessons are also taught before a beginner can start this activity. The first time I came to know about this activity was when I watched a Hollywood movie in my childhood. Since then, I became fascinated about this sport and wanted to try my hands on it. To participate in scuba diving, I had to either go to Goa or Andaman and Nicobar Islands. These two places offer professional experience of this sport.

I have seen a lot of videos on internet about the scuba diving. Some even make video of their expedition. The world under water looks so amazing and different from our world. Whenever I see those videos, I imagine myself swimming in water along with fish and other species. I have also searched on the internet regarding the best companies that offer this activity. There is one in Goa that is licensed through the government and take care of safety norms. They also provide the best equipment for smooth experience. I have decided that I am going to pursue this sport through this company soon. So, this is the activity that I desperately want to try in the coming year.

Follow-up questions for practice

- Do you enjoy water sports?
- How water sports are different from other sports?
- Have you ever tried any unusual water activity?
- Have you ever been to a beach?
- Have you enjoyed a voyage in sea?
- When and where did you see ocean for the first time?
- What sort of activities do people do near sea?
- Do you enjoy visiting amusement parks?

IMPORTANT VOCAB FOR THIS TOPIC
- Exploring – discovering
- Fascinated – captivated / mesmerized
- Expedition – voyage / journey
- Safety norms – safety rules
- Desperately – urgently

Special date in your country's history

OR

Describe a significant historical event in your country

OR

Describe a National Day in your country

There have been hundreds of historical events and special dates that have taken place in the past in our country. We have learned a lot of things from these events and noteworthy dates. One of the special dates for all the people in our country is 15th August 1947. On this day, our country was freed from the Britishers after they ruled this country for more than 150 years. This event of independence brought smiles to all the people of India. This event made every Indian proud and filled their hearts with joy. Indians over the years suffered many obstacles under the imperial rule of the Britishers. Many historical movements started and ended in tragedy. Numerous freedom fighters were martyred during the struggle. There were huge protests that were held against the British rule for many years continuously. Most of the freedom fighters were imprisoned and killed. People feared speaking against the autocratic government. But persistent protests and certain policies by the Indian political parties and efforts of freedom fighters led to the independence of India and forced the British rulers to leave the country. This news of independence spread like a wildfire and people felt that they now have the freedom to live and work in their own country. But one unfortunate thing happened in the process. Our country was divided, and a new nation was born, Pakistan. It led to numerous riots and killing on both sides. An estimated million people lost their lives in India as well as in Pakistan. Today, this day is celebrated with great joy all over India. Processions take place in the capital of India. Prime minister of our country delivers speech on this day mainly highlighting the achievements of the past year. I think this event and date is carved in our hearts forever. This is simply the most unforgettable date in our country's history.

Follow-up questions for practice

- Is it important to celebrate national days?
- Which is your favourite national day?
- How do you celebrate you favourite national day?
- How do people generally celebrate national days in your country?
- What is the importance of celebrating past events?
- Do you know about a national day of any other country?

IMPORTANT VOCAB FOR THIS TOPIC
- **Noteworthy** – notable / remarkable
- **Obstacles** – barriers / difficulties
- **Tragedy** – disaster
- **Martyred** – killed / put to death
- **Imprisoned** – detained / jailed
- **Persistent** – relentless / continuing
- **Processions** – parades / marches

Describe a skill that is difficult to learn

OR

Describe a skill that takes long time to learn

Do you like acquiring skills?
Which skill takes long time to learn?
What are the benefits of learning this skill?

There are many things that are difficult to learn in life. I have tried my hands on several things, but I failed or quit doing it. Once, I took up guitar classes but after a while I gave up on it. Similarly, there are many skills that most individuals find hard to acquire. In my perception, the most problematic skill to learn is the art of public speaking. I reckon this skill requires great practice and discipline to master. I have seen many students struggling to speak in front of a group of people. There are many reasons behind that. The first one is that the group speaking requires a lot of confidence and courage. To be able to speak in front of more than ten or twenty people is not a cakewalk for most people these days.

This skill cannot be learnt in a day or two. There is no book or guide that you can read and become a good speaker. It requires hours and hours of practice every day. One needs to be determined to learn the art of public speaking. I have seen a lot of people standing in front of a mirror and practicing their speaking skills.

This skill is the most urgent requirement for the youngsters of today. I think this skill can take a person to great heights. You can see everywhere in the world that most of the celebrities and famous personalities will inevitably be good speakers. There are numerous benefits of learning public speaking. People can become more influential and trustworthy if they have this skill. A good public speaker will invariably have more friends and connections than ordinary individuals.

So, I ponder that skill of public speaking is one of the most difficult skills for anyone to learn.

Follow-up questions for practice

- What is the importance of learning skills in our life?
- Which are the easy skills to learn?
- Have you taught any skill to someone?
- What is the best way to learn a skill?
- Should we teach our kids the skill of art and craft? Why?
- Do you know any skillful person?
- What skills are required to be a good teacher?

IMPORTANT VOCAB FOR THIS TOPIC
- Perception – insight / observation
- Problematic – difficult
- Cakewalk – very easy
- Inevitably – certainly
- Trustworthy – dependable
- Invariably – always
- Ponder – think about

A game you played in your childhood

Which game did you play?
Why did you play that game?
How did you play that game?

OR

A video game / computer game / puzzle you played in your childhood

Childhood is a great time in which most of the kids are involved in playing hundreds of games. I was no different. I played all the games that were popular at that time.

The one which I played regularly with my friends was Mario. It is a video game which is produced by Nintendo and was invented in the 80s. This game took over the world by storm as everyone was indulged in playing it.

I remember when I cleared my fourth standard exams, I demanded a video game console and Mario game cassette from my parents. My father was kind enough to fulfil my demand and I remember that we bought it on my birthday which falls in April.

I was so excited as I unwrapped the box of the game. My father helped me in installing the game and taught me to do that as well. Once it was installed, I played it for more than six hours that day.

I played this game mostly in the summer holidays and not on the normal days. I was not allowed by my father to play this game on daily basis. Games can be very addictive, and I remember that three of my other friends use to come to my house in the morning and leave in the evening after playing the game.

Mario is made in such a way that you must clear all the stages to win the game. In this game there are several stages that you need to clear and reach the last stage where you save the princess from the evil dragon.

Every day we played that game for more than six hours. We played in a team and helped each other to clear the levels. Playing this game also created a special bond between us.

So, I can clearly remember that Mario was the best game that I played in my childhood.

Follow-up questions for practice

- Do the kids play different games these days than past?
- What kind of games did you play as a child?
- Did you play any sport in your childhood?
- Do you feel today's kids play a lot of video games?
- Are video games bad for the health of kids?
- What is the difference between playing board games and video games?
- Speak about your favourite video game you played in your childhood.

IMPORTANT VOCAB FOR THIS TOPIC
- Unwrapped – unpacked
- Installing – connecting / fixing
- Evil – vile / criminal
- Bond - union

Talk about a part of city that is changing

OR

Speak about any recent change or development in your hometown

Does your hometown have basic amenities?
Speak about the recent development
Has the recent development helped people?

I live in Chandigarh, and it is one of the most livable cities in my country. It is extremely neat and clean and there are numerous parks and facilities that makes people's life easy. On the other hand, there are not many public transportation facilities in our city, as a result, people are forced to use personal vehicles to commute from one place to the other. There have been huge developments in every corner of my hometown in the recent years. The most commendable is the construction of cycle tracks along the roads of the city.

This has been undoubtedly the best addition to the city's list of achievement. Everyone is praising this effort from the government. Not only the main roads but all the link roads and the city roads have been added with cycle tracks. This is a great bonus for people who like to do cycling and for people who use cycle as their main mode of transport. I think it is now safer for those who use cycles. I see that school kids are the ones who have benefitted the most due to this wonderful step. The cycle tracks are wide enough for more than two cyclists to pass by parallelly. The tracks have been carved alongside the roads by acquiring the open spaces on the sides of the roads. There were some places which had no room to make tracks. Instead of leaving the thought of making the tracks there, the government instead shortened the width of the road to accommodate cycle tracks. Most of the tracks have been marked in blue colour and the crossings with red. This is done so that the car drivers can easily see the tracks and make way for cyclists when required.

This shows how serious was the government on this issue. I thank the local authority for such a great step and expect same type of attitude in development in future as well.

Follow-up questions for practice

- How has your hometown changed in the past decade?
- What changes do you want to see in your hometown?
- Is transportation facility good in your hometown?
- Is there anything in your hometown that needs immediate change?
- Are you satisfied living in your hometown?
- What is the best thing about your hometown?
- Why are changes required in life?

IMPORTANT VOCAB FOR THIS TOPIC
- Commute – travel
- Commendable – praiseworthy
- Undoubtedly – unquestionably
- Carved – sculpted / made
- Alongside – along with
- Shortened – compressed

A lecture you remember

OR

An English lesson

Who gave you this lesson?
What the lesson was about?
What did you learn that day?

I have learned uncountable English lessons in my life as I studied in an English medium school. But the lesson that I am going to talk about is the lesson that I learned from my IELTS trainer. I took my IELTS coaching in Mohali, and I was fortunate enough to get astounding IELTS coaching from Aman ma'am. She is a wonderful trainer and a great human being. I remember when I went for the first day of my class, she taught us incredible things regarding English language. The moment our class began, she told us to focus on the English language rather than focusing on the IELTS modules. She explained that IELTS is a part of English and if we are good at English then we can reply to any question that is asked, and we can also respond to any essay topic that we encounter in exam.

When the class started, I thought that it will be regarding the modules of IELTS, instead it was a pure English language class. We were around 50 students in the class, and she started with vocabulary words for writing and speaking. She noted down more than 20 vocab words that were alien to me and most of the students in class. Then she told the meanings of those words and asked us to write one sentence each on it so that we could memorize those words. It was a wonderful exercise as it allowed me to learn 20 new words that day. Next thing that we discussed in the class was common spelling and grammatical errors that happen in English. When we finished this task, I was so impressed because no teacher had told me so many things in one English class before. I learnt a lot of things that day. This was not the end, after that she gave us few readymade introductions and templates for important essays of IELTS. I noted down all of them and have still got those notes in my notebook. Those lines were beneficial in the exam. I think this was a complete English lesson that I learnt recently.

Follow-up questions for practice

- Do you like attending lectures?
- Which is the best lecture that you have attended in life?
- What are the qualities required in a good lecturer?
- Do most people pay attention towards the main topic of a lecture?
- Why is it important to learn English?
- Have you attended any political lecture recently? What was it about?

IMPORTANT VOCAB FOR THIS TOPIC
- Fortunate – blessed
- Astounding – surprising
- Incredible – amazing
- Encountered – confronted
- Alien – strange
- Templates – patterns

A live match you have watched

OR

Describe a sports event you have seen

Where did you see that event?
What was it about?
How did you feel after watching that event?

I have seen numerous sporting events in my life but most of them were cricket matches. I have seen a couple of hockey matches as well but the event that has a long-lasting impression on my mind is the 2011 cricket world cup semi-final played between India and Pakistan. In 2011, the world cup was co-hosted by India, Sri Lanka, and Bangladesh. Everyone expected India to lift the cup as the semi-final and final were scheduled to be held in India and our players knew the conditions well. India eventually went on to win the cup, but I am going to talk about the semi-final match as I saw it live at the PCA stadium, Mohali.

I live in Mohali, and we are fortunate enough to have an international cricket stadium there. I have seen several live cricket tournaments at this venue. This was an important match and all the top leaders and celebrities from India and Pakistan were present at the stadium. The environment was amazing and there was a lot of buzz long before the start of the match. The match was scheduled to begin at 2 PM but people queued up outside the stadium as early as 8 AM. We reached at 10 AM and it took us around couple of hours to enter the stadium. When we entered the arena, practice session was going on in the ground and we got a chance to see a lot of our favourite players from close quarters. India won the toss and decided to bat first. India put up a decent total to defend but Pakistan had a flying start to their innings. They scored 70 runs in no time without losing a wicket. Then suddenly our bowling clicked, and we start taking wickets at regular intervals. In the end, we won the match. Sachin Tendulkar scored the highest number of runs in that match. We were so excited and stayed in the stadium till mid-night and celebrated the victory with other people. On our way back, we saw people dancing on the streets and celebrating the victory. This is the sporting event that I saw, and I can never forget it my whole life.

Follow-up questions for practice

- Do you regularly see live events?
- What is the difference between witnessing a live event over a broadcast?
- Who's your favourite sportsperson?
- Do you watch sporting events of other countries?
- Why do people watch sporting events?
- Have you ever participated in a sports event?

IMPORTANT VOCAB FOR THIS TOPIC
- **Numerous** – several
- **Impression** – idea / notion
- **Eventually** – ultimately
- **Buzz** – noise
- **Arena** – stadium
- **Clicked** – snapped
- **Witnessing** – watching
- **Broadcast** – telecasted

Describe a leisure activity near sea

OR

An adventurous activity you did

OR

Describe a scary activity you did

I am an adventurous person and like to do all kinds of activities. I have been to beaches a couple of times. The last time when I went to a beach was in Goa. It is in the western part of India. It's a beautiful place with a lot of beaches lined with lush green trees. I have been to Goa twice. When I went there last time, I did a lot of sea activities. One of the most popular activities near sea is the para sailing. It is adventurous as well as scary. I had never heard about this activity before visiting this beach. I saw people flying in the air with a parachute tied to their backs and connected with a boat that was sailing recklessly in the sea.

First, I thought of skipping this activity but after some time I was eager to do it. We went to the activity center and deposited 2000 rupees. Then I was given some instructions by them, and I had to wait for 30 minutes as other people were in queue. My turn came after 30 minutes, and they tied harness and safety equipment on my waist and shoulders. The person who was assisting me wished me good luck and then I was ready to go. When you parasail, you must run when the boat starts moving otherwise you could get bruised or fall on your face down. The guy at the activity zone shouted me to run when the boat started moving. In a matter of few seconds, I was suspended in air and felt adrenalin rush. The world looks so different when you fly. I was in the air and enjoyed the eagle's eye view of the ocean and the beach.

To my left, I saw people on the beach and on the right-hand side there was the never-ending ocean. I felt on top of the world that day. The ride lasted for about 10 minutes, and it ended so quickly that I hardly realized. When I landed, I thanked everyone who assisted me, and I was really impressed with their professional work. I think if anyone gets a chance they should go for this activity.

Follow-up questions for practice

- Why do people attempt adventurous activities?
- What are the risks involved while participating in adventurous activities?
- Have you ever participated in an activity near sea?
- Do you like water sports? Why?
- How do you feel after completing an adventurous task?
- Do you feel we should not attempt adventurous tasks?

IMPORTANT VOCAB FOR THIS TOPIC
- Lined – covered
- Recklessly – carelessly
- Skipping – hopping / missing
- Harness – hitch / safety ropes
- Bruised – injured / hurt
- Suspended – dangling / hanging
- Assisted – helped

A person you admire from a foreign country

Do you admire personalities from abroad?
Speak about that person
How has that person inspired you?

OR

A person who has inspired you from abroad

OR

An international leader or politician you like

I admire several personalities from foreign countries. I love to appreciate great personalities from all over the world like Barak Obama, Bill Gates, Jack Ma, Steve Jobs but the person I admire the most is Nelson Mandela. I wish I could meet him, but he died in December 2013. I came to know about him through his book. The name of the book is 'Long walk to freedom'. This is an autobiography which was published after he became the President of South Africa. In this book, he gave detailed insights from when he was born to till, he became the President. He also included the years when he was imprisoned and wrote about his family and friends. Nelson Mandela was a freedom fighter for more than five decades before he became the first black president of South Africa in 1994. He stayed in the prison for about 3 decades. He and thousands of his fellow freedom fighters were imprisoned by the white government. Some were executed and others were sent to the jail for lifetime. Nelson Mandela was one of them. He stayed in the jail for so many years, but the struggle continued outside the jail and as a result the white government was forced to release the political prisoners and Mandela was freed in 1990. He continued with his freedom struggles after his release and participated in the first ever fair election in South Africa as the president of the ANC. This was the first time that the majority blacks could cast their votes. In 1994 the election results were declared, and Nelson Mandela won by unanimity of the people of South Africa and became the first black President of South Africa. This story had a long-lasting impression on me, and I never knew anything about Nelson Mandela before reading this book. From that day onwards I admire him as the greatest leader and symbol of peace and reconciliation.

Follow-up questions for practice

- Do you like politics?
- Who is your favourite politician?
- Do you admire people from foreign countries? Why?
- Do you feel politicians make good role models?
- Who's your favourite actor from foreign country?
- Will you ever join politics?
- Why should we admire people who have achieved big things in life?

IMPORTANT VOCAB FOR THIS TOPIC
- Appreciate – be thankful for
- Autobiography – life story
- Insights – visions
- Executed – murdered
- Reconciliation – compromise

A book you have read

OR

A book you have read that made you think a lot

Do you generally read books?
Which is the best book you have read that left an impression on you?
Whom will you recommend reading this book?

Book reading is one of the best activities that a person can have. I am a book lover. I have around 50 books in my personal library at home. I generally love to read all kinds of books, but I am always inclined towards the biographies and autobiographies of famous personalities. I have read the autobiography of Mahatma Gandhi, Albert Einstein, and many influential figures but my personal favorite is the autobiography of Nelson Mandela. The name of the book is 'Long walk to freedom'. This is an autobiography and was published after he became the President of South Africa. In this book, he gave detailed insights when about his childhood till, he became the President. He also included the years when he was imprisoned and wrote about his family, friends, and freedom struggle. Nelson Mandela was a freedom fighter for more than 5 decades before he became the first black president of South Africa in 1994. He stayed in the prison for about 3 decades. He and thousands of his fellow freedom fighters were imprisoned by the white government. Many were executed and few of them were send to the jail for lifetime. Nelson Mandela was one of them. He stayed in the jail for almost 28 years, but the struggle continued outside the jail. As a result, the white government was forced to release the political prisoners and Mandela was freed in 1990.

He continued with his freedom struggles after his release and continuous negotiations with the government led to the first ever fair election in South Africa. This was the first time that the majority blacks could cast their votes. In 1994 the election results were declared, and Nelson Mandela won by unanimity of the people of South Africa and became the first ever black President. I learned all this information from the book.

This book had a long-lasting impression on me, and I never knew anything about Nelson Mandela before reading this book. This inspired me to read more such books. Mostly, I read books in the morning time. I like to wake up early in the morning and read books for around 40 minutes. This is a great habit as it gives you a lot of knowledge and you can also improve your reading skills. I highly recommend kids to read this book as it will teach them the real-life struggles of a great leader and will also inspire them to wait for the results of their hard work patiently.

Follow-up questions for practice

- Do you like reading?
- How has reading helped you in life?
- What are the benefits of reading books?
- How many books do you read in a year?
- Should children read books apart from their syllabus?
- What sort of books do women read in your country?

IMPORTANT VOCAB FOR THIS TOPIC
- Influential – leading
- Imprisoned – jailed
- Unanimity – unity
- Negotiations – talks

Talk about a time when you visited somewhere and lost your important thing there

Where you went?
What had you lost?
How did you lose that thing?

I have lost a couple of things in my life. Today I would like to tell you about a thing that was very dear to me, but I lost it in a wedding, and I still regret it. I went to my cousin's wedding in Delhi last year and lost one of my most precious possessions. I lost a smartwatch gifted by my sister.

I wear that watch even when I sleep because it tracks my sleep as well as activities for the whole day. It also shows me how many calories I have burnt and how many steps I have taken in a day. That watch also shows me the notifications for my phone calls and the messages.

I lost it, and I was so upset after this incident. I will share the whole story that why and when I lost that watch. The watch was given to me by my sister on my birthday. I was so attached to it that I used to never share it with anyone.

That day I was wearing that watch on my left wrist. I remember when I reached at the wedding, I was sitting on a huge couch with my relatives. We were having some snacks and conversing about the event. At that time, I recall that I was still wearing the watch.

But after some time, we all decided to go on the dance floor and express our happiness towards the occasion. We started dancing and I felt a bit irritated by the watch. The watch was clinging on my jacket. So, to get rid of that, I untied the watch and kept it in my jacket.

To my surprise when I came back from the wedding, I could not find my watch. I was so worried and started searching it in my jacket and other pockets. I felt so sad when I was not able to find my watch. I called my cousins to ask them whether they have seen my watch or not. But I could not find it at all.

I was so angry and blamed myself for the loss. I wouldn't have lost it if I was still wearing it. It was an expensive watch and I had never lost something that costly before. I felt so embarrassed that day, but my family consoled me after that incident and told me not to worry about that.

Follow-up questions for practice

- Do you often lose things?
- Why do you think people lose things?
- What do you do when you lose things?
- Have you lost an expensive thing in the past?
- How do people feel when they lose things?
- What precautions can be taken so that a person doesn't lose things?
- How do you react when you lose things?

IMPORTANT VOCAB FOR THIS TOPIC
- Precious – precious
- Possessions – belongings
- Clinging – grasping
- Embarrassed – ashamed

Describe a person who apologized to you

How is the person related to you?
Why did he/she apologize?
Did you forgive or not?

There have been few instances in my life when people have apologized to me for certain things. On some occasions, people were at fault but on the other occasions their actions were unintentional. Today, I would like to tell you about one incident in my life when a person sought an apology from me.

The name of that person is Rajiv, and he is one of my old friends. This incident happened when I was in my 10th standard. Me and Rajiv went along extremely well. We used to sit together in class and shared a lot of things and secrets with each other. One day, we both were playing a game in which we had to tell about one of our secrets. We promised each other not to reveal those secrets to other friends. While playing the game I was asked to tell one of my secrets. I told him about one of my pet names kept by my friends in my colony. The name was very comical, but I knew that Rajiv would not tell it to anyone in school as we had promised each other and had faith among us. But what came to my surprise was that everyone in the school was teasing me with the same pet name. Following this, I was really upset and angry with him. Upon asking him about it, he kept on telling me that he has not done it, but I knew that this secret could only be leaked by Rajiv as no other student knew about it. I changed my sitting plan with another student at school and stopped talking to Rajiv for what he did with me. I could see from his face that he was apologetic and feeling guilty. Afterall we were good friends before that incident.

One day he came to me quietly and said sorry for what he did. He admitted that he was the one who told my pet name to one of his friends, who spread it like a wildfire. I accepted his apology and told him to not repeat such behavior with anyone. After that we became friends again but from that day onwards, I never shared any of my secrets with him.

Follow-up questions for practice

- Have you ever apologized to someone?
- Why do people apologize?
- Is it crucial to apologize after committing mistake?
- Do you feel elders should also apologize to the youngsters?
- What are benefits of apologizing to someone?
- Do you feel one should not apologize if the mistake is not big?
- Is it important to forgive people?
- Do you feel forgiving people will make them realize their mistakes?

IMPORTANT VOCAB FOR THIS TOPIC
- **Unintentional – accidental**
- **Apology - sorry**
- **Reveal – exposed**
- **Comical – hilarious / funny**
- **Guilty – embarrassed**
- **Wildfire – something that spreads rapidly**

Talk about a time when you unexpectedly met someone

Who do you meet?
Why was it unexpected?
What did you do?

There have been a lot of instances in my life when I met people unexpectedly. Once I was totally surprised after meeting one of my childhood friends after 10 years.

I was astonished because I was meeting my classmate after so many years and I could hardly recognise him from his appearance. This happened when I was travelling in a train to New Delhi. I boarded an express train which takes three hours to reach Delhi from Chandigarh.

I had taken the window seat and after some time, a person quietly sat on my adjacent seat. He introduced himself as Harman. Every now and then he was looking at me and I was doing the same. The reason I was doing so is that I thought he and his name resembles my childhood friend from school.

After a while I asked him about his primary schooling. I was amazed to hear that he was the same person whom I was thinking about. I told him my name and after a few seconds he recognised me as well. We shook our hands tightly and laughed for a while.

I never expected to meet him in a train in India. The reason is that he studied with me till the class 4. After that he moved to United States of America with his family. I was stunned to meet him after so many years in a train journey.

I asked him about his life and shared a lot of things with him. He told me that he had come to India after 5 years and was now going back to USA. He had to catch a flight from New Delhi Airport. I really enjoyed my time with him in the train.

We chatted on length about our childhood and school. We talked a lot about our colleagues and teachers. Soon the journey was about to get over. So, he asked about my contact details. We exchanged our numbers and addresses. I also connected with him on social networking sites.

In the end we bade goodbye to each other at the New Delhi railway station. It was a great meeting with an old friend. Even now I am in touch with him through the internet.

Follow-up questions for practice

- Why do people meet each other?
- What do you do when you unexpectedly meet someone?
- Do you often meet people unexpectedly?
- Do you feel that people these days meet less than in the past?
- What do you do when you meet your friends?
- Is it always a good moment when you meet someone unexpectedly?
- What do you do when you meet people after a long time?
- Do you like meeting people whom you know from your childhood?

IMPORTANT VOCAB FOR THIS TOPIC
- Astonished – shocked
- Adjacent – adjoining / near by
- Amazed – surprised
- Stunned – shocked / horrified

Talk about a performance you gave at school or college

Did you often participate at school?
What was the performance about?
Did it go well?

I was not someone who gave a lot of performances at my school time. However, I remember one of the performances that I am going to share with you today. Once I participated in a skit that was performed on the annual day function of our school. Me and four of my other friends from my class were the part of the act. The performance included different characters inspired from animals and sea creatures that would demonstrate the effect of plastic waste on them. Many people are not aware about the fact that thousands of animal species die due to pollution from plastic in the ocean and on land. So, our teachers decided to do this skit with students. First, they took a screening test with more than 20 students and then finalized five students from our class. The function was organised in our school's auditorium. It was a big hall with a seating capacity of over 500. I was feeling nervous at the start but slowly gained confidence as the skit went on. Everyone had to perform for about a minute and lecture about the cause. We all had to dress up like different animals and creatures. One of our friends became a Penguin and told the audience about the deadly effects of plastic straws on Penguins. He explained that the Penguins eat straws mistaking it for food and choke themselves to death in the ocean. I was dressed as cow and told the spectators that throwing away plastic or polyethene bags are deadly for cows. There are thousands of stray cows in India. They gobble plastic with their feed which can stuck in their internal organs or throat. This cause severe problems and even some cows die because of that. One by one we came at the centre of the stage and gave our one-minute speech. The audience were looking extremely interested in the information given in the skit and applauded loudly after our performance was over. The act went extremely well, and we were all contented about it. We also got recognition from the principal for bringing up such an awareness. So, this was one of the performances that that I gave at school.

Follow-up questions for practice

- Do you feel nervous before giving a performance?
- Do you feel that giving performance increases the confidence of a person?
- How often did you give performances at school?
- What is the biggest fear while performing in front of the audience?
- How do you overcome your fear or anxiety when you perform in front of public?
- Do you feel that all children in schools should perform in front of the audience?
- Do you feel that performing in co-curricular activities is a waste of time?

IMPORTANT VOCAB FOR THIS TOPIC
- Skit – satire / act
- Demonstrate – explain
- Spectators – observers
- Stray - homeless
- Gobble – eat up
- Contented – satisfied

Describe an important journey that was delayed

Why was that journey important?
Where were you going?
Why the delay happened?

In the given topic I am reminded of a situation that occurred in my life and from which I learned a great lesson. I am talking about a journey that I had to make early in the morning and reach Jaipur for an important scholarship exam. This exam was held by the Rajasthan government and students who would score good in the exams would be handed over scholarships to study in the top universities for free of cost. I came to know about the exam through the internet. I filled the form and took my father's consent to go there. I started preparing for the exam as soon as I booked it. I was very well prepared for my exam and hoped to score good. I was getting ready for my exam and packing for the trip a couple of days in advance. Jaipur is located 500 kilometres away from Chandigarh.

I booked a flight ticket that takes one and a half hours to reach Jaipur. I was excited for the journey, but one silly error proved to be a menace for me. My exam was on Sunday at 10 AM and I booked the flight for Saturday, so I was scheduled to reach a day before the exam for which I had also booked a hotel.

The time of my flight was 7 in the morning, but I had mistaken it for 7 in the evening. When we reached the airport in the evening, I was shocked to know that the flight had already left in the morning. I was dejected as I had prepared for the exam so hard, and I was ready to give my best. I started weeping at the airport, but my father consoled me and quickly sorted the issue. He quickly booked a taxi on the phone and decided to go with me to Jaipur. It took us 10 hours to reach Jaipur and another hour to find the exam centre. I reached at the venue just in time and gave the exam. My exam did not go well as I was so tired after the journey. But my father supported me and told me to learn a lesson from this mistake. I could not clear the exam but learnt a great lesson that day. From this incident, I learned to always check the departure and arrival timings of the railways or the flights so that I would never miss them again.

Follow-up questions for practice

- Why do you think people get late for journeys?
- Do you often get late for your journeys?
- What do you do at first when you get late for a journey?
- Do you book your tickets and hotels well in advance before a journey?
- What preparations do you do while going on a long journey?
- Which mode of transportation do you prefer for your journeys?
- Which is the fastest and most convenient mode of transport in your country?

IMPORTANT VOCAB FOR THIS TOPIC
- Menace – danger
- Dejected – unhappy
- Consoled – comforted
- Departure – leaving
- Convenient – accessible

Describe your dream workplace

Why is it your ideal workplace?
Do you wish to work there one day?
Are most people able to work in their dream workplace?

My ideal workplace would be working as a Travel Video logger, popularly known as Vlogger. The reason behind this is that I love traveling, and I like to see new place. I get excited when I see new people and interact with them. My ideal working place would be all over the world.

I wish to work as a travel vlogger every day of my life. I know it is not an easy job and one needs to be highly motivated if he/she wishes to work in such an industry. A Travel vlogger needs to be travel fit and should be open to any kind of challenge while travelling.

There are many famous Travel Vloggers in the world like Drew Binsky and Renata Perrera. I am a huge fan of these vloggers and I never miss a chance to see their videos. They make superb quality travel videos and engage their viewers in an extremely interesting manner.

I wish to work as a Travel Vlogger for my YouTube channel. I would like to travel the world and visit the most exotic places. I will tell people about the country, culture, and region I visit. In my travel vlogs I will give information on how to travel to new places and what are the things to keep in mind while travelling there. What are the places to eat and where to do shopping?

In my travelling vlog, I will plan to visit every country in the world. I know doing this will take a lot of money and efforts, but I am making plans for that. After doing a job or business for 5 years, I will work as a full-time Travel Vlogger. I will also look for sponsors for my online travel channel.

In my opinion most people are not able to work in their dream workplace. I think the main reason behind that is money. People these days run after money rather than passion. I am lucky enough to have parents who support me in any decision I make. I would rather choose passion over money.

Follow-up questions for practice

- Describe an ideal job?
- Why do you think travel vlogger (or any job you have explained in the topic) is an ideal job?
- Why do you think people want to work in their dream workplace?
- Is money more important than having a dream job?
- Do you most people are not able to find a dream workplace? Why?
- What sort of workplace do you like? why?
- Is it easy to get a job in your country?
- Are you planning to take up a job or do business in your future?

IMPORTANT VOCAB FOR THIS TOPIC
- **Interact – communicate**
- **Superb – excellent**
- **Exotic – glamourous**

Describe a company which employs many people in your hometown

What that company is about?
Have you ever visited that company?
Tell about that company in detail

There are two or three huge companies that employ a lot of people in my hometown. There are companies like Mahindra & Mahindra and Infosys. But I would like to speak about Reliance Industries. Reliance is one of the companies that employ thousands of people across our country.

There are many subsidiaries of Reliance Industries. This company is one of the largest brands in India. The name of the owner of Reliance Industries is Mukesh Ambani. Reliance industries provide hundreds of services to the people of our country.

One of the newly launched services by Reliance industries is JIO. This service provides fast speed internet and satellite channels at low cost. They have employed thousands of people in this field over the past few months. I have met a lot of people who are working with Reliance Industries in my hometown.

Apart from this, Reliance has thousands of clothing and groceries stores all over the country and my hometown. You can find their store in literally every city of India. Not only this, Reliance employs thousands of people in petroleum and yarn industries as well.

There are Reliance digital stores in my hometown that deal in electronic gadgets. There is a huge Reliance Mart near my house that sells groceries on wholesale rate. There are many stores and offices of Reliance industries in my hometown, and I believe they generate tremendous amount of employment.

I have been to most of their stores in my hometown. There is one store that opened recently by the name of Trends. It sells latest clothes and garments. I went there last week and bought a pair of jeans. Moreover, Reliance has myriad retail stores of groceries around my town.

I admire this company a lot as they have certainly employed millions of people across India and thousands in my hometown alone.

Follow-up questions for practice

- Which are the largest companies in your country?
- Do you believe it is the sole duty of the government of a country to employ its people?
- Do you feel private firms generate more employment than government?
- Are there many big firms/industries in your hometown?
- Have you ever visited a huge industry in your hometown?
- What sort of industry is there in your hometown?
- Do you feel huge companies and retail stores must be located outside the centre of the city?
- Do you feel foreign firms generate more employment than local firms?

IMPORTANT VOCAB FOR THIS TOPIC
- **Subsidiaries - firms**
- **Groceries – rations**
- **Literally – exactly**
- **Tremendous - immense**

Describe a bicycle tour you took

Do you often ride bicycle?
What was the tour about?
Who were the other participants?

I have a bicycle at my home, but I do not ride it often. I go on a ride a couple of times in a month. I like riding the bike when I am free but I hardy get a chance due to my busy schedule. Recently I saw one guy who rides bicycle every day in my colony.

I connected with him, and he told me about his group. He has formed a group of around 20 people who get up early in the morning every day and go for cycling. They go on different routes and do cycling for about an hour. The name of his group is cycler's corner.

I was impressed with his idea and asked if I could join the group and go on a cycle tour with them. He instantly agreed and added me to his chat group. He introduced me to his other friends and told me about the timings and place of gathering a day before the tour. I had previously told him that I would not be a regular member but would love to go on the bicycle tours when I get time.

Next morning, I was ready to go on the tour at 5 AM. We all gathered at a nearby landmark and began our journey. Our leader led us to a garden nearby where we breath in fresh air. After that we went to the Sukhna Lake which is in the east side of my hometown.

After cycling for about half an hour, we all took water break and continued our journey. We took the best roads in the town that are integrated with a cycling track. After a few minutes we reached near our assembly point and parked our bikes there.

One of the group members then took out his phone and start clicking selfies of all the riders. We talked to each other for about 5 minutes, and everyone started going back to their destinations.

I thanked the leader and told him to keep me informed for the weekend tours. I thoroughly enjoyed that day and will never forget it for a long time.

Follow-up questions for practice

- What are the benefits of riding bicycle?
- Is walking better than cycling?
- Do you feel cycling is getting popular in your country nowadays?
- Do you feel more and more people should use bicycle within cities?
- Is riding bicycle dangerous?
- Do you feel government should spend more budget on building infrastructure for bicycle?
- Is there any infrastructure for bicycles in your hometown?
- Do you believe bicycle is the future of transport?

IMPORTANT VOCAB FOR THIS TOPIC
- **Integrated** – incorporated / combined

Describe a night when you could not sleep at all

Why could you not sleep that night?
Do you often feel insomnia?
Did you wake up well the next morning?

There have been few nights in my life when I was not at all able to sleep. The one that I remember the most is when I visited a foreign country for the first time.

This happened a couple of years ago. My father gave us a surprise holiday package. Me, my father, my mother, and my younger brother were set to visit Dubai for the first time. This was the first foreign trip for all of us.

I remember I started preparing a month before as I was feeling enthusiastic for the trip. A couple of days before the trip, I finished my packing and was eagerly waiting for the trip to get started.

I remember one night before the trip when I could not stop thinking about Dubai. I just could not sleep even for a minute. I was so curious for the tour that I could hardly stop thinking about that.

I tried hard but I was feeling highly insomniac. However, I was also aware that if I could not sleep well tonight then I will find it difficult the next day. So, I decided to try some method to get myself some sleep.

I tried reading some old books and listening to some old songs but that too did not help. I also called my father to help me in sleeping. He told me to do light exercise in order to get some sleep. I did some exercise for 15 minutes but that did not work either.

I was so frustrated with the situation that I decided to stay awake. Decision of staying awake was not a good one because the next day when all were fresh and ready to go, I was feeling sleepy and tired.

There have been some sleepless nights in my life but none like this one.

Follow-up questions for practice

- Is restlessness a common problem in your country?
- Why do you think people get restless?
- What do you do to get rid of your restlessness?
- Is being restless good for health?
- Do you get anxious when you are not able to sleep?
- Do the youngsters in your country sleep late at night? Why?
- Why do you think that people get stressed?
- Is stress a common issue nowadays?
- Do you blame working hours for restlessness?

IMPORTANT VOCAB FOR THIS TOPIC
- **Enthusiastic – passionate**
- **Insomniac – sleepless**
- **Frustrated – angry / annoyed**
- **Restlessness – impatience**

Describe a person who likes to travel by plane

Why that person travels in plane?
Does he/she travel frequently in plane?
Do you like to travel by planes as well?

I know a few people who like to travel by plane. Today I would like to speak about my cousin who loves to travel by plane. His name is Ashish, and he lives in New Delhi. He is working in a multi-national company there. His favourite hobby is to book a plane ticket and travel the world. He often takes sabbatical to go around the world. He has visited more than 30 countries over the past few years. He is a frequent traveller by plane. He journeys more than five times through plane in one year. He says that he feels rejuvenated when he travels by plane. He has collected all the plane tickets of his past journeys as a memoire. He is so obsessed with travelling by plane that he books plane tickets to even places which are easily accessible by train or bus. Recently he flew to Jaipur from Delhi just for leisure. The reason he did so was that he only wanted to experience a short flight. The distance from Delhi to Jaipur is hardly 250 kilometres which can be covered in merely four hours by car or bus. But he chose to travel by plane just to experience a short plane journey. Recently he completed his 100th journey by plane. He tells about that to everyone with a sense of pride and achievement. I have never seen a person in my life who loves to travel by plane so much. His love for planes is amazing. He has even bought a huge replica of Boeing 787 and kept it in his house's lobby. I am not as crazy as him when it comes to travelling by plane. I do not relish the plane travel much as I feel it's quite tiring and congested.

Follow-up questions for practice

- Why do people travel by plane?
- Is travelling by plane the best way?
- Do you feel that travelling by plane is the safest option?
- Do you like travelling by plane?
- Why do some people do not like to travel by plane?
- What are the advantages of travelling by plane?
- Are plane fares cheap in your country?
- Are the main cities in your country well connected by airports?
- Do you feel that more and more people in your country will travel by planes?

IMPORTANT VOCAB FOR THIS TOPIC
- Sabbatical – vacation
- Frequent – common
- Rejuvenated – refreshed
- Memoire – journal
- Accessible – available
- Merely – only
- Replica – copy
- Relish – delight
- Congested – crowded

Describe some advice you received on your subjects or work.

OR

Describe some good advice about choosing a job or subject.

What advice did you receive?
Was the advice helpful?
Do you often take advice on your subjects or work?

I have had wonderful people around me who have supported me in all aspects of life and have given me words of wisdom when needed. I have received many useful and some great advice from people around me. One advice that I remember I took from my elder sister proved to be vital in my life and career. I remember when I was studying in 10th class, I never thought of choosing my subjects for senior secondary. But my sister always encouraged me to choose the subjects while studying in 10th class so that I could plan my future well in advance. When I stepped into 10th class, I was confused about choosing subjects for my further studies. I understood my sister's thoughts about choosing the subjects in advance. This allows a student to manage his/her future in a better way. I was confused between choosing medical or non-medical. I thought I was good at medical subjects but that was not the case. To be successful in medical field one needs to be good at memorizing thousands of terms and medical substances. I thought I was good at biology, so I was restricted to only that subject. Moreover, I am not the kind of person who could sit for long hours and study same subject repeatedly. I was muddled and looking for someone to guide me and help me chose a better option. So, my sister came to my rescue. She explained me about the current scenario of subjects and bright future in the field of non-medical. She also told me that non-medical is not restricted to only one type of job like the medical field is and gives you more choices after the senior secondary level in India. She also gave me examples of people who excelled in this field. I felt inspired and there was clarity in my mind regarding the subjects. After discussions with my sister, I chose the non-medical field and felt quite confident about it. After that I never looked back and worked hard on that subject. So, I believe that her advice in choosing my subjects proved fruitful.

Follow-up questions for practice

- Do you often take advice from others regarding your studies?
- Is it crucial to take advice from elders or seniors before choosing subjects for higher education?
- Do you believe taking advice can sometimes confuse a person?
- Is taking advice from others a good habit?
- Do you feel taking advice from others help you chose the best options?
- Do the kids in your country consult their parents before choosing subjects?
- Do the teachers in your country help kids choose their subjects?
- Do you feel kids should not take advice regarding the choice of subjects and should choose subjects themselves?

IMPORTANT VOCAB FOR THIS TOPIC
- **Wisdom** – knowledge
- **Muddled** – confused
- **Scenario** – situation
- **Restricted** – limited
- **Fruitful** – prosperous

Describe an experience when you were with people and got bored

Where were you and why did you get bored?
Did other people get bored as well?
Did you do anything to get out of that boredom?

I remember one instance in life when I was surrounded by a lot of people and got really bored. This happened a couple of years back when I was going to Mumbai to my aunt's house for a holiday.
I had to board my flight from New Delhi, so I reached the airport 2 hours before the departure. I checked-in my baggage and went to the boarding gate to wait for the flight's departure. I was waiting there and was well on time. I saw a lot of people coming there one by one. There were still 30 minutes to departure but there was no sign of flight gate opening. I asked a person at the inquiry counter about the flight departure, but he did not give me any information regarding it. He told me to wait for another 10 minutes.
After some time, an announcement was made that the flight was delayed by 3 to 4 hours due to a technical slag. I was disappointed for the delay as I was thrilled for my trip. I went to the inquiry desk in anxiety and asked about the issue. They assured that the flight would not be cancelled but the delay will surely happen. That wait at the airport proved to be extremely boring for me. There was no entertainment source at the boarding gate. The TV and the WIFI at the airport were also not working. I felt jaded at that time. I did not have a book or a movie in my mobile to kill time. I was looking at the faces of people around me and I could sense everyone's frustration and boredom. There were about 300 people who were waiting for the flight to depart. I could not connect with anyone as they were all strangers for me. I was feeling alone and fed up with the situation. I tried many things to get out of boredom, but none worked. I can easily say that it was one of the most boring moments in my life when I was surrounded by people.

Follow-up questions for practice

- What causes boredom to you?
- Do you easily get bored?
- Why do you think people get bored?
- What do you generally do to get rid of boredom?
- Do you think boredom can be useful?
- Should boredom be avoided?
- Which places generally make you feel bored?
- Is there a friend or a relative of yours who makes you feel boring?

IMPORTANT VOCAB FOR THIS TOPIC
- **Boarding** – entering
- **Thrilled** – delighted
- **Jaded** – tired
- **Boredom** – dullness

Describe a time when you first met someone OR A famous personality you have met.

Who was the person?
What did you do in that meeting?
How do you react when you meet a person for the first time?

I have met many people for the first time in my life, but I can hardly remember about most of them. However, there are some people who leave a strong impression on you. I would like to tell you about a person whom I met, and he had a great influence on me. I am talking about Sachin Tendulkar. He is a great personality in India and around the world. He was the best Cricket player of his time. He had broken numerous records while playing cricket for India.

I was extremely fortunate to meet him in Mussoorie. Mussoorie is a quiet hill station situated in the northern part of our country in Uttaranchal Pradesh. I went there with my family and was staying there for a week.

On the second day of our trip, we were roaming in the market in the early hours. There was no rush as it was an early morning of a winter day and there was a lot of snow everywhere. Suddenly I saw someone coming from the other side of the road. That man was wearing a blue woollen cap and as he came closer, I recognised him and loudly took his name. At first, he ignored, but I chased him and told him that I had recognised him. He stopped and acknowledged my greetings. I told him that I was one of his biggest fans and always dreamt of meeting him one day. I shook his hand tightly and hugged him. I asked for a selfie, and he smiled to my request. I requested him to stay with me for a minute as my parents were also coming from behind. The next moment my parents were there, and they were shocked to see him. They could not control their emotions and we again clicked a few pictures with him. After that we bade goodbye, and I can never forget his smile and modesty during that meeting. That day he inspired me a lot and I learned a great life lesson that regardless of all the success and despite of having everything in life, he was so humble and down to earth.

Follow-up questions for practice

- How do you react when you meet famous people?
- Have you met many famous people in life?
- Do you think famous people are different than normal people?
- Do you believe people should not disturb famous personalities for pictures and autographs in public places?
- Do you believe media interferes in the life of famous personalities?
- Are there any famous people who live in your locality?
- Why do you think people become famous?
- Would you like to become famous in your life?
- What are the advantages and disadvantages of being famous?

IMPORTANT VOCAB FOR THIS TOPIC
- **Fortunate** – lucky
- **Modesty** – simplicity
- **Interfere** – affect

Describe a time you were sleepy but had to stay awake

Why were you feeling sleepy?
Why did you stay awake?
How did you manage to stay awake?

There have been many instances in my life when I had to stay awake. But on those occasions, I remained awake intentionally. Either I was with my friends enjoying or I was in a party and came late. But I remember one situation when I felt the need to sleep but had to stay awake for the whole night. This happened last year in summers. There was a power cut in our area due to a periodic maintenance. The electricity did not show up till afternoon and upon calling the electricity department, we came to know that this issue would be resolved by evening. We patiently waited till evening, but the electricity was not yet there. We were extremely frustrated as the electricity complaint department had stopped picking up calls from the locals. Summers in India can be exhausting and imagining life without an air conditioner is hard. We were at least able to get fan air as the inverters were still on. But unfortunately, the invertor batteries went down in the evening, and we all were sweating and felt irritated with the situation. I was feeling so helpless and frustrated. I called the electricity department again and this time they picked up call and told that there was a major fault in the electricity grid of our colony, and it would take another 10 or 12 hours to get the things repaired. As the night fell, I was feeling tired because my daytime was extremely hectic. I tried sleeping but could not as I was choking with heat and drenched in sweat. So, I decided to sit outdoors and sleep on the chair. But after some time that did not work as well. I was feeling sleepy, but I could not sleep as the heat was too much for me. I started getting scratches on my neck and back due to excessive sweating. Finally, I decided to go for a drive in my car with my brother. We went on a long drive with its Air conditioner on full power. We drove for three hours and came back early in the morning. To our surprise the electricity was still not there. Eventually I decided to get some rest, but I was still not able to sleep.
Luckily at 6 in the morning, the electricity was supplied, and everyone breathed a sigh of relief. But it was already time to get ready and go to work. So that was the day when I felt sleepy but could not sleep.

Follow-up questions for practice

- What is the best way to get rid of sleep?
- Is sleep crucial for good health?
- Do you feel that today's people do not get as much sleep as people used to get in the past?
- Why do you think that people's sleeping patterns are changing these days?
- How many hours do you sleep each day?
- What are the disadvantages for excessive sleep?
- What do you immediately do after you wake up from sleep?
- What is the best time to wake up in the morning?

IMPORTANT VOCAB FOR THIS TOPIC
- **Exhausting** – tiring
- **Choking** – suffocating
- **Relief** – respite / rest
- **Excessive** – extreme

Talk about a person in news whom you would like to meet

Who's that person?
Why do you want to meet him/her?
What will you do when you meet that person?

There are many famous personalities these days in news who are worth meeting. However, if I intend to choose one person then it would be prime minister Narendra Modi. He is the current prime minister of our country and is one of the boldest and dynamic leaders of our times. He is always in news as he is the prime servant of our country. He is known for his extra ordinary speeches and work since he took the office in 2014 as the Prime Minister. I have read about him and his early day struggles. If I am given a chance to meet one person in news, then it would be Narendra Modi. He has inspired millions of people in our country and around the world as well. I want to personally meet him and learn a great deal of things from him.

I will ask him a lot of questions when I meet him. I guess I will learn myriad of things from him. He is an experienced leader and can teach me a lot of things that are required to lead a great life. He is a fantastic leader and after meeting him I can seek some advice on leadership.

Mr. Modi rose from a very humble beginning and reached the pinnacle of politics. He used to sell tea at a tea stall with his father and later with his brother at railway station. Despite being short of resources, he fought his way up in politics.

I want to learn everything from him about life and how to acquire certain traits that he has. He is the person who is almost every day in news due to important decisions that he makes for our country.

So, if I am given a chance to meet someone in news then it would be our prime minister, Narendra Modi.

Follow-up questions for practice

- What kind of persons are generally seen in news? Why?
- Do you believe some celebrities do certain things that helps keep them in news?
- Do you trust news channels and newspapers in your country?
- Do you feel editor of news channels sometimes goes over the top in reporting news for maintaining viewership? Why?
- Which is your favourite news channel? Why?
- Do you feel most news channels on internet report fake news?
- Which is the best source of getting news? (TV/Newspaper/Internet)
- Do you feel that people are more interested in negative news?

IMPORTANT VOCAB FOR THIS TOPIC
- Intend – plan
- Extraordinary – remarkable
- Humble – respectful
- Pinnacle – top
- Acquire – attain
- Traits – qualities
- Fake – replica / bogus

Talk about a meeting you attended at your school or workplace

What was that meeting about?
What was your contribution in the meeting?
Do you like to attend meetings?

I have not attended many meetings during my school time. But there was an instance when I was involved in a meeting. At that time, I was the monitor of my class and other monitors from different sections were invited in that meeting. The meeting was about preparing for the sports event. All the monitors from 10th class were selected as the event managers from their respective sections. We were five monitors in total and were given certain responsibilities. We were supported by our corresponding class teachers, and we were also allocated some capital for the same.

The meeting was called upon by the principal of our school. Our principal Ms. Shalini is an inspiration for many. She is very dynamic and full of life. She placed trust in us and gave us all the responsibility to manage and organise the annual sports day. I was given the responsibility of arranging the trophies and medals for the participants and the winners. In total there were twenty events, and the number of participants were 300. In meeting, the principal gave us different responsibilities and asked us about any suggestions that we can give.

I was given particulars about the participants and the events. I had to buy medals and trophies for all. I gave suggestion to the principal about the trophies. I told her to buy only medals instead of trophies as the medals would cost less. Everyone in the meeting agreed to me and the principal was impressed with my idea and gave me a go ahead. Yes, I like attending meetings because it gives a person many ideas for a certain thing or event. People in meetings share different ideas with one another and I feel that participating in meetings enhances the maturity level of a person.

Follow-up questions for practice

- Is it crucial to reach in meeting on time?
- Should a person go to a meeting fully prepared?
- Do you feel that a person learns something from meeting different people?
- Are people punctual for meeting in your country?
- Why do people get late for meetings?
- Are meetings all about presentations and discussions?
- Do you like attending meetings?
- Do you feel that meetings sometimes can be boring?
- Do you feel that keeping meets and discussion sessions improve the working environment between employees?

IMPORTANT VOCAB FOR THIS TOPIC
- **Respective** – corresponding / separate
- **Allocate** – allot / assign
- **Dynamic** – energetic / vibrant
- **Particulars** – facts
- **Maturity** – experience

Talk about a time when you used a foreign language to communicate

Why have you had to use a foreign language to communicate?
Did you communicate well?
Do you often use foreign language to communicate?

I generally speak decent English but when I communicate with a native speaker then it can be a bit of a challenge because I am not a native English speaker. I want to tell you about an instance when I had to communicate with a foreigner in English. I often use English in school and in daily life while studying. Although I have studied all my life in English medium schools but when it comes to communicating with a foreigner in a foreign language, it can get a bit difficult as their accent can be a lot different than us.

A few months ago, I was roaming in the most famous commercial area of my hometown with my friend. There, I saw some foreigners looking for help regarding something. They hesitantly approached me and asked me about one of the cafés in that area. They were looking for the Indian coffee house. It is one of the oldest and famous cafes in our city. They asked me about the directions to the café. They were also curious to know about the local transportation in the city. I was happy that they approached me, and I was eager to help them. I gave them much needed information regarding the local transport and how to bargain for the fares. I was roaming there in my free time, so I told them to follow me to the café. After ten minutes we reached there, and I also told them few local delicacies to order.

They were very generous and invited me and my friend to join them. We agreed and I ordered some of the local dishes. They enjoyed the food, and I did all the conversation with them in English. We talked on length about my life, and I also asked them a lot of questions about theirs. They told that they had come from England for a holiday. We had a great time together and conversed with them well. I can never forget that day. This was the first situation in my life when I had to talk with someone entirely in a foreign language.

Follow-up questions for practice

- Should people learn foreign languages? Why?
- Which foreign language do you like most? Why?
- What are the benefits of learning a foreign language?
- Do you agree with people who say that learning foreign language will make people forget their own culture?
- Is it important to learn the language of a country where you are visiting for study/work? Why?
- How many languages are spoken in your country?
- Do you feel that there should be one world language?
- Why do people learn multiple languages?

IMPORTANT VOCAB FOR THIS TOPIC
- Native - local
- Roaming – travelling
- Hesitantly – doubtfully
- Eager – keen
- Bargain – good deal
- Fares – charges
- Delicacies – treats
- Generous – substantial / large
- Conversed – chatted

Describe a wrong decision you once made

What was the decision?
Why that decision went wrong?
Did you correct it after that?

Many of my decisions and actions in life have proved fruitful but there were some decisions that did not go well. One decision that I regret the most is deciding the dates for my holidays.

I was in my 10th class when me and my family decided to go on a vacation in winter breaks. We planned to go to Dubai and thought of celebrating Christmas and New Year there.

At first, I thought it was a great decision by me, but we were not aware about the consequences of it. Our flight was scheduled on 23rd December in the evening. After reaching the hotel in Dubai, it took us so long to check-in to the hotel room. The reason was that was the peak season and millions of travelers had flocked to Dubai for Christmas and New Year.

Next day we were greeted in the morning by the tour company and the guide took us to the malls and famous attractions on that day. Wherever we went, it took us long time to buy tickets and we had to wait in long queues to see the attractions.

We faced huge rush in every mall. People were all over the place. I felt that my decision to visit Dubai in the month of December was not good. For the simple reason that I do not like huge crowd. I like quiet places and places that have less people.

Due to the rush of tourism in that period, everything was overpriced. It was even hard to find a taxi. Even if we found one, it was expensive than normal days. All the prices of souvenirs went up due to the high season.

I learned a huge lesson of life from that trip. Now I never suggest visiting tourist places near Christmas and New year for the obvious reasons. Although we enjoyed our trip, but it could have been better if we would have planned it at some other time of the year rather than December. So, I feel that this was the decision that went wrong for me.

Follow-up questions for practice

- Who takes important decisions in your family? Why?
- Is it necessary to consult elders in the family before taking any decision?
- Do you take your own decisions, or you consult someone?
- What are the benefits of taking your own decisions?
- Have you ever regretted any decision in your life? Why?
- Do you feel only mature person can take better decisions? Why?
- Is it crucial to analyze your decision once you take them? why?
- Do you feel successful people take prompt decisions?
- What are the advantages and disadvantages of taking quick decisions?

IMPORTANT VOCAB FOR THIS TOPIC
- **Fruitful – abundant**
- **Regret – sorrow**
- **Consequences – effects**
- **Flocked – assembled**
- **Queues – lines**
- **Overpriced – expensive**
- **Souvenirs – mementos / reminders**
- **Obvious – apparent / clear**
- **Prompt – quick**

Describe something that helps you in concentration (yoga/meditation)

What is that thing?
How does it help you to make concentration?
What breaks your concentration?

I know a few methods that helps me to improve my concentration. One sure shot method is doing Yoga or meditation early in the morning. This is the best activity that helps me build concentration.

Not only this, yoga and meditation also help me in maintaining good health and temperament. I usually do yoga in the early hours of the day. I have learnt certain postures of Yoga from my mother as well from television.

I see videos of Yoga specialists and have tried to learn the positions and exercises to improve concentration. Distorted concentration is one of the most common problems that people face today, especially the youngsters.

Even I was facing this issue in the past. But since I started Yoga, I started improving my concentration. I do Yoga and meditation early in the morning. I usually get up at 5, then I do certain postures and take deep breath. There is one exercise that I do the most. In this exercise I sit on the floor with my legs folded. Then I keep my index finger on my forehead and rest of the fingers over my closed eyes. I use my thumb to close the ears.

Then I inhale and exhale for at least four to five minutes continuously without interruption. This exercise really helps me in improving my concentration and it also reduces my stress levels.

There are certain things that breaks my concentration. While studying I need pin drop silence. Previously I was disturbed by even the slightest of disturbance, but now I have changed. Due to Yoga and meditation, I can bear distortions without breaking my concentration.

I recommend everyone to do Yoga and meditation to get rid of concentration problems.

Follow-up questions for practice

- What disturbs your concentration? Why?
- What do you do to get back your concentration?
- Do you feel today's youngsters struggle more with maintaining concentration? Why?
- Is there any food that help maintain concentration?
- Why do people generally lose concentration?
- Do you feel exercise helps in maintaining good concentration?
- Do you know a person who has tremendous concentration levels?

IMPORTANT VOCAB FOR THIS TOPIC
- Temperament – personality
- Postures – poses
- Distorted – biased / altered
- Inhale – breath in
- Exhale – breath out
- Interruption – stoppage
- Slightest – smallest

What makes you angry

Do you often get angry?
What are the things that makes you angry?
How do you get rid of your anger?

No, I do not often get angry. But there are few things that disturbs me and can also make me angry. I do not like people telling lie and I get annoyed of someone who is behaving in an amateur way other than kids.

But one thing that makes me livid is the wastage of valuable resources. I cannot simply tolerate the wastage of natural resources. When I see someone misusing water, electricity, and wood, I get very angry.

I can never see wastage of water. I see many people washing their cars with flowing water. That makes me very angry. I have had many altercations with people who do such activities. There was one guy in our colony who used to wash his car daily and wasted hundreds of liters of water on one wash.

I explained him the importance of water, but he refused to listen. I always keep all the fans and lights switch off when not required. I get angry when any of my family member keeps the lights on when not in room.

This kind of attitude irritates me to a great extent. Sometimes I explain myself that it is not a thing to be angry. But I cannot resist myself from getting angry if anyone is wasting natural resources.

I feel these resources are very expensive to produce and once exhausted, we will not be able to get them again. Resources such as water and fuel are limited hence, we should be responsible in using them for the future generations.

Follow-up questions for practice

- Do you often get angry? Why?
- What are the negatives of being angry?
- What causes people to get angry?
- How do you control your anger?
- Is it crucial to remain calm in every situation? Why?
- Can exercise and yoga help in controlling anger?
- Do you feel a person's behaviour changes when he/she is angry?
- Should there be anger management sessions at school for kids? Why?

IMPORTANT VOCAB FOR THIS TOPIC
- **Often – frequently**
- **Annoyed – frustrated**
- **Misusing – exploiting / abusing**
- **Altercations – clashes**
- **Refused – rejected**
- **Resist – refrain / survive**

A female leader you would like to meet

Do you follow politics?
Why would you like to meet that leader?
What will you do when you meet her?

There are quite a few female leaders that I would like to meet in my life. I like Michell Obama and Angela Markel from outside India. But if I am given a chance to meet a female leader in my life then I would love to meet Mamata Banerjee. She is the 9th and current Chief minister of West Bengal.

She is one of the most powerful female leaders in our country. She is currently serving as the Chief Minister of the state of West Bengal from the year 2011. She has been the most successful leader in West Bengal till now. She was the first women chief minister of West Bengal. She is popularly known as 'DIDI', an elder sister. Previously she also served as the Minister of railways for two terms in the central government. She was also the first women railway minister. She held several ministries and positions previously in the central government. She started her political career with congress and soon rose the ranks and became the head of youth and women congress in west Bengal. After some controversies with the congress party, she left the group and formed her own party in Bengal by the name of All India Trinamool Congress in 1997. After that she defeated her rival in 2011 and became the Chief minister of West Bengal for the first time.

She continued her success and won the recently concluded elections in 2021 and is still the Chief minister of Bengal in 2022. She adorns a simple and light coloured Saree and lives a modest lifestyle. She has achieved many landmarks in life. She has reached the pinnacle of politics in India. She is also considered as one of the most powerful women in Indian politics. If I meet her then I would first greet her with utmost respect and will ask about the secret of her success. I will ask about all the things from which I can learn to lead a great lifestyle as her. I admire her as a leader and will like to meet her if given a chance.

Follow-up questions for practice

- Do women indulge in politics in your country?
- Is there any successful women politician in your country from present or past?
- Do you feel politics is still dominated by men all over the world? Why?
- Is there any women world leader you admire? Why?
- Do you feel societal position of women in your country is getting stronger?
- Is there any gender discrimination against women in your country?
- Are women of your country self-sufficient?
- Do you feel women should do jobs in tough fields such as Army and police?
- Do you feel a women can lead a society better than men?

IMPORTANT VOCAB FOR THIS TOPIC
- **Controversies – debates**
- **Rival – competing**
- **Adorns – decorates**
- **Societal – social**
- **Self-sufficient – self-supporting**

A piece of clothing you received as a gift

OR

A gift that made you happy

Do you often receive gifts?
What type of attire was gifted to you?
Did you like that gift?

Yes, I often receive gifts from my loved ones. I generally receive gifts on my birthday but a piece of clothing I got as a gift was not on my birthday. I got a jacket gifted by my aunt who returned from Canada. She lives in Canada from the past many years. She is my beloved aunt and I have a cordial relation with her. She is my mother's sister. Whenever she comes to meet us, she brings a lot of gifts from Canada. Last time she came to India in December. She brought a beautiful jacket for me. As soon as she handed me over the gift, I quickly opened it and thanked her for that. It was a blue-coloured leather jacket of xxxx brand.

She has a great sense of choice in selecting clothes for everyone. I instantly liked the jacket and tried it in front of them. It fit me properly and I was looking good in that. I stood in front of the mirror and checked my looks. I was looking more sophisticated in that than my usual clothing. The brand of the jacket is famous worldwide and is also expensive. There were many pockets in and out on the jacket. All the pockets were lined by a steel zip. The colour of the jacket was bright and the leather had a crumbly texture.

This texture gave it a great look. It was a full sleeves jacket with an option of removing the sleeves and converting it into a sleeveless jacket. I had never seen a jacket like that before. There was a zip on the shoulder that could be opened to remove the sleeves. The zip on the shoulder was nicely tucked by an overlapping seal. There was a removable hood at the back of the collar as well. I was so impressed with the jacket that I used to wear it every second day of the winters. I flaunted that jacket to all my friends in the neighbourhood. They also liked it very much.

Follow-up questions for practice

- Do you feel that it is better to gift something else than clothes to someone?
- Do you like getting clothes as gift? Why?
- Have you ever gifted someone a piece of clothing as a gift? Why?
- Do you feel that people have different choices regarding clothes?
- What is the best gift that you can give someone? Why?
- On what occasions do people generally give gifts to each other?
- Do you like receiving gifts?

IMPORTANT VOCAB FOR THIS TOPIC
- Cordial – amiable / friendly
- Instantly – rapidly
- Sophisticated – refined
- Crumbly – flaky
- Texture – surface
- Tucked – put
- Overlapping – covering
- Flaunted – showed

Speak about a time when you felt anxious

Do you often get nervous?
Speak about when you got nervous?
How did you feel?

Emotions are a wonderful thing as they reflect the state of our mind. Through emotions we can judge a person's thought process. There are a wide variety of emotions that people run through every day and nervousness is a very common sign that can be seen on the people's face or in their actions.

I get nervous on several occasions but the time when I got overly nervous happened when I was waiting for my class 12th results. The thing is that I was not very well during my exam days, and I thought my exams did not go well. Although I was well prepared during the exams as I studied regularly throughout the session rather than studying more in the exam days.

I was suffering from mild fever during the last three exams of 12th class. These subjects were important, and it was necessary to score good in them as I had to apply for a student visa abroad.

One of the subjects was English. I did not prepare for this subject during the session, so I thought of preparing it during the exams.

But to my bad luck I could not get any time and intent for studying it during the exams. I was suffering from viral fever and was unable to concentrate on my study. I hardly read about the English syllabus. I was worried on my exam day as I was not prepared for the exam at all.

The result was to be declared in a couple of months after the exam. On the result day, I was apprehensive about my scores in English exam. The result was scheduled to be declared in the evening. So, from morning itself, I was anxious and barely relaxed. I just could not stay calm throughout the day.

As soon as I received the result, I was relieved, and all my nervousness was gone. Although I did not score high in that subject, but I was satisfied with average scores given my preparation and health. So, this is the time I remember when I was very nervous.

Follow-up questions for practice

- Do you generally get anxious?
- Why do people get nervous?
- How do you get rid of your nervousness?
- How can people stay calm in troubles?
- Have you seen someone who is always anxious?
- What are the negatives of being anxious?
- Do you get nervous when you meet strangers?

IMPORTANT VOCAB FOR THIS TOPIC
- Anxious – nervous
- Overly – very / excessively
- Mild – moderate / slight
- Intent – purpose
- Apprehensive – anxious / uneasy
- Barely – scarcely / just
- Relieved – comforted / eased

Describe a good law for women

When was it introduced?
What is there in this law?
Why you like it?

Well, it's quite unfortunate that the status of women in my country is not yet good as our country is mostly male dominant. But now the situation is changing, and the government is introducing various laws to uplift the position of women in society.

One such law that needs to be appreciated is the law against female foeticide introduced by the state a few years ago. Actually, India is a male-dominated society; parents always wish to have a baby boy than girl. Earlier, the parents used to get the sex determination test while the foetus was still in the womb.

Most people used to abort their baby if a girl child was detected. The situation got worse as the huge imbalance was witnessed in the gender ratio of males and females in our country.

Understanding the gravity of the situation, the government has now enacted the law against female foeticide.

Under this law, sex determination test is completely banned, and if anyone is caught, they are bound to pay huge penalty as well as imprisonment in some cases. The best thing about this law is that it is being implemented strictly. This is perhaps the reason the situation has changed greatly.

Now, society's perception has also transformed. People happily accept the birth of baby girls in their homes. In fact, the situation has improved as in many regions of India, females are outgrowing the number of males.

I really appreciate the government for coming up with this law and implementing it strictly because it has improved the situation of women in society. Since this law has improved the status and position of women to a great extent, it is good law in favour of women, and I admire it the most.

Describe a village near hometown

What is the name of the village and how far is it?
What do you know about it?
Do you like it or not?

I live in the north part of India where you will find thousands of villages and very few metropolitan cities. Most of the people reside in villages in this area. Although I live in a city, but a village is never away as my city is surrounded by many of those. Here I would like to take the opportunity to talk about one village which I find interesting to visit, and it is hardly 5 kilometres from my hometown. The name of this village is Chat, and I got to know about this place when one of my friends recently shared a post on social networking site.

He shared pictures of a gorgeous lake with hundreds of palm trees lined behind it. There were other pictures of the village that made me curious to know about it. I was astonished to see the beauty of it and started searching about that place. I was shocked to know that the village was bordering my city and I had never heard about it.

My first impressions of the village were positive. I noticed that the village had a public school, a college, multi-speciality hospital and other facilities that most villages in my region do not have.

From the locals, I came to know that many youngsters from this village live in foreign countries, for that reason, it is also known as NRI's village. Well-settled people from foreign countries send a lot of financial aid to the village, and the management utilizes those funds in a superb manner.

While I was roaming around this wonderful village, I was told by a local that it is one of the only self-sufficient villages in terms of energy production, and the villagers also harvest the rainwater. I was stunned to see the cleanliness in the village. People living in that village were quite friendly and guided us towards every attraction. In the end, we went to that lake which I saw in the photograph. The lake was magnificent, and I could not resist myself from clicking a few pictures of it. It is a natural lake that is well maintained by the locals. I think we must learn from the people of this village. The way they have kept the nature intact and streets clean is simply commendable.

After I returned from my visit, I told my other friends and relatives about it. Even they were feeling excited and wanted to visit that place.

A foreign personality who motivates you to do well

OR

Describe a foreign person who you have heard or known that you think is interesting

Who this person is and how do you know this person?
What kind of person is he/she?
Why do you think this person is interesting?

With globalization and increasing use of social media networks, nothing and no one is alien to people of any country. We live in a world where we can get access to unlimited information. I admire many foreigners and try to learn great deal of things from them.

Today I would like to talk about an extremely interesting person who is actually the richest man on this planet right now in 2022, Elon musk.

He is the person who always remains in the limelight as the media tries to bring everything related to him in public. At the same time, he remains extremely active on social media, especially Twitter. Several things make Elon Musk quite interesting.

Firstly, his curiosity towards space travel. He owns the company named SpaceX with a mission to make it possible to travel to space and settle permanent colonies on mars. His imagination has no boundaries, that's why he often comes up with ideas that others find interesting and unrealistic.

He is often invited as a guest lecturer, and I always listen to his speeches available on internet, which are extremely knowledgeable and motivating. He also believes that technology is going to change the world completely in the future. He also owns Tesla, which is the leading manufacturer of electronic cars and trucks.

In addition, Elon Musk is interesting because he has a comical nature, and he even jokes about technology and its future. I was watching one of his interviews recently when he was asked whether there are aliens on this earth or not? He jokingly replied, yes! Why not? I could be one of them. The audience laughed out loud after listening to his remarks. He is not only interesting but extremely hardworking as well. He is someone whom I admire pretty much. He gives me motivation and positivity to do well in life.

A quality or skill your friend has that you want to adopt

OR

Describe a habit your friend has, and you want to develop

Who your friend is?
What habit he/she has?
When you noticed this habit?

I am quite a watchful person and like to adapt good habit of others. I have noticed that most of the people have habits that are worth learning. Here I am going to describe a good habit of my friend. Reading books is his best activity and it is inculcated in his DNA. He simply cannot let a day go without reading. He has abundance of knowledge on any matter as he reads quite a lot.

He has been reading books since I have known him, and now he is addicted to this activity.

Where most of the youngsters of today are busy on social medial platforms, playing games and wasting their precious time on unproductive activities, he is always immersed in reading books. He is always reading about great personalities, history, and science. Secondly, through reading, he acquires knowledge of different domains, and this is perhaps the reason why he is one of the most active students I have seen.

He is also quite proficient in English and in using vocabulary as he reads most of the books in English. Considering all these factors, I think I should also develop interest in reading.

This is the habit that I always wanted to develop but could never do it. This time I am determined to build this habit as it is one of the most productive habits.

I hope this habit will help me to sit and study for long hours, which will ultimately improve my academic performance as well. It is the habit that my friend has, and I, too, wish to develop.

Describe a creative person whose work you admire

Who he/she is and how do you know him/her?
What creative things he/she has done?
And explain why you think he or she is creative?

Not everyone is blessed with creativity, but I know few people who have extremely creative and innovative minds. Here I am going to talk about my science teacher Mr. Harrison whom I believe to be the most creative person I have ever come across.

I feel fortunate to be his student during my school days. Science is one of the most difficult subjects, and majority of students face trouble understanding it, but our science teacher is a true genius who always had innovative ideas to make students understand the concepts and nuances of the subject.

He used to accentuate more on practical learning than theoretical part, and for this, he frequently took us to school's science laboratories for practical learning.

In addition, there are some topics related to physics that are highly impractical to comprehend by solely reading books and to clear such concepts he used to teach us with the help of technology.

For example, by playing videos and showing 3D images. In fact, it was also a fun way to learn for students, and we never felt bored in his class. Moreover, Mr Harrison was deeply involved in teaching us the practical uses of science. For that, he used to make working models of different concepts and would teach with the help of those models.

Last but not least, he also used to request school management to organize some excursions to keep the fun element in education. He was such a genius that he always had ground-breaking ideas to bring improvements to the school and the way education was delivered. I had a wonderful experience of learning at school, especially the science subject, and the credit goes to the science teacher Mr. Harrison.

Describe a time when you were waiting for something special to happen

What you waited for?
Why was it special?
Explain how you felt when you were waiting?

I am an optimistic kind of a person. I always expect good things to happen. There are many occasions in my life when I was waiting for something special to happen but today, I would like to talk about a recent experience. This happened a few months back when I was waiting my holidays to start. I was extremely excited for the holidays to begin as I had planned a lot of things to do. It is kind of a tradition in our family to plan holidays in the winter breaks. I have a huge family and we mostly go out on excursions and trips together.

I was having my exams in November and the holidays were scheduled to start in December. I was eagerly waiting for the holidays to begin as this time, we had planned to visit Dubai to witness the beautiful country as well as the World Expo 2020. I was so excited about the trip that I could not even prepare for my exams well. I love travelling and whenever we plan for travelling, I always get excited about it. The highlight of the trip was the World Expo as it was one of its kind. It was going to be the world's largest expo in which every country would participate.

Unfortunately, there was a rapid increase of Covid-19 cases in my country and soon a lockdown was announced. Even most of the countries banned the flights from India as we struggled a lot with the Covid situation. I was dejected as all my plans went in vain. The World Expo was announced four years back and I was so thrilled for it since then. I never thought that I would see the day when I would not be able to go there. Not only this but the World Expo event was called off and postponed to a different date.

So, World Expo was the special even for which I waited so long and expect to witness it in person, but it did not happen in 2020.

Describe a time you bought something from a street or outdoor market

When was it and where was the market?
What did you buy?
And how you felt about it?

I do not shop from the outdoor markets generally as I believe that the products there are not of good quality and there is no warranty either. But there were few occasions in my life when I had to buy something from a street market.
This happened when I visited Thailand last summers. Thailand is a wonderful country with great food and humble people. One day I was roaming around Bangkok, a city in Thailand and found a colourful and vibrant market on the roadside. I was stunned to see the arrangement and how nicely it was managed by the organisers. From locals I came to know that it is a weekend street market that is organised every Saturday and Sunday at different locations in Bangkok.
The street market was pretty long and had everything from food, gadgets, clothes, and toys. When I saw a few shops, I realised that the quality of products was reasonable, and prices were low.
At one stall, I was impressed with the gadgets they had. I needed an international travel adaptor that charges multiple electronic devices of any country and voltage type. When I asked about the price, I was surprised as a similar product in my country would cost three times more. I bargained a bit and paid a reasonable price for the international travel adaptor.
I was satisfied with the purchase as this was something that I was looking to buy for a long time. I have been using this adaptor since then and it has been a great buy for me. From that day my perception about street / outdoor markets also changed.

Describe a cafe you like to visit

Where it is and what kinds of food and drinks it serves?
What do you do there?
And explain why you like to go there?

Well, it is pretty common these days to visit cafes to have a cup of tea or coffee. Here I would like to talk about a cafe I regularly visit. The name of the café is French Press Café. It is located in the centre of the city and is quite popular among the youth of my city.
It is a laid-back kind of a place with quiet ambience. The café has a huge variety of Italian and French cuisines. Moreover, it is famous for its delicious coffee. I generally go there with my friends especially on weekends. We sit there for hours and chat about our lives on length. At café, they have relaxed sitting options with wide sofas and comfy chairs.
The staff at this café is wonderful as they greet us with smile every time we go there. The staff is well trained and explains the menu in detail to the new visitors. As the menu is full of foreign dishes, it is quite confusing for first time goer. But the staff handles it nicely.
The reason I love this café is that they make the best coffee in our city. I am a coffee lover, so I always order coffee latte. It is a sweet and creamy coffee with amazing fragrance. Another thing that I order every time I visit there is pasta and Croque.
I like ordering white sauce pasta with mushrooms. A croque is a French sandwich mostly infused with feta cheese and mozzarella on top. Although they have huge list on the menu, but these are the two things that I always order.
On top of that, this café is built in a way that you will feel that you are sitting in a café in France. The ambience is great, the food is palatable, and I cannot resist myself from going there again and again.

Describe an article which you have read about health

What was it and when did you read it?
Where did you read it and why did you read it?
Why do you think it was an interesting read?

I love reading articles about health online as I am keen to change my diet and include exercises in my routine that boosts health. I came across an article last week and I found it intriguing. I read an article about intermittent fasting on an online version of the Morning Herald newspaper.

I have struggled with eating a healthy diet and keeping my weight in control. I wanted to make desperate changes to my diet and physical activities. But I was not getting motivation at all.

So, for that reason, I started reading many articles and watched a ton of videos regarding health care and dieting.

I read the bold heading, intermittent fasting. I was allured by the term as I was hearing about it for the first time. I started reading the article and gained a lot of knowledge about the benefits of this type of fasting. The article explained that intermittent fasting meant fasting for 16 hours every day. This can be done by eating dinner at 8 in the evening, skipping breakfast, and having the first meal at noon.

The writer suggested that people can start fasting for 12 hours and gradually increase to 16 hours.

This helps in losing weight as, during fasting, glucose gets depleted, and our body starts burning the deposited fat to get energy.

Before reading this article, I thought people only fasted for religious reasons, and there were no health benefits to it. I previously thought it was important to eat three meals a day and never miss breakfast as eating breakfast boosted our metabolism. The article also mentioned that other than weight loss, fasting every day also reduces the risk of many diseases like diabetes, Alzheimer's, and some cancers.

I found all this information fascinating and began following this diet. It was hard at first, and I almost gave up, but I was beginning to see amazing results, and that kept me going. I am at my desired weight now, and I am glad that I came across this article. I have shared this article with so many friends who are trying to lose weight.

Describe a time when you felt proud of a family member

When it happened and who is this person?
What the person did?
Explain why you felt proud of him/her?

There have been numerous occasions when I felt proud of my family members. But today I am reminded of a time when not only me, but all my family was proud of my brother.

Actually, my brother Amit studies in 8th class, and has a friend named Raj who is quite a brilliant student. Unfortunately, he comes from a poor family, and his parents find it difficult to pay his school fee. Last month his father met with an accident, and because of that, a lot of money went into his treatment. For that reason, Raj's parents were unable to pay his school fee.

The school management was quite unsympathetic, and they issued a notice to Raj stating if the school fee is not paid on time, Raj will not be allowed to sit in the exams. But Amit assured Raj that he will pay his fee and he should only concentrate on preparing for the exam.

Amit paid Raj's fee from his savings and did not tell anyone about this. But some time ago, when Raj visited our house, he came with a flower bouquet to thank my brother, and during this time, he revealed the entire story of how Amit helped him.

That time, we all got emotional and hugged Amit tightly, and we were all feeling proud on him. It was really a proud moment for the entire family.
I never though that a kid of his age could do this kind of favour to his friend. But that day I was extremely proud of my brother.

Describe a person who impressed you the most when you were in primary school / childhood

Who he/she is and how you knew him/her?
Why he/she impressed you the most?
And how you feel about him/her?

I hardly remember anything from my primary school, but I cannot forget Miss. Leena who impressed me the most in my childhood. She was a wonderful teacher who motivated me to do well in life.
I can recall that I was a naught kid and used to play a lot of video games and with friends outdoors. I was not at all interested in doing homework as I found it quite monotonous. So, my mother decided to enrol me to a tuition taken by Miss Leena who used to live nearby our home.
I was not satisfied with the decision as it would cut my play time in the evening. But after attending her class for the next few days, I started gaining interest in studies as she was an amazing teacher.
She had a knack of teaching in a way that everyone liked. She used a lot of practical learning techniques to make children understand the concept of the subject. She never told us to memorize maths tables or English phrases, instead she used to play educational games with us which helped us learn different subjects in a fun way.
Not only studies, but she also taught me so many different values and ethics of life. I cannot thank her much for her contribution in my life.
I was also impressed from her as she used to dress in an appropriate manner and has a great accent to her language. She was soft spoken and humble to everyone.
She was so close to all the kids in class that we used to share all our issues with her. Miss. Leena is someone who impressed me the most in my primary school.

Describe an activity that you usually do that wastes your time.

What is it and when you usually do it?
Why do you do it?
And explain why you think it wastes your time.

In this fast-paced era, not many people have much spare time which they can waste on a certain activity. Still, I believe that there are a lot of activities that take up huge time of individuals.
Here, I would talk about an activity that I do, and it wastes a lot of my time. I am talking about spending time online on social networking sites and youtube. Every day I use these platforms for my entertainment, and I always decide to stop within an hour, but this is not the case.
Once I start using these sites, I am bombarded with the latest videos and posts from my friends and relatives. I cannot resist myself from seeing all those pictures and videos. I also like to comment on those posts as it keeps me closer to my friends and relatives abroad.
Staying on these sites for long also keeps me updated about the lives of my loved ones. I enjoy spending time on these sites as it keeps me virtually connected with all my old friends from school as well as childhood.
The moment I start using these sites, I lose the track of time. Sometimes I feel that I am doing the right thing but, on many occasions, I believe that it is a total waste of time.
I am sort of addicted to this activity as I spend around three to four hours of my daytime on this. I reckon that I can use this precious time on certain activities like reading, playing sports and spending time with my friends and family.

Describe an occasion when many people were smiling

When did it happen?
Who you were with?
What happened and why many people were smiling?

I think people these days hardly smile as we live in such a world that is full of stress and competition. It becomes crucial that we smile often to keep ourselves mentally fit. I love listening to people who make me laugh.

Recently I came to know about a concert that was scheduled in my city. In that program, one of the most famous comedians of our country Johny Liver, was going to make people laugh in a stand-up comedy show. The ticket was a bit pricy, but I did not want to miss the chance to see him perform live in front of me. He has acted in more than 400 movies in India and is highly respected for his comic timing and face expressions.

I went there with my friends, and we reached at the venue an hour before to grab the front seats. We were lucky and got the second row. The show began with one of his trademark jokes and all of us started to laugh out loud. There were about 500 people in the auditorium and no one there could control their laughter. All were smiling and it looked that they have forgotten their worries. As the show went on, Johny Liver cracked some of the most hilarious jokes that I had never heard in my life before.

During the whole show, everyone was smiling and applauding Johny Liver for his delightful comedy and jokes. I had never seen such occasion where so many people were smiling.

A house you visited but you would not want to live in.

Where is it situated?
When did you visit that place?
How did you feel about it and why don't you want to live there?

I have visited many types of houses, but I would like to speak about my friend's house that I recently visited. I liked the house as soon as I entered it. His house is in one of the posh colonies of our city. It is a gated society and has tight security.

He lives in a four-bedroom apartment that is situated on the top floor of the building. Anyone would dream of living in a house like that. The apartment has five balconies that oversee the beautiful Shivalik hills.

The location of the apartment is tremendous as it is in the heart of the city. Most of the main attractions of the city are nearby. The bedroom size is big, and the hall is spacious. The kitchen is modern and includes all the latest amenities in it.

The interior of the house is stunning with maximum utilization of space. I had never seen such a beautiful house before. Not only this but the apartments boast of social and club facilities where residents can enjoy gym, pool, and common lobby at the ground level.

Most people would love to live in a house like this, but I am the kind of a person who do not like apartments. Because apartments are like a closed unit, but I like living in open spaces, like an individual house. Most apartments would not give you a personal parking space, open spaces, roof, and space for gardening.

Even after liking this house so much, I would never want to live there.

Describe your favourite curtain

Which curtain is it?
When and where did you see it?
What it looks like and why you liked it so much?

Last year, I went to Dubai for a family holiday trip. There we stayed at a five-star property by the name of TAJ. I was stunned to see the beauty of that place as the hotel was decorated and modelled like a King's palace.

There were ultra-modern amenities in our room like automatic lights, robotic room service and a remote control to operate almost all the features of the room.

As soon as we entered the room, I grabbed the remote and started experimenting with it. I switched on the AC, lights, and TV from that remote. Soon I noticed that there were other switches on the remote that controlled different functions. I saw this button with a curtain sign and pressed it in excitement.

Upon pressing the button, the curtains on the side of the room swayed away like the ones in a theatre. First, the initial layer opened that partially lighting up the room. On pressing the button again, the second layer exposed the window to the beautiful view of the city.

I thought it was an amazing feature because I had never seen it before. I could not stop myself from opening and closing it again and again. The back curtain was plain white which was letting some light in the room and the curtain at the front had a beautiful floral design with robust stuff.

I think everyone should have this type of curtain at home. It is so convenient and easy to operate. From that day onwards, those automatic curtains became my favourite ones.

A time you had to wait in a queue / long line

When was it?
What was it about?
How long the queue was and how you felt about waiting there?

I live in India, and we are a nation of a billion people, so it is not uncommon to wait in long queues for your work. I can remember numerous occasions when I had to wait in long queue but today, I would like to speak about a time when it was necessary to wait in the queue and I can never forget that day.

I am talking about 2015 when the Prime Minister of our country announced that the government has decided to demonetize the ongoing currency and especially the bank notes to replace them with new ones to control the corruption.

Everyone was afraid and in utter shock and did not know what to do. The government also announced that people can deposit their old bank notes in the bank and can get the new ones in a limited quantity.

The maximum withdrawal of new note was 4000 rupees at one time per week which was not much for an individual or a family. We had no new bank notes and most people refused to take the old ones for any transaction. We required some cash immediately and for that my father told all of us to go to the bank and bring the new ones. You would not believe what I saw upon reaching the bank.

There was a long line of people wanting to withdraw the new currency notes. The line was so long that you could hardly see the bank from the end of the line. I could not give up as we required the cash urgently. I waited in the queue for at least 5 hours in direct sunlight without water and food. After so much struggle, I managed to get the new notes.

This was a common sight in front of every bank across India . People struggled to get new notes as the availability was limited and population of country is high. It was so hard to wait in the line for this long, but the situation became better after a week as there was more availability of the new bank notes.

Your favourite wild animal

Which animal do you like?
Where did you first see it?
What did you know about it and why do you like it?

I have huge interest in studying the wildlife and like quite a few wild animals like Tiger, Lion and Leopard. But the one I like the most is Elephant.

There are many reasons behind my liking. I clearly remember when I was 5, I went to a circus and saw elephant for the first time. I could not believe my eyes when I saw this gigantic creature. I was a bit worried as well as excited to see such a huge mammal.

The ring master at the circus was instructing the elephants to do certain things that would make the audience laugh. First, they instructed them to make a painting with their trunk and then the elephant was told to play football. The elephant did a lot of stuff to make people happy. I could not believe that such a huge animal was so funny and did things that are not expected of wild animals.

When I grew up, I came to know that elephants are indeed one of the most intelligent wild animals in the world. They are also known to have sharp memory and great sense of friendship. Old tales have revealed that elephants and humans have lived together in harmony for years. Across many countries including some parts of India, elephants are worshipped and taken care of. In Thailand and Sri Lanka, there are Elephant orphanages and Elephant care centers where abandoned elephants are treated and kept in safe conditions.

The reasons I like this animal the most is because this wild animal signifies intelligence and power. And they are generally not too aggressive as other wild animals.

Describe a job you would never do

What is the job?
Why don't you want to do it?
How you feel about the job?

I love travelling and like to see new places, meet new people, and try new food. If given a chance, I would always prefer a job that includes a bit of travelling. I hate sitting jobs and would never do them even if I am offered a good salary. I would never do an IT job as I have seen many people struggle with their routine who are involved in IT jobs. I am not against people who do these kinds of job but the job itself is quite demanding.

You must spend at least 8 to 10 hours on a PC or laptop when you are in this kind of a job. Using gadgets for this long not only affects your health but puts a lot of burden on you mentally. I have experienced this situation firsthand as my elder brother is in the same field and he simply hates it.

Although he cannot leave his job, but he is not at all satisfied with his routine and workload. He has dark circles under his eyes, and his eyes usually turn red that irritates him a lot. He is not able to give proper time to his family and kids. He does not have a day off as he is also working on Sundays. He does not have a fixed time schedule as most of his clients are from another country. So, he usually works at nights and gets very little time to rest in the day. Most IT jobs disturbs the work life balance of a person. This is not the plight of my brother alone, but of the most people involved in IT jobs.

Moreover, IT jobs are boring as it hardly involves travel. You just need to sit in a room full of computers and gadgets that really annoys me a lot. I think that IT sector jobs is not my cup of tea, and I would never do that.

A poisonous plant you know

Which is the plant and how do you know about it?
How the plant looks like and what are its characteristics?
Have you ever seen that plant?

India is rich in flora and fauna. There are millions of species of plants that a person can spend his/her entire life counting them all. I know about a handful of plants that are harmful or poisonous. The one which I am going to talk about today is Wild Carrot. It is one of the most poisonous plants that are found in my country. This plant was first found in temperate regions of Europe and Southwest Asia. This plant can also be found in some areas of North America and Australia. I came to know about this plant when I was in school. I had participated in a botanical exhibition where schools from all over my state had come there to participate in that exhibition. Our teacher selected me and one of my friends from our class to participate in the exhibition.

Our teacher told us the details of the plant and the school administration arranged it for us. That plant does not look so big. It is only a foot tall over of the ground. The leaves of the wild carrot are very thin and spiky.

The leaves are of light green colour and has small flowers on it. The colour of the flowers is white and pale yellow. It has a solid but thin stem that supports hairy like leaves at the top. The leaves are very thin and curved at the edges. The leaves are like a needle, thick at the bottom and it becomes thin at the top. This plant blooms in summers and just before the winters start. Its leaves are also allergic and can cause irritation to the skin when held in hand. This plant is very rare, and people can also mistake it for the real carrot that we eat. The plant is similar in size, but the carrot's texture and colour are different.

I had never seen such a plant in my life before. We handled that plant with care and explained the features to everyone in the exhibition. We used surgical gloves to touch the plant as a mere touch can sometimes cause serious allergy reaction.

(Note: You can also search and speak about Tobacco – as the poisonous plant)

Describe an environmental law in your country

What the law is about?
How you first learned about it?
Who benefits from it and explain how you feel about this law?

Our country was not at all concerned about the environment in the past but now the things are changing. With growing awareness among individuals and government's concern have brought about many new laws that are made to protect the environment. There are strict laws made recently that curtails the use of fuel in cars, lower emissions for vehicles, growing of trees but I would like to speak about my favourite environmental law, the ban of single use plastic. This was a long pending law that was not being implemented for so long. But the government of our country has taken a bold decision to ban single use plastic across all states. Single use plastics are toxic for our nature and environment. It not only creates a lot of pollution but is also the cause of many animals being choked to death when they accidently swallow it. Under this law, if any shopkeeper is found selling or use any type of plastic for packing, will be fined heavily, and could also be jailed. The license of the shop could also get cancelled. It is not only about bringing this law to the public, but the police and government are forcing the law and taking every necessary step to curb the use of single use plastic. I have seen many people now using recyclable jute bags and purses made from linen. People are now becoming more anxious and feel that it is the need of the hour to cut down the use of plastic in society. This is one of the most required and necessary laws introduced by the government that will help in protecting our environment.

A bag you want to own

Which company's bag is it?
Why do you want to own it?
What are some of the special features of the bag?

I love to own bags as it gives us utility to carry certain items on the move. I love travelling and have a collection of bags at my place. I love to carry bag even if I am going for a small outing as it gives me a space where I can keep my water bottle, laptop, or important documents without any hassle.

Recently I was searching for a new bag for short term travel, so I went to a bag store in a mall. I always purchase Supreme company bags as they are one of the most durable and good-looking bags in the market. Although they are on the expensive side, but I still choose to buy them.

I went to the showroom and told the sales executive about my requirements. She showed me the perfect bag that I was looking for. It had the option of three colours but I wanted to buy the blue one.

The bag looked extremely durable with lots of zips and hidden pockets. There were two water bottle holders on either side of the bag with lock to keep them in place. Inside the bag, there was a dedicated space to keep laptop, tablet, and a phone. Apart from this, there was a provision of changing the size of the bag as per the requirement. It was primarily a shoulder carry bag but could be converted to a small travelling bag with a single zip pull action.

Not only this, but the bag also had a variety of other utility pockets and spaces for different purposes.

I fell in love with that bag but soon I was disheartened after I came to know about its price. It was the latest model and costed around 8000 rupees. I was on a budget and could not spend more than 4000. So, I had to leave the idea of buying that bag.

I loved everything about the bag except its price, but I am also not in the mood to buy any other bag. So, whenever I have enough money to spare, I will surely buy this bag.

Describe an item on which you spent more than you expected

What it is?
How much did you spend on it?
Why you bought it and explain why you think you spent more than expected?

NOTE: You can start with the same answer mentioned in the above topic (a bag you want to own) and end it a bit differently like this:

When I asked about the price, I was shocked to know that it was 8000 rupees. I was stunned because I was expecting it to be around 4000 or maximum 5000. But the price was way more than I expected. I had no option but to buy that bag as I had simply fell in live with it. Although I love my bag so much, but I still think that I paid more for it, and I had never expected it to be so expensive.

Your favorite item of clothing

What is the importance of clothing?
Speak about your favourite clothing item?
Why it is your favourite?

Clothing is a basic need of human beings. But now it has become more than a basic need. It has become a style statement. Nowadays people spend more money on clothes than ever. Numerous brands and stores are in existence everywhere in the world. I like to be updated with my clothing and I am very conscious of the latest trends. I generally like to wear informal clothing in my daily routine. A pair of jeans along with a decent shirt or a polo. I like to keep my clothing comfortable rather than body fit. I think I like every item of clothing, but I have to say that I like a pair of jeans the most.

I have around six or seven pair of jeans in my wardrobe. I like to buy only Wrangler and Levi's jeans. These two brands are on the top when it comes to jeans. I like to wear dark colored jeans as it can be worn on a stretch for many days without even washing it.

I read somewhere that Levi's was the person who invented the jeans for the construction workers as they wanted something durable and clothing that do not easily get dirty. So, Levi's came up with an idea of jeans and gave workers a new type of clothing. Today, Levi's is one of the top brands across the globe that manufacture's jeans. The story is so inspiring. There are several advantages of wearing jeans. Most of the jeans go with every kind of shirts and uppers. There is no need to wash the jeans after every use. You do not even need to iron most of the jeans. The life and durability are also the best when it comes to jeans. I mostly like to buy blue and black jeans. These colors suit me the most.

Jeans can also be worn with formal shoes, and it also looks good with the casual ones. This is the beauty of jeans; it is extremely versatile. I have a knack of buying jeans whenever I feel bored from the old ones. Recently I bought the most expensive jeans that I have bought till date. It costed me around 5000 rupees. Buying jeans give me immense satisfaction and it is certainly my preferred type of clothing for most occasions.

An occasion when you helped someone

How does helping someone feels?
How did you help that person?
How did you feel after helping him/her?

Helping someone gives immense pleasure. It is great to have done voluntary work in life. It does not give you money, but it gives you innate peace and joy. I am fortunate enough to have received help from a lot of people in my life when I needed it and I have also helped a few people when they need it.

I remember helping an old man who lost his way. This happened last year when I was waiting for my bus at the bus stop and an old person came to me and asked for help. He told me that he was going back to his hometown, but he mistakenly got off the bus at the wrong station and his belongings were left in the bus. He was looking worried and helpless as he had also forgot his wallet in the bus. He also told me that he was feeling very hungry and could not eat anything as he does not have money.

I calmed him down and offered him some snacks at a nearby restaurant. He was extremely old and was using a stick to walk. So, I decided to take him to the restaurant and his home myself. I took him to a restaurant and ordered tea and some snacks. We had the food and I asked him to come with me. We waited at the bus station for about 20 minutes before the next bus came. I boarded the bus with him and paid the bus fare. Then I started asking about him and his family. He told me that he had gone to his village to attend a funeral of one of his childhood friends and now he was returning to his son's house where he originally lived.

We talked a lot on the way and soon we reached our destination. I escorted him out of the bus and said goodbye, but he convinced me to come to his home to meet his family.

So, I decided to accompany him to his house as he was extremely tired by then. When we reached his home and he told the story to his family members, they thanked me and give me a gift as a token of love and appreciation which I could not refuse.

On that day, I was so happy and when I told my parents about this, they hugged me and told me to help people in future as well.

Speak about one of your future plans

OR

Something you planned to do but have not done yet

What is that thing?
Where do you plan to do it?
How will you do it?

Well! This is a very interesting topic because I love to do new things every now and then. There are so many things in life that I have planned to do but I am waiting for the right time and funds. The thing that I have planned to do before I die is sky diving.

It is one of the extreme sports that many people do not even dare to attempt. There are select people who chose to do sky diving and I am one of them. I planned to do sky jump last year along with my best friend. I searched on the internet about the best places from where we can perform this activity. I found that Gujrat, Thailand, and Dubai are the best places for sky diving according to the reviews and suggestions from the people on the internet.

So, I decided to call the one in Dubai as I was always excited to visit that country. They were very responsive and told that they have different packages with diverse tariffs. The best package that I found included the skydive experience with an expert and video recording was to be done by them as well. They explained that they would record the whole experience in the form of videos and photos. The price of the package was exceeding my budget, so I decided to know about the other places.

Then I followed up the one in Thailand and found that the package inclusions were like that of Dubai, but the price was almost half. I got excited to know this and decided to immediately book the package and flights. But after discussing it with my parents my dreams were shattered. My father had invested a huge sum in a property recently so I could not get the money for this, but they assured me that whenever they have extra money, they will surely give it to me for skydive.

This is my long-cherished dream and the day I get time and money to do it, I will go for it.

A car journey you remember

OR

A long road trip

Where did you go?
Who accompanied you?
What was special about that journey?

I have journeyed in car many times. The one that I remember the most is when I went to Jaipur, Rajasthan with my family last year. This was the longest road trip I have ever done. My elder brother drove the car along with my father and my mother was the fourth member. We were travelling by an SUV car so there was no problem of extra room. We had three full sized luggage bags as we were planning to stay in Jaipur for a week.

Jaipur is around five hundred kilometers from where I live, and it took us ten hours to reach there. We had a couple of rest stops during the journey. We left for Jaipur early in the morning at about 5 AM. On our way we did not see much traffic as we departed quite early.

There was a bit of fog on the way as the highway to Delhi is surrounded by farms. The reason we were taking a stop at Delhi was to rest for a bit. Delhi is located on the halfway to Jaipur. So, we reached Delhi in only three hours. We parked our cars in a restaurant and did breakfast. We chose traditional breakfast that includes stuffed bread and butter. It was so delicious that all of us could not restrict ourselves to overeat. After some time, we decided to continue the journey.

The highway to Jaipur is wide with neat and clean roads. We were cruising to our destination, but we had to take another stop as my brother was feeling sleepy. So, we decided to have a cup of tea. We stopped at a kiosk on the roadside and enjoyed our tea.

After that it took us only one hour to reach Jaipur. All of us enjoyed the journey to the fullest. We had so many conversations during that journey that we generally do not have at home. So, this is the car journey that I can never forget. That journey was long but it was enjoyable.

An important letter you received

Do you generally receive letters?
Speak about that important letter.
Did you respond to that letter?

These days the trend of writing letters is vanishing day by day. People nowadays are using e-mails and other electronic stuff for interaction. I used to send and receive letters from one of my pen friends in my childhood, but it's been a while since I have received a letter.

I can never forget the letter that I received last time. It was very important for me. The letter was regarding the cash prize that I won during a lucky draw.

This lucky draw happed because I went to a shopping mall few days back and there was a counter at the exit of the mall where a lot of people were gathered. There was a lot of chaos, and people were looking excited.

I went there in anticipation and asked what was going on? The person at the counter told me that it was a lucky draw for the customers who shopped at the mall. I told him that I bought certain items and would like to participate in the draw. He told me to fill up the form and put it into the lucky draw box. I wrote the details like phone number, name, address, and gender on the form and put it into the box and waited for the result with excitement.

There were a lot of cash prizes and numerous other items to be given away by the mall. The lucky draw scheme was to commemorate the completion of 5 years of the mall. I was excited and on the other hand I was a bit pessimistic on whether I would win it or not?

But to my surprise, one day I received a letter and before opening it I had no clue regarding the lucky draw as it was nearly a month since I had gone to the mall. The letter stated that we are happy to announce that you have won a cash prize from the lucky draw. I was astonished to see that.

The cash prize was 20000 INR which was a huge amount for me at that time. I was so happy after reading the letter. It also stated that you must collect the cash prize from the mall office. So, I went to the mall and got my cash from there.

That is the letter that I think was very important and if I had not received it, I would have regretted.

A time when you teamed up with an old person

Why did you team up with an old person?
What happened?
Will you team up again with the same person?

Teamwork is crucial in achieving success. I have teamed up with a lot of people in my life, but I always enjoy the company of my grandfather. I have played a lot of table tennis matches and tournaments with him over the last few years.

My grandfather is a champion player himself. He had played at national level during his young days. He is extremely fond of playing table tennis. We have a proper table to play table tennis at our home. I have learnt the sport from him 6 years back.

First, I was not interested in playing the game but one day I picked up the bat and never looked back. I learnt a lot of tricks from my grandfather, and I used to beat a lot of my age group players at school and locally.

One day my grandfather told me about a table tennis competition that was to be organized in our locality. It was a doubles tournament in which you must team up with one player and play against the other two. We decided to team up and play that tournament as there was no age restrictions for participants. I knew that we had good chances of winning the tournament.

There were 10 days to prepare for the competition, so we decided to practice table tennis every day for at least an hour in the night. We used to play single games, and, on some occasions, I used to call my friends so that we would have four players to practice the double's game.

On the day of the final match of the tournament, my grandfather was feeling tired, and some cramps were disturbing him. So, I decided to take the lead and play to my full potential. In the end, we won the tournament, and the credit goes to our teamwork. I would love to team up with my grandfather for more tournaments like this. So, this was the time when I teamed up with an old person and enjoyed very much.

An achievement

OR

Speak about a time when you participated in a competition

How and when did you achieve the feat?
How did you feel after the achievement?
Did you learn something from the whole experience?

I have not been able to achieve a lot of accolades in my life but there are some achievements that gave me confidence. One achievement which I am going to tell you about is when I was in school.

This happened when I was studying in 10th class. In that year, there was a compulsory debate and speech competition organized by our school in which more than 200 students from our school participated.

I was extremely shy in nature but there was no escaping. Everyone in our class had to participate. It was a compulsion, and no choices were given. I was anxious when I came to know about this debate competition because I was really introvert and could hardly speak a word in front of 10 people. The debates were to be performed in front of more than 2000 students and teachers.

There was only one week to prepare, and we were given a choice of three topics. We selected one topic and started rehearsing on it. It took me around 4 days to even speak in front of 10 students while practicing. Slowly and steadily, I gathered my courage and prepared the speech topic. On the competition day I had mixed feelings. I was excited as well as timid. Once my name was announced, I rushed to the stage and took a deep breath.

I started with my speech topic, and I thought I spoke very well. I had practiced hard due to the fear of failure, and I think it really helped. When my topic was over, I took a huge sigh of relief. I came back to home and realized that I had achieved a huge thing. I believed that now I could stand in a group of people and speak my mind. However, I did not win the competition that day but the courage that I won was a big achievement for me.

Your ideal home

Is home important for people?
Describe the ideal home
Describe all parts in detail

Having a house of own is the biggest dream of every person. I live in a medium sized house with decent construction. I would like to have a house of my dreams which would have all the amenities in it that I want.

An ideal house would be difficult to describe but I will try to define it in my own version. An ideal house would probably be big. Its exterior will be of plain white color as this color sooths my eyes and it gives positive vibes as well. It should be a multi-storied house with a lot of big windows and airways for great ventilation and sunlight.

The main entry gate of the house should be huge with wooden work on it. There should be huge space for car parking. At least 3 to 4 cars should easily accommodate within the residence. Apart from this, there should be a minimum of 6 to 7 rooms where everyone in the family can have a private or separate bedroom.

Moreover, the house style should be duplex in which the upper floor can be accessed from the inside of the ground floor. There should be a lot of wooden work as it looks classy. A big kitchen should be there with a large dining table having at least 8 chairs.

At the entry of the house, there should be a small garden where colorful flowers could be planted. An ideal house should be in a posh locality as there will be more security and the area would be neat and clean.

I would want my ideal home to have a terrace garden or an artificial turf. Some plants on the terrace will surely increase its beauty. I am a sports lover so I would like to have a gymnasium room or a games room where I can spend my leisure time.

At last, I feel that an ideal house is a house that has all the facilities and luxuries of life.

Your favorite sports

Is sports culture popular in your country?
Describe your favorite sport in detail
Do you play this sport?

India is a big nation, and we play most of the sports on international level. I love most of the games and sports as I am a big sports lover. Hockey is a team sport that is native to India but other sports like football are also picking up the craze. I would like to mention that I like cricket the most. Cricket is considered like a religion in our country. Most of the youngsters play this sport in our nation. India has won two 50 over and one T20 world cup titles in the past three decades.

Around the world, cricket is played by more than 30 nations. I have played this sport since my childhood. This is played between two teams having 11 players in each team. There are different formats of cricket, the longest being the test cricket and the shortest is the twenty-20 cricket match. The most prevalent is the 50-over one day match. In cricket, one team bats first and sets a target for the other team to chase. The other team must chase the target in the given 50 overs or as per the format of the game. The team that scores more runs, wins the match.

Cricket is played primarily between 10 nations and some domestic leagues are also popular across the globe. One of them is the IPL (Indian Premier League). This is held every year in April. In this tournament, cricketers from over 12 prominent nations participate every year.

The one-day cricket world cup is mostly held after four years, and the twenty-20 cricket world cup after two years. There is a huge frequency of the number of matches these days as cricketers are the highest paid athletes in our country. I like this sport very much and I have seen numerous live cricket events and contests in my life.

A product of your country

Does your country produce local products?
Speak about a local product
Is it popular in your country or abroad?

India is such a huge country, and we have a lot of products that are produced and grown locally. Be it aromatic spices in the southern part of the country or the colorful saffron in the north part of India.

India is also famous for red chilies that are grown in the west regions but today I would like to talk about the Assam tea which is grown in the eastern part of India. Although tea is also grown in other states like Himachal Pradesh and Uttarakhand, but Assam tea is the finest.

This tea is grown in the state of Assam as it provides the best weather for the growth of tea buds and the landscape is suitable for tea plantation. The workers who work in the tea gardens often experience drowsiness while working in the farms as the tea leaves contains sedative compounds.

Most people of our country consume this tea. There are a lot of varieties that are grown there. Huge industries are set up there to produce enormous amounts of packed tea. A large ratio of production is exported all over the world and sold as premium tea in many countries.

Assam tea is the most aromatic and palatable tea. Most of the tea companies in our country source the premium tea from Assam. The Assam tea is pure, and it is one of the tastiest teas around the globe. Recently I read somewhere that this tea is exported to more than 80 countries across the globe.

Tourists can also take a tour of the tea gardens and can see the production and packing at the local factory. When tourists visit the factory, they are welcomed by great variety of tea.

I have never been to Assam, but I have seen the pictures on the internet. It looks beautiful and serene. The tea gardens look marvelous and lush green farms are a sight to watch. If I ever get a chance, I would like to visit the Assam tea farms.

A big company/organization near you

Are there many big companies in your area?
Speak about the company/organization in detail
Do we learn something by visiting such places?

I live in Mohali which is not famous for big organizations and industries. It is well-known for its greenery, neat and clean roads. Infrastructure is fabulous and the life in Mohali is royal.

There are few medium sized organizations and industries and a couple of big ones as well. Today I would like to talk about Mahindra Swaraj Tractor division that is situated in Mohali. This is a huge industry and has its branches all over the state of Punjab and India.

The one which I am talking about is famous for producing Swaraj tractors for farming. It is one of the most renowned brands in our state. I visited this industry as my uncle works here and one day, he told me to accompany him as he wanted to show his office and factory where he was working.

I was also excited to visit as it was my first visit to such a big organization. We went there in the morning and were greeted by few security men who gave us the pass and allowed us to enter the premises.

As we entered, I saw a big assembly area. On the way to the office, there were a lot of flowerpots that were placed along the walking path in a stylish manner. Then we entered the main complex of the organization. It was a huge compound with a big screen welcoming the visitors.

Then my uncle took me to his office where I was received by his colleagues. I was offered some snacks along with a cup of tea. Then I was taken to the workshop where the farm tractors are manufactured. It was a humungous workshop and numerous tractors were lined one after the other.

After that I went to the testing area where the finished product was tested by the experts. After visiting all the sections of the factory, we came back, and I was feeling so tired. It is such a big organization as it took me around 3 hours to see the whole area.

It's great to visit big organizations as we come to know about the workmanship of such a great company and learn a lot from there.

A businessperson you admire

Who's that person?
What does he/she does?
Why would you like to meet him/her?

OR

A business tycoon you want to meet

I have always dreamt of being a business tycoon in my life. If given a chance I would like to start a business rather than doing a job. There are several big shots in our country, but I am a huge fan of Mr. Ambani.

Mukesh Ambani is one of the biggest businesspersons all over the world. He is the largest shareholder of Reliance group, and his company has also featured in the fortune 500 companies. Once, he reached the pinnacle of the world when he became the world's richest man for a brief period.

Reliance industries deals mostly in refining, petrochemicals and in the gas and oil sectors. Its other subsidiary is the reliance retail which is also the largest retail chain in India.

Mukesh Ambani was born on 19th April 1957 and has three siblings. He did his schooling in Mumbai and completed Chemical Engineering. I admire him to a great extent as he has achieved a lot in his life.

Although he inherited everything from his father Mr. Dhiru Bhai Ambani, but he worked day and night to take his industries to the top.

Currently he lives in Mumbai. His house is Antilia which is probably the biggest and the most luxurious house in our country. Antilia is the world's second most valuable property after the Buckingham Palace of United Kingdom.

He has also bought a cricket team by the name of Mumbai Indians in Indian premier league. He is a sports lover and can generally be seen supporting his team in the crunch matches. He has stretched out in almost every field and continues to grow. Few years back, Mukesh Ambani launched a telecommunication service by the name of Jio. It has spread in every corner of our country like wildfire which provides great services to its customers at reasonable cost. I wish I can become like him one day and rule this world.

A holiday you enjoyed

Are holidays important in life?
Speak about your holiday
Which places and attraction did you see?

Certainly, holidays play an integral role in our life. It gives us a chance to relax and a break from the monotony. I have been to a few places and enjoyed holidays with my family in India and abroad. I would love to speak about a family vacation that I enjoyed with my family members when I passed my tenth class.

We decided to go to Dubai. Dubai is a city in the United Arab Emirates. It is one of the fastest growing cities in the world and has provided a lot of jobs and opportunities to the deserving people from all over the globe.

Dubai is such a wonderful place that you do not want to come back from there. We landed there on 24th of December, a day before Christmas. The atmosphere was amazing throughout the city. The main parts of the city were decorated with the themes of Christmas.

On Christmas day we went to Dubai mall which is the biggest mall in the world, and we spent our whole day there. This was our second day of the vacation.

On the next day we went on a city tour in which we saw the main attractions of the city. We went to see the Burj al Arab, which is a seven-star hotel. We also went to the JBR Beach and enjoyed a lot there. At night we strolled around the downtown area of the city.

The next day we were scheduled for desert safari. We were picked up from our hotel in an expensive SUV car. We were taken to the middle of a desert and did dune bashing. In this activity, the driver of the car drives through the desert dunes and makes the ride adventurous.

At night we went to the Dubai creek cruise. We took the boat which went through the creek, and we enjoyed buffet dinner on it. The next day we planned a visit to Abu Dhabi which is a city in UAE. It took us 2 hours to reach there.

In Abu Dhabi we visited the Ferrari world which is the biggest Ferrari Museum in the world. There are few roller coasters rides that we took and one of them was the world's fastest one.

Next day we came back from Dubai. I have to say that it was a great experience, and I will never forget my visit.

A faraway place you want to visit

OR

An interesting place in your country that tourists do not know about

Are there many interesting places in your country?
Speak about the place in detail
Will you recommend it to others?

I live in India, and everyone knows that it's a huge country. We have a lot of natural marvels that people from around the world come to see. I will not talk about famous places like Goa, Jaipur, or Mumbai but I would like to share an interesting place which most people in my country are not aware of!

I am talking about Andaman and Nicobar Islands. It is an archipelago of over 300 islands famous for its palm lined white sand beaches. This is an Indian Union territory and is in the Bay of Bengal. These islands are famous for diving and snorkeling as there are abundance of coral reefs which supports the marine life.

The area of Andaman is far away from the mainland Indian territory. The islands are located near Thailand on the east coast. Port Blair is the capital but Havelock, and Neil are the more famous islands among the few tourists who manage to go there.

In the bygone years, this island was used as a cellular jail where most of the freedom fighters were imprisoned in the British era. Havelock is the largest island and is famed for parasailing, scuba diving and other sea activities.

The bustling city of Port Blair gives you the local feel and you can also witness few historical sights, architectural monuments. You can reach this place through air. There is an airport in Port Blair that serves as the main airport for people who are travelling to these islands.

This part of our country is least explored by Indians as well as the foreigners. The cuisine here is a must try as it is entirely different from what you get on the mainland India. People generally use a lot of coconut in their dishes and the main course is usually the sea food.

I have never been to these islands, but I have seen a lot of videos and searched on internet regarding this. I would recommend anyone who wants to visit a unique place in India should go to the Andaman and Nicobar Islands.

Describe a piece of art (statue or painting)

Do you like art?
Describe the statue/painting in detail
What does that piece of art symbolize?

Not many people these days love art. But I am the kind of a person who relishes art in every form. I remember when I was at school, I always participated in most art competitions. I loved doing painting and draw sketches in my free time.

The piece of art that I am going to describe today is the statue of Unity which is erected in Gujrat. This statue is of great freedom fighter Sardar Vallabhbhai Patel. He was also the first home minister of independent India. He was hugely respected for his efforts in uniting the 562 princely states to form a single union of India.

The statue of unity is situated in a river delta in front of the Sardar Sarovar dam on river Narmada. The nearest city is Vadodara which is located at about 100 kilometers in the Northwest direction of the statue.

The construction of the statue began in 2013 and was inaugurated by the Honorable Prime minister of India, Narendra Modi in 2018 on the 143rd birth anniversary of Sardar Patel. This is the world's tallest statue that encompasses a height of 182 meters.

This is a humungous piece of art that includes five zones. Three of these zones are open to public in which there is a museum that describes about Patel's contribution towards our country and about his early life.

There is a huge viewing gallery at the height of 153 meters from where people can see a 360-degree view of the nearby places. The lifts are swift and smooth and take up to 26 people at one time.

This statue symbolizes the contributions of Sardar Vallabhbhai Patel towards our country. It also inspires the current generations to learn from the sacrifices and hard work done by the great man.

On the contrary, the government of Gujrat also faced some criticism due to the huge expenditure on the statue, but the matter suppressed with time.

Describe a time when you went to a crowded place

Do you like visiting crowded places?
Why was that place crowded?
Did you face any difficulty there?

I have been to a lot of jam-packed places, although I do not like visiting such places. But you cannot avoid crowded places when you live in a country like India. Today I would like to speak about a sports event that I have seen. I am talking about a Hockey match between India and Australia.

I experienced a huge crowd during the Champion's cup match in 2015 that happened in India. I am a big fan of sports especially hockey. This match was scheduled to be played in the Hockey stadium, Chandigarh.

I booked the tickets for me and two of my friends online at a reasonable price. We bought the VIP tickets that had the best view according to the website. I remember the ticket price was around INR 200 for the normal and INR 500 for the VIP ticket.

The Hockey match lasts 70 minutes with quarters of 15 minutes each divided by short breaks. The match was scheduled to start at 8 PM. So, we decided to reach at the arena at 7 PM to avoid any delays.

But to our surprise, the event was sold out and there were long queues even for the VIP block. We stood in the line for at least 45 minutes before we could enter the stadium. Standing there was not boring as people were chanting for the support of the Indian team.

As soon as we entered the stadium, we were filled with excitement. There were songs that were played on the loudspeaker, and everyone was dancing to its beats. The match began at sharp 8 PM. In the first half Australia were leading 1-0.

The crowd was so tensed and started cheering loudly for the Indian team. The stadium was packed with supporters. In the second half, the momentum shifted towards India, and they scored 2 back-to-back goals.

In the end we won the match by 2-1 margin and the crowd was extremely joyous. There were around 30000 people who came to watch the match. Despite that, it was very well managed, and we never felt rushed or cramped. The arrangements were made superbly to handle the crowd. I had never seen such huge crowd at one place before.

Favourite author

Do you like reading books?
Speak about your favourite author
Describe a work of that author

I like reading books in my leisure time. I would not say that I am a book bug, but I have around ten books at my home, and I pick them randomly when I have free time. I mostly read autobiographies and inspirational books.

A book that left a long-lasting impression on me is the 'Magic of thinking big' written by David J. Schwartz. He was an American motivational coach and writer. He published this book in 1959. Since then, millions of copies of this book have been sold across 150 countries in more than 25 languages.

He has written numerous books but the magic of thinking big was his best-selling book across the globe. I admire him because he was a wonderful coach and a great motivational speaker. The way he has explained different things in his book is amazing.

He has covered all the aspects of life. He constantly motivates his readers to be positive in every situation. In one chapter he has described how we can achieve greatness by repeating positive words and concentrating on good rather than bad.

He constantly tells his readers to concentrate on the things you need rather than the things you want to avoid. He has written this book beautifully with tremendous conviction to the readers. The language used in this book is simple, so I think that it is the perfect book for all age groups.

He led a great life and inspired millions of people through his writing, lectures, and workshops. He used to be an early bird and helped many people change their lives. Many bestselling authors praise his work as well.

I believe that he is one of the best authors of all time. He has changed the lives of many people through his book. I gained a lot of things from his book, and I recommend everyone to read this book at least once in their lifetime.

Something that you bought online

Do you generally buy things online?
Which product did you buy?
Was it worth buying online?

Shopping online is the leading trend these days. There are thousands of e-commerce websites from where people can buy anything from a needle to a car. The most prominent websites are Flipkart, Amazon and Myntra.

I usually buy a lot of things from these online platforms. I see a lot of people complaining about the quality and authenticity of the products online, but I have never experienced any shortcoming from these websites.

Normally I buy clothes, shoes, and electronic gadgets through online shopping. The recent product that I bought was an IPhone. I bought the latest model of the IPhone from Amazon.com. My experience was remarkable while buying this product.

There was a sale on the website for selected customers. I participated in the sale in which I had to answer five questions that were related to general knowledge. I completed the survey and gave all the answers correctly, so I was selected for a special discount on certain products.

I was given a list of products along with their maximum retail price and discount offered on them. Suddenly, my eyes were stuck on the column that read 25 percent discount on the IPhone. I was stunned to see this offer as this product is never on discount in India due to its heavy demand.

I had long imagined of having an IPhone. So, I asked my father about it. He was reluctant at first but later agreed to pay for it. I quickly paid through my father's debit card and thanked him for the wonderful gift.

The delivery took around four days to reach our doorstep. I eagerly opened the package and switched on my brand-new phone. There was a congratulatory letter along with the delivery box on winning the discount. I felt lucky that day and thanked the website through an e-mail for their wonderful gesture.

You were going on a tour and your vehicle broke down

Do you generally go on tours?
How did the vehicle break down?
Did it get repair?

I like travelling a lot with my family and friends. There have not been many instances where our vehicle broke down, but I remember one occasion when our car broke down partially.

Last year, an incident happened when we were going to Shimla with my friends on my father's car. We were four friends in total and one of my friends was driving the car. The highway to Shimla was under construction at that time.

There were some large potholes and diversions on the way to our destination. At one blind curve my friend slowed the car and turned it smoothly, but it bumped into a sharp piece of stone, and we heard a loud bang from the bottom of the car. It was so loud that it sounded like a bomb blast.

We got panicked and immediately got out of the car and inspected the damage. We found that the radiator which is in the front of the car was punctured from bottom and it started leaking. I was afraid and thought that we have incurred a huge loss.

We had no clue about that place and could not locate a workshop there or anyone who could help us in this regard. The nearest town was 10 kilometers away but there was a risk of engine getting seized if we would have driven without the coolant in the radiator.

But one of my friends had good knowledge of automobiles and told that if we keep the coolant level in the radiator up to the mark and drive slowly then there is no harm in driving the car until we find a workshop. So, we carefully drove the car and kept refilling the water in the radiator from time to time and reached the town. There we found a workshop and got the car repaired. I was so relieved as it required a minor repair which only took one hour. After that we happily continued our trip and came back.

A national building in your country

What is the history behind that building?
How the building looks like?
Do a lot of people visit there?

Our country has a rich history and there are numerous monuments and national buildings which are preserved over the years. The building that I am going to talk about today is the Red Fort. It is situated in the capital of India. It used to serve as the main residence of the Mughal dynasty emperors for two centuries.
It is built in the center of the city and houses a bundle of museums. Apart from accommodating the emperors, it was a major political center of the Mughal rule. It was built over a period of 9 years. The exterior of the fort is made of red sandstone hence giving it the name, Red Fort. It is a massive structure with giant walls just like any other Fort.
Its unique architectural design influenced other builders in the states of Punjab, Rajasthan, Delhi, Kashmir and elsewhere. When I went to the Red fort, I felt remarkable. Nowadays, there are several souvenir shops that are built inside the fort.
We also went to one of the museums inside the Fort and learnt about the history of the Red Fort. There is a massive flagpole which supports a gigantic Indian flag which is built at the front side of the Fort.
Every year on 15th August, the prime minister hoists the flag in front of thousands of people gathered for the Independence Day celebration. This program is also telecasted to millions of watching at home and on this day, the prime minister delivers a speech on National harmony and peace.
The fort looks magnificent from outside. There is a lot of security in and out of the Fort and I also saw several CCTV cameras installed in the premises of the Fort. Unfortunately, there was a terrorist attack on the Fort in 2000 that resulted in the death of two soldiers and a civilian.
When I visited the Red Fort, I learned a lot about its history and construction. I must give credit to the government for maintaining the cleanliness and I hope they continue to do the same in future as well.

Favourite weather

What sort of weather is there in your country?
Why do you like this weather?
What do you generally do in this weather?

In my country, there are basically four seasons throughout the year namely, spring, autumn, winter, and summers. All the seasons have their own atmospheric conditions. People like weather as per their comfort and choice.
For me, winter is the best season as it stays for long time with low temperatures. I like cold weather than hot and humid summers. High temperature causes sweating and I do not like it as it causes various skin problems. Summer in our country is very hot and sometimes unbearable.

While cold weather here is just cold but not intolerable. Early mornings and late nights are probably cooler than the rest of the day but that is endurable to the body. Cold weather in our country starts from November and lasts till February while, December and January are the coldest months of the season.

The weather pattern changes every year as per the Himalayas atmospheric conditions. It's very cold only in few parts of the country during this time whereas many cities record pleasant weather. In my city, it is quite cold in the winter season.

I really like this season because one can have variety of hot food, drinks and get cozy in the blankets. One can even go out during the daytime as sunshine appears to be a delight for the body. I love to wear jackets and scarves in this season, so it remains to be my favorite one. I usually visit hill stations in this season to enjoy the falling snow.

The cold weather is very suitable to my skin and makes me extremely glad. Well, I am a great coffee lover so, I love to have a sip of coffee every day in the morning in cold weather.

One thing which makes this weather difficult to bear is when it fogs. There is too much fog and mist in the air during night which causes difficulty in driving and there are many cases of accidents reported every year due to it. Even then, I eagerly wait for this weather to arrive every year.

A tranquil place you enjoy going to

Do you love peaceful places?
Which place do you visit for peace?
How do you feel when you visit this place?

I am a peace-loving person and like visiting peaceful places in my leisure time. One such place is Dagshai which is in Himachal Pradesh. As I am a resident of Chandigarh, places in Himachal are never away. It takes about ninety minutes to reach Dagshai from where I live.

It is a cantonment (Army) area and is nicely preserved by the government. This small town is situated in Solan district. It's extremely easy to reach there as the roads are well maintained. There are many attractions that can allure people.

First, it is famous for Dagshai public school. It is one of the best residential schools in the state. Dagshai is a quiet town with lots of greenery. It is located on the peak of a hill, so the climate remains cooler even in the summers as compared to the plain areas.

Another thing that this place is famous for is the graveyard. There is an old graveyard where solders from World War 1 and 2 are cremated. The graveyard is in the south side of the town and is visited by limited people. Thus, making it a tranquil place.

Apart from this, there is a Dagshai jail that was built in the nineteenth century by the Britishers. That jail is preserved well and is converted into a museum for the visitors to see. That jail has been recreated in the same way it was in the bygone era.

At the corner of the town, there is a football field that is built at the top of another hill. From there one can see great views of the valley. I have met many locals and felt they were humble. I go there at least 8 or 9 times a year, and I find eternal bliss and tranquility.

Sometimes I just go there to relax my mind and to get positive vibes. I always feel peace at body and mind when I go there as there is hardly any traffic or crowd.

A foreign dish you want to eat

Do you try different cuisines?
What is that foreign dish made of?
Would you recommend other people to eat that dish?

I am not a foodie, but I like 0new dishes and cuisines whenever I get chance. I have never visited a foreign country, but I have tried a lot of foreign dishes that are available in my country. I have had a chance to eat most of the famous dishes from around the globe but there's one dish which I have not eaten yet.

The name of the dish is Panini. I came to know about this dish from TV. I was watching a travel program and the host was praising this dish. It is one of the most common dishes in Italy. Many people eat it on daily basis. It's an Italian dish that is primarily made of Italian bread and stuffing. I have not seen any of the restaurants in India that are offering authentic Panini dishes. It's my dream to visit Italy one day and eat a traditional Panini.

Panini in Italian means small bread or bread rolls. It is basically a sandwich that is usually served warm by grilling or toasting. Panini is not sliced sandwich, rather it is filled with some ingredients. The filling can range from meat, beef, chicken, fish, cheese, or vegetables.

I like the cheese Panini. This type of bread is generally filled with different vegetables along with mozzarella and cheddar cheese. After filling the fresh bread with all the stuff, the bread is grilled and warmed to an optimum temperature. Panini can be served with a lot of side dishes. I like potato fries and coleslaw with it. I have seen a couple of restaurants serving Panini, but I feel that it is nowhere near the traditional Panini that is found in Italy. If I am given a chance to eat a foreign dish, then I want to eat the authentic cheese Panini.

A musical instrument you like to play

Do you like music?
Which instrument do you play?
What things must be kept in mind while playing this musical instrument?

Music is one of the most beautiful things in life. It infuses a person with wonderful feeling. People listen to music to calm their nerves. Some even say that music can heal mental issues. I like listening to music in my free time or whenever I am feeling anxious.

I have dreamt of playing a musical instrument fluently since my childhood. I had joined guitar classes last year and for that I bought a guitar. I enrolled in a musical institute nearby my residence for a month's basic course. During that period, I was also busy in my studies so I could not go to the class regularly. However, I learned a few tips to keep in mind while playing the guitar. I learned how to hold it first and how different strings are to be treated differently. There are several aspects that must be taken care while playing this instrument. I learned a couple of chapters and after that I did not go to the classes for a week. At the time of joining, I had bought myself a basic medium-sized guitar.

This type of guitar is best suited to the people who are learning this art for the first time. Although I left the classes midway, but I kept on practicing the basics at my home. I downloaded a couple of video tutorials from a website and started spending some time in learning it.

It is difficult to learn anything on your own, but those lessons were quite helpful and simple due to which I could play the guitar. That practice helped me to learn the basics of guitar. I am not a perfectionist, but I can play a bit of it.

So, whenever I am free or feeling stressed, I just take out my guitar from the bag and play some songs and tunes that sooth my mind. Playing this instrument gives me immense satisfaction and it also rejuvenates my mind.

A historical building you have visited

Do you like visiting historical buildings?
Speak about the historical building in detail
Should we keep historical buildings intact?

I am very fond of visiting historical places. I have seen numerous buildings that hold great significance in our history and culture. I recently visited one building that is in Jaipur, Rajasthan. It is a palace that was built in 1799. The name of this historical building is Hawa Mahal. This name translates to Palace of the Breeze in English. This historical landmark was constructed primarily of red and pink sandstone. This palace is located on the edge of the City Palace.

This palace was built by Maharaja Sawai Partap Singh and was designed by Lal Chand Ustad. It has five stories that resembles a honeycomb. The windows of the palace are decorated by superb artwork. This building is designed in such a way that maximum air passes through it. The passage of air keeps the palace cooler than rest of the buildings and surroundings even in summers.

When you enter the building, you can see fountains in the center of each chamber which further helps in the cooling effect. The entry of the palace is from the side where City palace is located. The huge door of Hawa Mahal opens into a courtyard. There are doubled storied buildings on the three sides of the courtyard. There is an archeological museum in the yard as well. The Hawa Mahal is built on the eastern side of the premises. This place was the favourite resort location for the previous emperors as Jaipur gets extremely hot during summers and this palace could provide the perfect stay for them.

Now this building has been turned into a historical museum that is open for the people to see. The entry ticket to this palace is of nominal cost. Hawa Mahal is one of the most interesting historical buildings that I have seen.

I believe that it is the duty of the local government to maintain and preserve such places of great importance. Keeping these types of buildings intact can provide economic help to the government as well as the locals.

A speech you heard recently

Where did you hear that speech?
What was the speech about and who delivered it?
How did you feel after hearing the speech?

I have heard numerous speeches, talks and lectures since my childhood. Today I would like to tell you about a speech that inspired me to do well in my life. I cannot forget that speech as it still echoes in my mind. This speech was delivered by the honorable Prime minister of India, Narendra Modi. He never uses slips or premade notes in his speeches. So, I feel that the talk comes directly from his heart.

One such speech that left a long-lasting impression on me was the speech that he delivered when he became the Prime minister for the second term in 2019. He was elated by the landslide victory over his opponents, so he could not hide his pleasure in that speech.

He thanked everyone who voted for him and who gave him a chance to serve the nation second time in a row. He spoke about the things that he fulfilled in the first term and talked about the things that he was not able to do. He was extremely confident of the fact that we are in the race to becoming a country with all the facilities and safety. He also guaranteed that he will control inflation in future.

He assured that he will fulfill all the promises of the manifesto and will take our country to new heights by his leadership. He also assured that minorities of this county will feel safe no discrimination against minorities will be tolerated. When he speaks, he connects with the common people. He is from a humble background but has reached the pinnacle of politics. He has a wonderful way of presenting things through his speech. He has also influenced the youth of the country to do well. I was moved by his speech as I heard it live and still remember most of the points, he made in it.

What kind of job you would like to do in future?

Does everyone get his/her dream job?
What should be the characteristics of your preferred job?
Will you be able to get it in future?

Everyone wishes to have a dream job in their lives, some get it, and some don't. I have made a checklist of the things that my dream job would provide. I think that there are number of things that I would want from my job. First, my job should be highly paid because only good paying jobs can give satisfaction of work. I reckon that high pay will also make me feel secure in this expensive era. I would like to earn anything between 4 to 5 million a year.

The second thing that comes to my mind is the timing of the job. Work is only a part of life, so it should be treated like that. Work is not life, there are several other aspects of life that needs to be addressed like family and friends. I believe that I should work anywhere between 6 to 7 hours, not more so that I can have time for other things. I am a travel freak so I would want my job to be related to that. I would love to work in tourism industry where I can get a chance to see the world. I want a job that allows me to grow as a person. Travelling is one activity that makes a person smart and sharp.

Apart from this, I want an appraisal system in which salary would increase every 6 months by at least 15 percent. The increase should depend on the quality of work I deliver. I would like to work in an environment where everyone encourages each other, and the team members respect each other's opinion.

Lastly, I would like to have a decent boss who is encouraging and polite. I will not work to impress him rather work for the company and betterment of the quality of whatever we deliver. So, these are the things that I am looking for myself in a future job. I hope that I get this kind of a dream job one day.

A prize/award you want to win

Have you won any award in your life?
Which award would you want to win?
How can you win that award?

I have dreamt of winning several prizes in my life but there is one that I have long tried but could not win. I would still like to win that prize if I am qualified to take part in it. I am talking about the Cadbury Bournvita Quiz Contest that began in 1972 and was sponsored by Cadbury, India. This show is one of the most famous quiz TV shows in India. This show is witnessed by huge audience across our country. Through this show, one can learn numerous things about the history of our country and about science and technology.

Previously it was conducted live in different cities across the country but later it became a radio show. Eventually in 1992, this show was telecasted on television for the first time on Zee TV channel. In this show, the host asks some questions regarding different fields to a group or team of students one by one. Children with most correct answers are qualified for the next round.

This show was last hosted on colors TV. In this, students from across the country participate in a round robin of quiz contest. Then the winners move to the advanced rounds where they face other winners in knockout rounds. From there the losers are eliminated and the last standing team wins the competition.

The number of members in team are two or three, depending upon the format of the quiz and episode. Most part of the show was hosted by one of the famous personalities in India, Derek O'Brien. To be eligible to take part in this competition, the teams from the quiz show pick most awarded students in reputed schools across India. Children who take part in the show must be able to present themselves clearly in Hindi or English. All the contestants who reach the finals on national level, are presented with an iPad along with some gifts from Cadbury.

This show is amazing as it gives you a platform on national level. I tried hard in my school time but could not get an entry in the show but if I am given a chance, I would try my best to win this prize.

An occasion where you arrived late

Do you generally get late?
Why and when did you get late?
Did you manage to reach at your destination?

Generally, I am punctual and like to be on time for my appointments and meetings with friends and family. But I can remember an occasion when I arrived late and was embarrassed for that.

Last year, I was scheduled to go to Goa for a destination wedding of my cousin. Me and my family members packed our bags in excitement as we received all the tickets of flight and hotel bookings sponsored by my uncle.

There were two functions that were planned, the first one was the engagement and the second one was the main wedding function. We were supposed to reach there on 1st December to attend both the functions on 2nd and 3rd December. Our flight was scheduled in the morning from Delhi airport as I live in Chandigarh and Delhi airport is the nearest one from where we can get a direct flight to Goa.

When we got the boarding pass from the ticket counter, it was announced that the flight will be delayed due to heavy fog and extreme weather. Generally, there is thick fog in the north part of our country during this time.

We were extremely concerned as we were scheduled to reach there on time as all our relatives had already gotten there and we were still at the airport waiting for our flight to take off. The flight got delayed by almost 24 hours as all the flights from Delhi airport were cancelled on that day.

When we reached there, the functions had already begun, and we were feeling guilty about it. My uncle was upset from us for reaching late but we explained him the whole story. He was supportive and told us to not to bother about that and advised us to enjoy the rest of the functions.

Speak about a time when you participated in a competition

Did you normally participate in school competitions?
What was the competition about?
What happened at the competition?

I was not great at co-curricular activities in my school time, but I always participated in cricket and activities associated to it. I remember once in my tenth class I got a chance to participate in a cricket competition.

This tournament was on national level that was conducted for tenth class school students. Schools from all over India partook in that tournament. There were around 100 schools that participated in that competition.

I remember that how I was selected for this elite competition. Best cricket players from schools were told to assemble in the school ground. There we went under trials in which we were given a chance to show our skills with the bat and ball.

I was selected along with 16 other players for the squad. After a few days of practice at school, we left for Delhi to play the tournament. There we were provided with kits and other amenities. We stayed at a decent hotel that was sponsored by the organizers.

This was a knockout tournament in which a team would be eliminated as soon as it loses. We had to play five matches before we could reach the finals. We won all the matches and the mood in our camp was exuberant. The final was to be played on Sunday. Due to this, there was a huge local crowd that came there to cheer us and to witness that game.

The number of overs for each side was 15 in the initial stages but it was increased to 20 for the finals. However, that day, there were a bit of clouds, and the field was also wet due to early morning showers. So, the match started late, and it was reduced to 10 overs each side.

It was not a great day as we lost the finals, but we were still contended that we won the runners-up trophy from over 100 schools. When we came back to the school next day, we were awarded some cash and all the students welcomed us with a lot of warmth and respect.

An animal you like most

Which animal do you like?
Why do you like this animal?
Is there any importance of this animal in your society?

I am a huge animal lover. I like all animals and I frequently visit zoos to see different kinds of animals and observe their behavior.

I am fascinated by zebra because of its striking looks. I also like camels due to their distinctive body structure but my favourite one is cow. Instinctively, cows are not aggressive. It is a friendly animal and seldom attacks humans. There are different varieties, sizes, and colors of cows in India.

Cow is given the designation of a mother in our society. It is considered as a sacred animal in some religions as well. Many people in my country worship cow. People feed special food items to cows on some occasions and festivals. The reason it is given the designation of a mother is that it gives us milk. Its milk is digestive and is full of calcium and essential nutrients. There is a yellow tinge in the color of the cow's milk.

Most farmers in our country keep cows for milk and other purposes. Cow's dung is another useful product that is used as a fuel. People burn traditional clay style ovens by using cow dung. You will be surprised to know that after cow's death, it is left for the hungry birds to be eaten up and decay. After that the skeleton is bought by pharmaceutical industries as they use it to make some medicines.

There are many cow shelters around our country where cows are taken care of, and they are fed properly. Present government has taken a lot of initiatives to protect cows as cow killing in our county is illegal.

Some people also drink cow urine as they believe it cures a lot of diseases and keeps a person fit. Cow is a versatile and loving animal, so I like it very much.

A bird you like

Have you seen that bird?
What are the characteristics of that bird?
Why is it your favourite bird?

I am a nature lover and love to go out in the woods and witness natural flora and fauna. I see so many different species of animals and birds there. I like birds for their ability to fly. I always wanted to be like birds as I desire to fly like them.

I like pigeon the most. They are firm-bodied birds with dwarf neck. Their main source of food is seeds, fruits, and plants. Pigeons and doves come from the family. They are the most common birds in the world. They are found in all the continents and possibly in all the countries around the world. It is quite common to find pigeons in the region where I live. I love to feed them as many pigeons gather at our balcony in the daytime.

Dove is generally referred to pigeon that is white or nearly white. In scientific world, dove is used for the smaller species and pigeon for the larger ones. Pigeon is a French word and dove is a Germanic word. Pigeons build relatively fragile nests, often using twigs and other wreckage.

Unlike other birds, both sexes of pigeons produce milk that is fed to the young ones. They have short legs, small heads on large and firm body. The wings are large and has eleven main feathers. The muscle of the wings is also strong that comprises of 35 to 45 percent of their total body weight. Body feathers are very dense and with large wings they can maneuver themselves easily in the flight. They can launch quickly and can escape from predators. Pigeons have a knack of remembering the paths of flight.

For this reason, they were used by the Australian, French, German, American and UK forces at the time of World War 1 and 2 to deliver sensitive messages and vital plans to Allied forces on the borders of Germany.

All the information that I have told you has been learned by me from a book that I read about the pigeons. I bought that book because I love pigeons so much.

A language you would like to learn (apart from English)

Which language do you like?
Why do you like this language?
Have you learned this language?

Language is a way to communicate our feelings with others through words, certain noises and pauses. There are thousands of languages that are spoken across the globe. Some are prominent like Chinese, French and Portuguese. Others are spoken by old tribes or by a handful of people and are not known to public.

If given a chance or if I have enough time, then I am prepared to learn Spanish. I am inclined towards that language since I saw one of the most prominent sitcoms, Narcos. This series was about the drug menace in Columbia and this sequence was made in Spanish with English subtitles. I watched the first episode and after that I could not stop myself. After I completed watching the series, I was so allured by that language that I promised myself to learn this language fluently.

That day, I logged into my you tube account and downloaded a couple of Spanish lessons by Spanish trainers with English explanations. I learned it for three or four days but could not study further because of my daily routine and busy schedule. Although I learned some common phrases and some greeting words. For example, Hola is hello and adios is bye. I also learnt that gracias is thank you. I am still in a mood to learn this language as it really excites me. The tone and words allure me instantly. I regularly watch movies made in Spanish and some Spanish sitcoms as well to learn the language.

I have also downloaded a mobile application by the name of duo lingo which helps to learn any language on the go, without any books or notes. So, whenever I get a chance, I would like to learn Spanish from an expert.

Exercises people do in your locality

What exercises people do in your locality?
Do all age groups do exercise?
Is exercise important in life?

Exercise is an essential part of our life. People do exercise to keep themselves fit. There are various exercises that people do according to their choice and age. I have seen a lot of people of all age groups do exercise in my area. I have seen people running, jogging, cycling and walking in my locality.

I usually get up early and like to go out for a short walk. I always see people do different exercises in the morning. The most common is yoga. I live in a society that has a big park and it is well utilized by the people of my area. Every day in the morning, generally people of middle and older age gather in one corner of the park and do yoga. Yoga is one of the most common types of early morning activity that people of my country do.

I also see many people running and jogging. I think this is the best exercise to keep yourself fit. There is a running track in the park which people use for running. I see people wearing sports shoes and fitness watch when they do exercise. People also like to do cycling as a part of their exercise. Myriad people burn their calories through cycling. This type of activity is generally preferred by the youngsters.

On the other hand, some old people do only walk and light exercises. They also participate in laughing exercise. In this, a group of people gather, and they laugh out loud for around 10 minutes. It is believed that this activity increases the flow of blood through the body. I think exercise should be a mandatory part of a person's life and I also reckon that people have become more aware about their health these days, that is why they do exercise.

Anything you would like to buy from foreign country

What product you want to buy?
Why you want to buy it?
How will you buy it?

I am the kind of a person who likes to shop a lot. I like to buy unique things that gives me satisfaction. If I am given a chance to buy something from a foreign country, then it would be white coffee from Malaysia. The first time when I tasted this coffee was last year when one of my aunts brought it from Malaysia. I fell in love with this coffee when I drank it for the first time. It was so delicious that I instantly asked for more of it. She said that all her coffee was now finished, and this was the last sachet that she had given me. I was so disappointed and asked whether she can arrange more in the future. She assured me that she would try her best. My aunt's sister lives in Malaysia, so she called her to ask about that coffee. Her sister told her that she would send it next week through courier. Fortunately, she kept her promise, and I received that coffee in a couple of weeks. I am addicted to this coffee, and I drink it every day. The coffee brand is OLD TOWN, and the type is white coffee. The price is also not that high, but the thing is that it is only available in Malaysia and a couple of other countries. If I go to Malaysia one day, then I will bring tons of this coffee with me. This coffee is so simple to make. You just need to boil water and empty the sachet into it. The premixed powder contains coffee, sugar, and powdered milk. Just stir it well and enjoy your coffee. If I have to buy something from a foreign country, then it would definitely be white coffee from Malaysia. I will either go there and buy it or I will ask my aunt to send it to me through a courier.

A season you like the most

Are there many seasons in your country?
Which season do you like?
Why do you like this season?

I live in the northern part of India, and I am lucky to experience most kinds of seasons that the Earth has to offer. Winter, summer, autumn, spring, and monsoon. I enjoy all the seasons, but the most favorites ones are when the main seasons are in transition. I like autumn the most. India is geographically located in the Northern hemisphere, so this season starts in September and ends in December. The reason I like this time of the year is that it is neither too cold nor hot. It is a part of temperate season.

This season is also known as fall in some parts of the world. Autumn marks the progression from summers to winter. At this time, the length of day starts to decrease, and the temperature starts to fall as compared to the summer season. I feel extremely happy in the autumn season as summers can be scorching while the winters restricts some outdoor activities. In summers, people generally do not roam in the day as its too hot. But in the autumn season, there is no such problem. Another advantage of autumn season is that there is reduced amount of energy utilized for heating and air conditioning.

I prefer spending more time outdoors in this season as there is perfect amount of sunlight along with moderate temperature. I can also have my favourite cold drinks as the weather is not too cold. This is the best time to do exercise in the morning as well as in the evening as there is always some cool breeze.

The day temperature is not that cold but it's not as hot as summers. On the other hand, nights are cooler with a bit of gust. I do not like hot weather or freezing winters. So, if I am asked about a wish to be fulfilled, then I would like to have autumn weather all year round.

A time when someone helped you

Why did you need the help?
Who helped you?
How he/she helped you?

There have been many situations in my life when I was helped by other people. One such instance happened in my life when I passed 12th class. I did my senior secondary in medical / non-medical / commerce .... After I gave the final exams of 12th class I was waiting for the results. I expected to score around 80 percent aggregate in that. After the result was declared, I got 77 percent and I was a bit disappointed as I predicted a better score.

After I got my result, I was in a dilemma weather to choose a degree program or to go for a more practical kind of a course. I believe that passing the secondary and choosing the right course after that is one of the most important tasks in one's career. I was so bamboozled that I could not make my mind whether to go for Indian college or to study in a foreign university.

If you go for the wrong course or the college, it can have a detrimental effect on your future. I believe it is good to take some advice from a senior teacher, friend or a relative to get information regarding suitable course. I did not go to any educational counsellor or free-lance advisor. I told my plight to my cousin and sought out advice on my career options. I went to my cousin for advice because she is extremely successful in her field. So, I thought that she would be the person to guide on my forthcoming development.

She told me the benefits of studying in a foreign university or college. She cited the reason that Canadian education is better than most countries in the world. She also emphasized the fact that I will get more exposure while living in a foreign environment. She said that studying in an international environment would get the best out of me.

After the meeting, I was so determined that I went to an educational consultant to decide the course and college for Canada. They suggested me to take the IELTS exam and score 6.5 Band score overall. I feel that she helped me in a great way as I was not able to decide about my future and I was also getting frustrated day by day. She came to my rescue and steered me towards a goal.

So, this was the time when I was helped by someone, and I will always be grateful to her for this help.

A quality that you appreciate about your friend

Speak about your friend
Which quality of his/her makes you appreciate?
Speak about an instance when he showed his/her quality

I do not have a lot of friends but there are a few whom I love very much. I would like to speak about a friend who has tremendous qualities. His name is Amit, and he lives in the United Kingdom these days.

I remember when we became friends in our school time. We were studying together since childhood but became good friends in the 10th standard. We used to sit on the same bench, and we shared a lot of things in common.

If I talk about his qualities, then I would have to write a big essay on that. The quality that I admired in him the most is his patience. He is an extremely patient guy and remains calm even in difficult situations. He is never too excited about anything, nor he is nervous in disturbing circumstances.

He is a great friend and keeps his composure in every aspect of life. I will give you an example of his patience. Once our school bus was struck in a traffic jam and everyone was getting annoyed with that. We were having an exam on that day, and everyone was praying anxiously for the jam to get cleared.

On the other hand, Amit was as cool as ice and was studying a book rather than worrying like others. I asked him that why he is not getting annoyed. He replied that I never worry about the things that are beyond my control.

I was taken aback by his level of patience and learned something interesting from him that day. From that day onwards I try to inculcate this quality in me as I feel that a calm person can win in every situation. We all were worried that day, but my dear friend utilized that time to study. He converted that worry time into study time.

So, this is the quality that my friend possesses, and I feel that this makes him stand out from others. I always appreciate this quality of him.

Describe a time when you complained about something

Do you complain about poor services often?
Why did you complain about that?
Was your complaint resolved?

I am the kind of a person who does not complain much until the water goes over the nose. There have been some occasions when I complained about certain things in my life. The one which I remember vividly happened recently.

I went to a restaurant and was highly unsatisfied. Last month, me and my family members went to a restaurant on a Sunday. The restaurant is nearby and the quality of food they serve is generally good. This is one of the most renowned restaurants in the city. It is a buffet style restaurant with a wide variety of options in cuisines.

That day was a holiday, and the restaurant was packed with people. The moment we reached there, the staff was bamboozled and took a long time to even prepare our tables. The preparation was so wicked that they did not even provide all the cutlery on the table.

Then the snacks were served in a haste. All the snacks were cold, and the taste was not up to the mark. After the snacks were over, we went on to take the main course. There were no plates on the station. I was so frustrated with this and called a waiter and complained about the situation.

He replied in a rude manner, so I decided to complain to the manager of the restaurant. The manager was kind enough to note my complaint and give me assurance that this kind of situation will not arise in the future.

He also waived off the food bill as we were not served with all the food items in the main course and the snacks as well. So, this was the time when I complained about something, and I felt that my grievance was taken seriously and worked upon immediately.

Remote place you wish to visit in the future

Do you like remote places?
Speak about the surroundings of that place
Have you been to that place?

There are many places that I want to visit in my lifetime. I love travelling to new destinations, and I always prefer to travel to faraway places with a lot of peace and silence.

A remote place that I would like to visit is Chail. It is in Himachal Pradesh and is one of the greener and cleanest places in that state. I have heard from many people that Chail is very remote, and the town is in the middle of a wildlife sanctuary.

I have searched on the internet about the things to see in Chail. There is a King's palace which is now an expensive hotel and a site for the visitors. It was home to Maharaja of Patiala in the past. The entry fee to the palace is only 100 rupees per person. The palace is made in Imperial style with a huge lawn in front of it.

The main city of Chail does not have all the amenities but is one of the most peaceful places. Not a lot of tourists go there even in the peak season. I guess everyone these days like hustle and bustle. But I am not one of them, I like tranquil places like Chail.

Chail is located at a height of about 2300 meters which is good enough to keep the weather cool even in the harshest of summers. It is away from the chaos of big cities. One can hardly hear any horns blown or vehicular noise.

There is no pollution at that place. I have been to Chail once in my life and I plan to visit in future as well. When I went there for the first time, I hiked the mountains and felt very close to the nature. I recommend everyone to visit this place at least once in life.

Describe a shop that recently opened in your locality/city

Are there many shops in your locality?
Speak about the shop
How has that shop helped you?

I live in Chandigarh, and I see a lot of shops that are opening nowadays. There are many local markets near the place where I live. Mostly there are grocery shops and some for clothes, electronic gadgets, etc.

Lately, a new shop was inaugurated in the main area of the city. The shop's name is Weekend Mart. It is a grocery shop that has stores all over the country. It is one of the renowned grocery stores across India. This shop is a great place for daily needs shopping.

This store is located at an arms distance from my house, and I came to know about its existence from a leaflet. It was a flashy page giving details about the shop opening and discount offers that will be available on certain products.

The opening date was 1st January 2022. I told my mother about this, and we decided to go there in the evening. When we reached there, I saw huge number of people in that store as if the grocery store was distributing free food, but this was not the case.

There were huge discounts on most of the items. So, we bought many things that day. It took us around two hours to collect the items and one hour for the billing itself. That day we got massive concessions on the items that are otherwise expensive.

The store was very well organized, and one could witness the great variety that they had. The store size is huge, and the staff is amicable.

This store has been a revelation as we can now buy groceries at competitive price with a wide variety of choice. From the past few months, this store has become the landmark of that area.

Describe an invention that has changed the life of people

Speak about that invention
What are the uses of that invention?
Has that invention changed people's life?

There are numerous inventions that has changed people's life in a positive way. Discoveries such as mobiles and computers have changed the way people live. I reckon that mobile phone is the biggest invention by mankind in the recent past.

Mobile phones have brought a revolution in the whole world. Mobile phones of this generation can do multiple tasks at one time. Smart phones have taken over a lot of other gadgets.

People used to carry a camera with them on the excursions but with the advent of mobile phones, there is no need to carry an extra device. Smart phones can click wonderful pictures with great clarity or even equivalent to the professional cameras in some cases.

One can also tune into radio with the help of mobiles. A mobile of this era can be used as a recorder. One can send or receive emails, or you can also download a song from the internet. Mobiles can also be used as a hot spot to run internet on other devices.

Certain mobile phones can also be used as universal remotes for a lot of other electronic devices. People also use it to play games. There is no need to have a separate music system when you have a mobile phone. A mobile phone can store thousands of songs and hundreds of movies.

People can also watch movies and any sort of videos on mobile phones. There are certain applications that help people to run live channels and live stream videos on mobile phones. I think that mobiles have taken over a lot of other things and in future there will be more functions in it that are still unimaginable.

There are unlimited purposes of mobile phone that makes it a unique device. I believed that mobiles have changed the world in a better way.

Describe a nation (not your own) that you know well

Give details about that nation
How that nation is different than yours?
Have you visited there?

I like to surf the internet a lot and I usually search different cities and places around the world. I have a knack of learning about the places that I would like to visit in my future.

One such country is Malaysia. I love this country very much. I have searched about the culture of that place, and I find it really alluring. It is a country in the south-eastern side of the globe. It borders Singapore and Thailand.

People of that country speaks Malay which is their mother tongue. They also speak good English as it is a compulsory subject in their primary and secondary education. The capital of Malaysia is Kuala Lumpur. It is a metropolitan city with different cultures and people from all over the globe living there together.

Kuala Lumpur is also known by the name KL. People of Malaysia are humble and amicable. One of my relatives is also living in KL. I have heard a lot of things from them. Kuala Lumpur is known for Petronas's twin towers which are the tallest twin towers in the world.

There are other cities that are famous for its culture and heritage. George Town and Melaka are well-known for its preserved heritage and culture. Both cities are declared as the UNESCO world heritage sites.

Malaysia has many towns that are in the highlands and many others that are on the seashore. Rice is the staple food in Malaysia and Nasi Lemak is the most common meal there. Nasi Lemak is basically rice cooked in coconut milk with spicy curry.

Malaysia is also famous for its rubber production. The quality of Malaysian rubber is the finest. Malaysia also deals in timber trade around the world. Malaysian wood is one of the best in the world and is found in abundance in the southern part of the country. Other famous product of this country is Batik silk. Moreover, some parts are famous for its tea and coffee plantation.

It is not much different from my country, but the size and population of Malaysia is quite small as compared to India. In India you have long queues wherever you go but this is generally not the case in Malaysia.

I have read a lot about Malaysia and if I am given a chance, I would like to visit it as soon as possible.

Describe an outdoor activity that you did for the first time

Do you like participating in outdoor activities?
Explain the activity
How did you feel after doing that activity?

I am the kind of a person who loves staying outdoors. I do not really like indoor activities much. Whenever I am holidaying or having a day off, I love to go outdoors and perform activities.

An activity that was outdoor and I did it for the first time was snorkeling. It is an activity in which one goes to a shallow water body, mostly a sea or a lagoon to explore the marine life.

I did this activity in Andaman and Nicobar Islands. I went there with my family members. We stayed in the capital city of port Blair. From there we went to Havelock Island. This island is surrounded by the Bay of Bengal and the Indian ocean. There are many beaches around this island.

We came to know about this activity from one of our guides. He told us that Havelock islands is famous for Snorkeling and Scuba diving. I opted for snorkeling as I am afraid of deep water and in scuba you go deep into the water using oxygen cylinders and a lot of other equipment.

In snorkeling you just need to put a face mask having a pipe on it for breathing through mouth. All my family members got ready to do this activity. I was excited for that, but I was a bit nervous as well. You can also do this activity even if you do not know swimming. This activity is done in the presence of experts and safety jackets are also provided during snorkeling.

This activity lasted for one full hour. We saw coral reefs around the island and a lot of other marine species that I could never imagine seeing in my life. We covered a lot of area while snorkeling. The sea water was crystal clear which allowed us to see many things underneath. The total experience was unique and exciting.

I was so glad after doing that activity as it gave me a lot of relief and mental satisfaction.

A time you had to search for information

Do you often search for information on internet?
For what purpose you had to search for the information?
Was the information helpful?

I like to search for any kind of information from the internet. I think internet has been a revolution in the past few years and has enable people to learn about anything in this world. whenever I get some free time, I like to browse for information.

Last time when I had to turn up to internet for info was previous month. I had to plan a holiday destination for me and my family. I know about certain places in our country that are amazing, but I wanted to go to a new place this time.

I had been to Goa and Jaipur before, and I did not want to repeat those locations for holidays. I started searching for some new destinations that are untouched and remote. So, I just opened my laptop and clicked on to the google browser. I typed tourist destinations in India. It showed a list of the prominent and common places, but I wanted something different. Thus, I added uncommon places to my search.

I got a list of so many places that I had never even heard of before. I was shocked to see some places that were totally unexplored. I browsed all the destinations in detail and chose five of them. I showed those places to my family members, and we chose one unanimously.

The location was Palampur. It is situated in the northern part of our county in the state of Himachal Pradesh. It is a quiet place with a lot of greenery. Palampur is known for its world-famous tea plantation. I also came to know from the internet that it one of the wettest areas in our country. It receives highest amount of rainfall throughout the state of Himachal Pradesh.

It is a quiet place away from the hustle and bustle of city which makes it a great place to relax. I read a lot of articles about Palampur and came to know that this place is one of the greenest and cleanest places in our country. I also inquired about the temperatures throughout the year in Palampur from the internet. In extreme summers, the temperature does not go beyond 30 degrees, which is extremely pleasant.

I also came to know from the internet that there is a huge tea producing factory that lies in the middle of the town. There, one can find huge variety of tea and can also buy it at a reasonable price.

After getting so much information about this place on the internet, I quickly booked the rooms in a hotel for four people and stayed there for 3 days. It was a great visit and the information that I searched on the internet helped me a lot.

Describe a building in your city

Where is this building located?
Describe different sections of that building?
Is it different from other buildings in your city?

OR

Describe a structure in your city

I live in Chandigarh which is in the northern part of the country. It is one of the greenest cities across India. More than 9 percent of the city area is covered in forest. Not only this, but Chandigarh is also a fast-developing city in our country with growing infrastructure and ever-increasing modern facilities.

The building that I want to talk about is the Secretariat building which is in sector 1. It was designed by the famous French architect Le Corbusier. It is a government premises that includes three buildings and three monuments.

The buildings are secretariat building, Legislative assembly building and the High court building. The monuments are open hand monument, geometric hill, and the tower of shadows. This is a huge complex and probably the biggest in city. It was built in 1953. In July 2016, this building was inscribed as UNESCO world heritage site.

This complex has the courts, offices and assemblies of both Punjab and Haryana. This building is well maintained and has unending sections. I remember visiting this building with my uncle. One of his friends was working there and he invited us to see the building on my request.

When we entered the building, just outside the entrance there were hundreds of security personnel and policemen who were patrolling the area. We were checked with metal detectors and other equipment for any objectionable material with us. The high security is there because a lot of ministers and VIPs are always present there.

There is a huge canteen in the middle of the complex and there are more than twelve floors that are packed with different departments and offices. My uncle's friend works in the courts, and he took us for a small tour. I was so impressed with the security and the system that government has maintained there.

The structure of that building from outside is huge. This building looks majestic and retro. It is unique in architecture as I have never seen a similar sort of building in my city or elsewhere. The colour of the building from outside is light tan. I felt so tired after finishing the tour of the building. It was a tremendous visit and I feel that Secretariat is one of the most iconic buildings in my city.

An advertisement you watched on TV recently

Do you like advertisements?
What the advertisement was about?
Were you influenced by the advertisement?

I am not a big fan of watching advertisements as it annoys me very much. Whenever I am watching TV and suddenly an advertisement pop's up, I just switch off the TV or mute the channel. But sometimes willingly or unwillingly we see certain things that can attract us.

One such advertisement came across me while watching a cricket match. The advertisement was regarding a mobile application that you can install on your phone to earn money while viewing cricket matches. The advertisement is performed by popular cricketer MS Dhoni.

He is the former captain of the Indian cricket team and in this advert, he tells people to use their knowledge of cricket and apply in the mobile application to earn money. In this advert, he explains how one can simply download the application and start playing a simple game to earn money. The name of the application is Dream 11.

In this application, a person must pick 11 players from two teams playing against each other. This can be played among two or even more friends. The winning amount can be set by the players of the game, and it is easy to play.

This advertisement is attractive as it uses mesmerizing background music with attractive themes. The designer of the advertisement should get a lot of credit as they have created such a wonderful advert. People who are acting in this advert are also famous personalities from different backgrounds. There are many versions of this advertisement.

This advert is quite frequent on every channel, and one cannot ignore it easily. The moment there is a break from any show, this advert pop's up from nowhere. This advert had a great influence on me, and I could not stop myself from downloading the application and start playing the game.

I think the company should lower down the frequency of their advertisement as people can sometimes get bored and irritated by it. But I still feel that this is one of the best advertisements that I have seen in a long time.

Describe a thing that has become a fashion or a matter of status nowadays

Why do people like to show their status?
Which thing do you believe is now becoming a matter of status?
Is it a positive or a negative trend?

People take pride in certain things, and I believe that it changes with time. In 13th century, clothes were a symbol of status and over the centuries, this has changed. People like to show their status because they earn huge amounts of money, and they want people to know about that from the expensive possessions they own.

There are numerous things that people of today's era like to own as a status symbol. Some of them are cars, sports bikes, watches, expensive mobile phones and so on. However, I reckon that keeping a dog as a pet has certainly become a status symbol these days.

I see myriad people keeping dogs as pets unnecessarily. Some breeds of dogs are so expensive that the same amount could buy you a decent car. Those rare species need special care and attention from the master. Not only this, but they also require substantial diets and regulated temperatures.

I would like to share an example with you, my friend bought a foreign breed of dog. The dog eats extensively and needs a cooler temperature than 20 degrees. We live in a country where most part of the year is more than 30 degrees. So, there is no point of keeping a dog that is not suited to our environment. It is just like keeping a showpiece at home that is of no use.

This trend is very dangerous as there can be some negative effects on the animals. They become lethargic and their mental state can get disturbed when they are not exposed to the outer environment. Moreover, it can lead to serious illness to the dog and may lead to fatal end.

I am totally against keeping dogs as a status symbol. As their job is not intended to just live in an air-conditioned room and eating loads of stuff. Instead, they are one of the friendliest species who like to spend time with the owner, and they are meant to be loyal and vigil.

So, keeping expensive pets has these days become a trend or even status symbol in some cases.

Describe certain laws of your country

What are the laws?
Which law do you like?
Are the laws strict in your country?

Laws are the rules and regulations made by the government of any country and it is the duty of its citizens to follow them. There are many laws that are fabricated in my society for the betterment of people. I would like to share some of those laws with you.

The law I like the most is the child labor law. This law suggests that no one can employ a child in a paid work who is under the age of fourteen years. I like this law as I feel that every child has the right to study and play in free time. By this law, parents of children cannot force them to do paid work under the age of fourteen. This is a tender age and children cannot be doing work at this stage. It is a time of life where children must enjoy and study.

The second law that I like in my country is the ban of smoking at public places. I have always felt that people get too annoyed by the smoke from the cigarettes. It is extremely harmful if children inhale this smoke. In this law, if a person is found smoking in a public area, then there can be imprisonment or a fine of 5000 rupees on the spot. Another law that I admire is the law of drink and drive. There is a huge fine for driving under the influence of alcohol in my country. I regularly see the barricades and policemen patrolling the signals and stopping random cars to check whether the driver is drunk or not. If found guilty, there is an on-the-spot fine of 2000 rupees.

Apart from the laws, there are several rights that are written in the constitution of our county which allows every citizen of India to practice whatever they want. There are six fundamental rights in total. The rights are as follows, right to equality, right to freedom, right to religion, culture, and education, and right to constitutional remedies.

Overall, the laws in my country are not that strict as the constitution of our country gives us rights and freedom to choose and do whatever we want.

An intelligent person you know

How do you know that person?
How has that person an influence on you?
Speak about the abilities of that person

I have come across many people in my life who are full of qualities and unique talent. I would like to talk about one of the most intelligent individuals that I have come across in my life till now. Arti is someone whom I admire from my school days. She is one of my best friends and we studied at the same school.

She was not in my class as she was 7 years older than me. She lives near my house, and we share a great mutual understanding and relation. She has sharp features and fair color. She is tall and can be easily recognized in the crowd.

She is a bit introvert, but she gets along well with anyone she knows. I remember that how she used to teach me in my younger days when I struggled in mathematics. As she was my neighbor, we were aware about her intelligence. One day my mother gave her the responsibility of teaching me at her residence. She agreed, and I found her to be one of my best teachers as well. In her school time, she used to top all the classes and was very well known at the school. She never bothered about her fame and continued to study hard.

She scored highest percentage in the matric exams in our city and was awarded with a prize money from the mayor. She prepared hard in the university exams and now she has passed her masters from IIT, which is one of the best institutions in our country.

After that she applied for a job in google and she got it. I have never seen such an intelligent person in my life. She never flaunted her intelligence and helped the weaker ones when required. She solves all the issues in a blink of an eye, whether it is work related or a personal one.

Describe a hotel you stayed at

Where is that hotel located and how did you come to know about that?
Describe the amenities at the hotel
Will you stay there again?

I have stayed in few hotels in my life but there is one that I will never forget. The name of the hotel is Taj Palace. It is situated in Dubai. It is a 5-star hotel, and my father took our family to a long-awaited vacation last year. We booked the hotel online after extensive research by me and my father on the internet. After short listing three hotels, we finally booked Taj Palace. Its price was in our range, and it is a 5-star property located in Deira, Dubai. When we arrived at the hotel at about 6 in the evening, we all were awestruck by its façade and decoration. As soon as we entered the reception, we were welcomed by the hotel staff and were served a traditional complimentary drink.

We were then asked for our passports for identification and soon we were handed over the key to our room. We had booked a suite for four persons. Our suite was loaded with all the modern amenities and the rooms were attached to a common lobby and a kitchenette.

We were surprised by the looks of our room. It was like a palace. There was a king-sized bed in one room and other room had two single beds. The lobby was quite big and had a couple of sofas in it. The kitchen was huge and was equipped with a refrigerator and other useful utensils.

There was free wi-fi in the room. We also discovered that on the 15th floor, there was a swimming pool along with a jacuzzi and gym. The hotel lobby was humungous with great amount of sitting capacity. The next morning, we took buffet breakfast at the hotel's restaurant. The breakfast spread was amazing and had variety of cuisines as expected from a five-star hotel. There were some Indian dishes that brought smiles on our faces. Our stay at Taj Palace hotel was memorable and I enjoyed every bit of it. I recommend anyone visiting Dubai to stay in this hotel for an unforgettable experience.

Describe a pet that you have or once had

How and why did you get that pet?
Describe the pet
How did you play with your pet?

I am a pet lover, and I had a beautiful pet last year. But I had to donate the pet in a kennel as I could not give it much time due to my studies and none of my family members had time to look after it. So, I thought that it was a good decision for my pet.

I had a great relation with my pet, and I kept his name Brownie. The reason I gave him this name was that his color is dark brown like a chocolate brownie. I miss it very much and I still meet Brownie in the kennel whenever I get time.

I wanted to get a dog as I used to be alone and had a lot of free time with me. We also used to live in an isolated area so having a dog is always useful.

Brownie was only a month old when we took him to our house. The breed is male Labrador. He was only a little dog and would roam in the house without any restrictions. He would get really scared when any stranger came to our house, but this changed when he grew up.

The first thing I used to do when I wake up in the morning was to feed him with his favorite biscuits. He loved them so much that he used to dance and run around me while eating it. Then I would get ready for my school and take him to a short outing.

When I would return from school, he would always greet me with warmth. He would jump onto me and lick my face in excitement. I used to feed him with his favourite dog food every time he learned something new.

Then the best time was in the evening when I would always take him to a nearby park and every day, we played with a ball. I used to throw the ball and he would bring it back to me. But when I was growing up, I could not give him much time. So, my parents decided to send him to a kennel. I can never forget the day when he was 5 years old, and we had to bade him goodbye.

I was so emotional, and I could get same vibes from him. This is the love that one gets from a pet. That day was one of the most depressing days of my life. I feel that everyone should keep a pet at least once in his or her lifetime.

A part of your rituals or customs that you do not like

Do people in your country follow customs and rituals?
Describe the ritual or custom
Why do you dislike this ritual or custom?

India is a land of religions, customs, and traditional rituals. There are so many different cultures that co-exist in our society. Every culture has its own rituals and traditions. Some of them are interesting and some are unacceptable, but people still follow them blindly.

Personally, I am not in the favour of following any rituals or customs as I believe they are a waste of time and energy. The world has evolved, and we do not really have time for this nowadays.

A ritual that I hate is Dowry. It is a valuable security, money, gifts such as furniture or a vehicle given by the bride's parents to the groom on the day of wedding or before that. Giving or taking dowry these days is an offence according to the Indian laws.

Dowry is such an evil that it has taken lives of many girls in the past due to the lust and pressure imposed on bride by the groom's side, but people are continuing this tradition which is beyond my weirdest of imaginations.

I think government should actively make some rules and regulations to control this ritual otherwise the situation can go out of hand. I reckon this ritual should be banned completely and should not be taken forward to our next generations.

Even the educated breed of people is following this culture and giving gifts to the groom in shape of expensive cars, property, and other things. This practice influences next generation in a negative manner. Some people have realized this over time and have stopped this ritual with mutual understanding between groom's and bride's family. I think this is a good step, and everyone should follow it. Lastly, I ponder we should all come forward and neglect this evil act.

Any souvenir that you bought during your holidays

Do you like buying souvenirs?
From where did you buy that souvenir?
How does it look like?

I like to collect souvenirs for the decoration of my house. I have bought numerous decorative items from tourist places. An item that I bought during my holidays is a replica of the building Burj Khalifa.

The souvenir is made from acrylic glass and is about the height of 1 foot. It has some LED lights at the bottom that shines through the model when switched on. It looks even more attractive with the lights on. It is the exact imitation of Burj Khalifa. It is the tallest building in the world till date. It stands around 850 meters above ground. I bought this souvenir from the building itself.

Burj Khalifa is in the heart of Dubai. I went there last year with my family on a holiday. I bought this souvenir when we went to the top of the tower. There is an observation deck that is meant for people to observe surroundings from 128th floor of the iconic building.

After we finished the tour, we headed towards the souvenir shop located on the same floor. There I saw many souvenirs that I thought were worth buying. I was flattered by the variety of items they had over there.

I went past one replica, and my eyes were stuck on it. I quickly made my mind to purchase that item. I asked the shop attendant about the price of that, to which he quoted 200 Dirhams which was about 3500 Indian rupees at that time.

I knew that it was a bit expensive, but I pursued my father to buy it. He liked the souvenir as soon as he held it in his hand. He was kind enough to give me money to buy it. I thanked him and took it home happily.

I have kept this in the living room of my house and whenever someone looks at the souvenir, they cannot take their eyes off it.

Describe a thing for which you saved money from a long time

Do you like saving money?
What was the purpose of saving money?
Were you able to save money?

There are many things for which I save money. I am a student, so I do not have a lot of money with me. I often save a part of my pocket money to buy expensive things or the things I like.

I remember once I saved some money to buy a laptop. The laptop was expensive, and I wanted to buy it as I like electronic gadgets. It was not my professional or educational need, but I just wanted to buy it for my leisure use.

So, I was promised by my father that he will contribute 50% of the money for my laptop but I must collect rest of the money. The cost of the laptop was 40 thousand rupees at that time. So, that meant I had to collect 20 thousand.

Then I planned to accumulate the sum of money in six months. I made a blueprint and started working on it. I cut down any unnecessary expenses off my pocket. I remember that I like chocolates very much and would buy one every second day. However, I had to sacrifice it for some months.

I also gave up eating outside food with friends as it would cost me a lot. I started walking more and avoided public transport to save some more money. By the end of six months, I was not able to save 20 thousand, but I managed to save 15000.

My father was impressed with my savings so he told me not to sacrifice anything else as he would lend me rest of the money. I was so glad and felt that how difficult it is to save money. It felt so good after buying laptop from the money I saved with so much struggle.

I bought the latest laptop with top configuration as it would help run every type of software and games. So, this is one occasion on which I saved money for a long time to buy something.

Speak about an interesting tour guide

Where did you meet this guide?
How that guide was interesting?
Did you talk to that guide?

I have been to a few tourist places in my life and the role of tour guides is impeccable there. I have come across some characters in my life, but I certainly feel that I cannot forget one tour guide whom I met in Dubai. I think it is great way to travel when you are in company of a tour guide. I went to Dubai last year with my family and we hired a tour guide from a travelling agency. They gave us his phone number and told us to contact him in the morning as he will come to our hotel to pick us up.

We called in the morning and to our surprise he could speak Hindi. I was curious to meet him. He arrived at the hotel at sharp 10 and greeted us with a broad smile and handshakes. He introduced himself as Akram.

He escorted us to a van in which we were meant to go on a full day city tour with him. He took us to renowned attraction of the city and told us about the history of Dubai. He explained about the past and present of this wonderful city. He was quite knowledgeable and humorous.

He instantly became friendly with us and treated us like we know him from a long time. He told us that he was an Iranian resident and was working in Dubai from the past 10 years. He also mentioned that he watches Indian movies and relishes them.

He took us to all the main attractions and landmarks of the city. We stopped at a local restaurant for lunch. He ordered some local food for us. We savored the food and went back to the van to continue the tour.

Then he took us to the beach where we spend about an hour. He was taking care of us in a great manner and would crack jokes every now and then. We all became amiable with him in a matter of few hours.

I think that he was the most interesting tour guide that I ever came across.

Speak about a family that resemble yours

Speak about that family
How that family resemble yours?
Do you have good relationship with that family?

I have not come across many families that resembles mine. But we were all surprised when our neighbors shifted to our colony last year.

I am talking about my neighbors who live across the street. I live in a joint family of 9 members and surprisingly they are 9 members themselves. They shifted in our colony last year and we quickly bonded well on every facet. I am the second child of my parents. I have an elder brother and a younger one as well. The same goes with them. DK Sharma, who has three sons. His wife is around 58 years old, and her name is Laxmi. Their eldest son is eight years older than me and is married since 2012. He has a son who is 6 years old. It goes same in my family where my elder brother is seven years older than me and has a daughter who is 5 years old.

Mr. Sharma's second son is a year older than me. His name is Amit and I like his company as we share similar interests and nature. I really get along with him well. We like to study together as he is a bit older than me so if I have any problem in studies, I like to discuss with him. My younger brother and their youngest son are of the same age. They share a good bond with each other. Their nature is strikingly same, and we all get surprised by this.

My father and mother are almost similar in age and nature as compared to Mr. and Mrs. Sharma. We all celebrate festivals together and like to dine together occasionally. They are a family that resembles ours and we all enjoy each other's company very much.

Speak about a time when you admired the sky

Do you often see the sky?
What did you admire about the sky that day?
Is it a wasteful activity?

In this fast-growing world, technology has taken over everything so much that we hardly get time to appreciate the natural beauty around us. One of the most beautiful things in this universe according to me is the endless sky above us, but unfortunately, I do not get time to look up and admire the sky often.

Today I would like to share a recent experience of mine when I was awestruck while looking at the sky. We travelled to the hills last week to celebrate my brother's first wedding anniversary. We went to Kaza which is a small, secluded town in Himachal Pradesh. This place is surrounded by beautiful valleys and mountains and has an amazing vibe. The atmosphere is extremely neat and clean, and air is pretty fresh because of the high volume of trees in that area. At the hotel, there was a big lawn, so we decided to spend most of our time there only. At night when me and my family were enjoying ourselves in the lawn, I looked up at sky and realized how enchanting it was. The bright twinkling stars seemed to be magical, and the moon were clearly visible. I loved the different patterns that stars made. I was trying to figure out the different shapes that was made by the constellation of stars.

Because of the clear sky, that night the moon appeared to be very close and extremely beautiful, so I kept on looking at the sky for a long time. Here in the big cities, it is very hard to find clear sky because of the tall buildings and a lot of pollution. But that night I realized the real beauty of nature. In my opinion, one should take out time from their busy schedule to admire the sky as it provides immense peace to a person and makes us believe in the power of God.

Describe a handcrafted item which you made yourself.

When you made the item?
Why did you make that item?
Were you pleased by your work?

From the very beginning I was fond of art and craft and used to participate enthusiastically in the art and craft class at my school. I studied in one of the best schools in our city, where they paid a lot of attention towards the non-academic activities as well.

To polish the creativity of students we were taught a lot of handicraft stuff like making paper bags, envelops, artificial flowers, jewelry box, photo frames, etcetera. But here I would like to talk about a unique thing which I made myself, that is a tea/coffee tray using newspaper rolls. I made this item for our school's exhibition when I was twelve. Our teacher taught us a new technique of hardening a newspaper by tightly rolling it on a table, several times and pasting the ends with glue.

By doing so, the newspaper turned very stiff like a wooden stick. Me and my classmates made hundreds of such sticks at first as we had to make 6-7 trays. It was a lot of fun rolling those and as kids it fascinated us how strong those sticks were from a mere newspaper.

After making the sticks and letting them dry completely, I joined the sticks together to form a firm base and then stacked them on all the four sides, giving it the shape of a tray.

Once all the trays were ready, it was time to beautify them by painting and pasting some glitters and stickers on them. Our teacher was impressed with our job and congratulated us for our efforts.

Even I was contented with our efforts. We made these trays as we had to exhibit something at the school's annual exhibition. We displayed our product and gave description to the audience. Everyone appreciated our work that day.

Describe a dish you like the most which is served during the festivals.

Is it a sweet or savory dish?
Is it served only during festivals?
Explain the dish and how it is made

I live in a diverse country where multiple festivals are celebrated at a large scale, and each has its own importance and value for the people of different religions and cultures. Every festival has a specific dish associated with it like Ghevar is prepared during Teej festival in Punjab and parts of Rajasthan as well, Biryani is famous during EID and Modak is another popular dish which is specifically made during Ganesh Chaturthi.

But the dish I like the most is Gujia which can be found in almost every sweet shop near the Holi festival. Holi is a famous festival in India, also popular by the name of 'festival of colors'. During this festival, the friends and relatives' gift each other a box of Gujia as a symbol of affection. Gujia is a sweet dumpling made of flour, stuffed with a mixture of dry fruit and solid milk. It is deep fried in clarified butter and then dipped in a sugary syrup. Mostly it is eaten cold or at room temperature. I love the texture of this dish; it is crunchy from outside and soft from inside. The filling melts in your mouth with the first bite itself. Also, the filling is not that sweet, this balances the overall flavor of the dish perfectly as the outer coating is glazed with caramelized sugar. The good thing about Gujia is that it is also available in every season at the sweet shops Gujia is not only eaten on Holi but on most of the other festivals as well like Diwali, the biggest Indian festival.

Gujia originally is an authentic dish of Madhya Pradesh which is known as the heart of India. Some parts of Uttar Pradesh and Bihar are also famous for this dish, but now it is prepared and enjoyed all over the country.

Describe a place full of colors

Do you like colorful places?
Speak about that place
Will you go there again?

I am a positive person and always get attracted by colorful things, be it beautiful flowers, a house, or a garden. Today I would like to talk about a place full of colors and that is the Diwali carnival, which is held every year in my city, Chandigarh.

Not only Diwali carnival but in general any kind of a carnival is extremely colorful with beautiful lights all around. So, I went to this carnival last month on the eve of Diwali. They always have a different theme for the entrance door and this year the theme was Disney Land which made it even more colorful and fascinating. The carnival was beautifully lit up by different colored bright lights.

Secondly the entrance gate was of bright purple and golden color according to the Disney theme. They had a huge red color carpet which covered the entire area of the carnival and gave the people a smooth surface to walk on. At the Diwali carnival, there were multiple games to attract children out of which my personal favorite was the "shoot the balloon". The theme and decoration of the carnival made it extremely colourful place. There was one wall that was completely adorned with numerous varieties of colourful flowers. Also, there was a section where street market was designated at the carnival that had everything to shop from clothes, jewelry, kitchen appliances, home decor, artificial flowers to lights etcetera.

Not only this, but there was also a huge variety of food to choose from different stalls. There were some vendors who were selling traditional sweets that were so vibrant in appearance. I had never visited such colourful place before in my life. This fare occurs every year in my hometown, and I eagerly wait for this event to happen.

Describe a product or application which is based on Artificial Intelligence

Speak about the product or the application
Have you ever benefited from it?
Is artificial intelligence a boon or bane for the humans?

Humans have seen massive developments in the field of technology in the past 100 years. The major development in the field of technology is the Artificial Intelligence. The AI is developing day by day and is becoming faster, smarter, and human-like. There are many products in the market these days that are based on artificial intelligence. I am using an iPhone so I would like to describe about SIRI. It is an Apple's personal assistant that is in-built in the phone and other products of Apple.

I interact with the friendly voice-activated computer on daily basis. SIRI helps me to discover a lot of information. In my phone I can simply ask her to give me directions of a particular place. I do not need to type anything. I just speak hello SIRI on my phone and give a command. Her job is to answer me anything I ask.

I can add events to my calendar by simply speaking to her. Even if I need to make a call, I can simply tell SIRI to dial that number for me. This has surely made life easier, but some people do not consider it to be a helpful thing. Instead, they think that Artificial Intelligence is interfering in the life of people and can be a threat in the future.

SIRI uses machine learning technology to become smarter and better equipped to predict and understand our natural accents and requests. It is like a magic that people would have only dreamt of in the past. It was unimaginable to think of such a discovery few years back. I think the artificial intelligence has surely benefitted the businesses, but it has also invaded the privacy of people in a lot of ways. I think that there should be some limits set by the government regarding the use of artificial intelligence.

Something kind that someone did for you

Who was the person?
What did he/she do for you?
How did you feel after that?

I have been fortunate enough to receive help from many people in my life. On one occasion I received a kind gesture from one of my friends in my school time.

He was my best friend and he helped in a situation when I needed the most. My friend studied in the same class as mine. His name is Ishwar, and he maintains a quiet nature. He is very sober and cool minded.

An incident happened with me when we were in school. I used to go back from school to my house on cycle. Ishwar accompanied me most of the times as he lived near my house back then. One day we were going back to house and suddenly a speeding motor bike passed besides me and due to that I lost my balance and fell on the side.

I sustained some injuries on my elbow and knees. But the most painful one was on the head. Ishwar quickly left his bike and held me in his arms. He asked repeatedly whether I was fine or not. I told him that I have a lot of pain in my head. Suddenly I felt blood oozing out of my head. Ishwar quickly took out his handkerchief and pressed it firmly on my head.

He called people around us and asked for help. One passerby stopped and laid me in his car. Ishwar left his cycle, bag, and other things at the scene and took me to a nearby clinic. There the doctor examined me and gave me some pills and soon after that he stitched the wound and put a bandage on it.

The doctor advised me to go home as there was no serious injury. Meanwhile, Ishwar had already informed my parents about the incident and soon my parents arrived there. It brought smile to my face. My mother hugged me, and I told her about how Ishwar took care of me and helped me to reach the clinic.

My parents thanked him, and we escorted him to his home. I can never forget that day and the kindness of Ishwar towards me. I am still in touch with him, and we often laugh when we talk about that incident.

Describe a time when you taught something new to an older person

Is it easy to teach the elderly?
What did you teach?
Was that helpful to him/her?

Believe me it is not an easy task to teach anything to elders. I live with my grandfather, and we share a great relation with each other. He is 80 but is very active in day-to-day chores. Despite his age, he is always keen on learning new things that he encounters in his daily routine. I have learned a great deal of things from him over the past few years. He has also asked me about things that he cannot do. I recently taught him several things like using a smart phone and operating emails by using it.

But there was one thing that made him struggle a lot and he could not learn it by himself. I am talking about a mobile app that helps you to book a taxi. The name of the app is Taxi. One day I promised my grandfather to teach him this skill on a Sunday.

First, I taught him to download apps on the mobile phone. Then I registered details in the application by using his phone number. I trained him to fill in the details in that app and then started it.

After that I showed him how to select the location where he wants to travel. Then I explained him the process of booking and choosing a taxi. I gave him some tips on booking cheap taxis as well. He was so keen on learning this application that he understood everything at once. He also booked a taxi to test whether he learned it or not. It took him some time, but he was able to make the correct booking.

This happens many times when he wants to go somewhere but he does not want to be dependent on anyone. That's why it was crucial for me to teach him the operation of Taxi app.

Describe an instance when you solved a problem using the internet

Do you often look for solutions on the internet?
What was the problem and how did you solve it?
Was internet helpful in solving that issue?

Yes, I look for solutions for most of the problems on internet. Internet is so easy to access, and I always find it a great place to look for answers to my problems. Internet has never-ending content and one can use it to solve most issues in day-to-day life.

The problem I was facing was in my laptop. I generally use my laptop to make presentations and projects. The major problem in my laptop was that it would restart itself anytime. Whenever I was doing something important, this issue would erase everything that I did in that period.

I searched on the internet about this problem and found a website where I shared my issue. They gave me an email id where I could tell about my problem and get it solved. I did not expect it to work but to my surprise, they replied swiftly with a solution.

They said, it is an internal issue and can be cured by self. They send me a series of steps that I needed to perform to get the problem eradicated. I followed those steps one by one, and it took me half an hour to resolve my issue. I was relived as I got rid of my problem and on top of that, I saved money.

The main problem was a virus in the software of my laptop. So, they instructed me to kill that virus by recovering the windows. It was very complicated, and I would have never been able to do it on my own. Or I had to get it checked from the market and it would have costed me a lot.

I am thankful to that website for helping me solve that issue. So, this is the time when I used internet to solve a problem.

A happily married couple

What is your relationship with the couple?
How they remain happy?
What do you like in them?

I have seen lots of couples in my life who are living happily in their married life. But today, I would like to talk about my sister and brother-in-law. Well, they are my favorite married couple not because she is my sister, but for the immense bonding and love they share with each other. They have a brilliant mutual understanding.

My sister got married three years back and since then I have never seen the couple arguing for any matter. No doubt, they sometimes disagree with each other on certain viewpoints, but they conclude and clear their differences quickly. Both have a mature and patient nature.

My brother-in-law is the best man for my sister. My sister always desired for such a partner in her life who could love her unconditionally and take care of her small and big needs. And undoubtedly, she got the right person in her life who never disappoints for her expectations. And the same goes for my sister too. She understands all his needs and precisely does all the things that could impress him in every possible way.

Whenever they go for any party, they are the apple of everyone's eyes as their internal love can be realized by everyone. People adore their bonding and cherish their togetherness.

I still remember when my brother-in-law faced terrible loss in his business, that time my sister supported him through the tough times. She is always with him in thick and thin. They support each other in every situation. I would also like to have someone special like this in my life. They always remain happy in every situation, and they are the most happily married couple that I have seen in my life.

Something you got for free

What did you get?
How did you feel when you got that thing for free?
How do you use it?

I have got many things in my life for free. One thing that I relish the most is the gift that I got from the restaurant owner. In this topic I will discuss the story about the thing that I got for free.

I am a big foodie and I love to visit different restaurants and taste variety of cuisines. Last week, I visited a newly opened Chinese restaurant nearby my place. I heard a lot about its upgraded food quality and decided to pay a visit to that restaurant. Thus, along with my brother I went for lunch at the weekend to the same food eatery.

As we were having our lunch, the owner of the restaurant came and greeted us. He asked for the feedback regarding the taste and quality of the food served to us. As the food was very delicious, I gave them positive comment and wished them good luck for the future of their restaurant. I also filled the feedback form of the restaurant and appreciated the things I liked.

The owner was really impressed with my reviews and to our surprise he gave us free discount coupons of 50 percent each for our future visit to the restaurant. In total he gave us five discount coupons. This was like a lottery for me as he presented us such a wonderful gift in return of a good review. These discount coupons could be cashed once at a time. I have already redeemed two of my 5 discount coupons as I visit that restaurant quite frequently. I love eating out, so these coupons save me a lot of money.

These coupons are one of my favourite possessions these days. Recently, my cousin demanded one coupon from me, and I did not hesitate to give it to him. So, this is the thing that I got for free.

An occasion when you received a lot of guests at your home

What was the occasion?
How did you feel about that?
How many guests did you receive?

Well, I am a jovial person, so I love attending parties and likewise, I generally throw parties for my friends and family as well. Last year, there was a huge party at my house celebrating the 25th anniversary of my parents.

It was a great event for them and for all the family members as they have happily completed 25 years with each other. We all were so excited about that occasion. It was a great day for us, so we invited all our friends and relatives.

We organized a dinner party for everyone along with music and dance. It was such a fun time. Whenever I look at the photographs of the event, I feel nostalgic. The occasion was a great success. All our guests were welcomed with a shower of flowers and attention was given to every guest so that no one felt isolated. All the guests were quite impressed with our arrangements.

All the things were planned by my mother so systemically that there was no confusion in any of the ceremony. There were dance performances, couple dance, rituals and much more in that occasion. Everything was just fantastic.

We hired the decoration team and best caterers for this occasion as many respected personalities were also invited to the party. Everyone appreciated our preparations and congratulated us for the huge success of the party. We received so many gifts as there were a great number of people in the event.

It was a tough task to unwrap all the gifts as it took us three hours to do that. I had never experienced such an occasion in my life before as we received more than three hundred guests at our home during this party.

A conversation with stranger

Where did you meet him/her?
What was the conversation?
Are you still in touch with him/her?

There are many strangers whom I have come across and made them friends. There is one such person who met me in a journey and we became good friends after that. I am talking about Amit. I met him in a train journey from Chandigarh to New Delhi.

I was going to my aunt's house to spend my holidays and on my way, I met this stranger. I had booked Capital Express which takes about three hours to reach Delhi. He was sitting on seat number 10 and mine was 11. I had the window seat, so I asked him politely to make way for me as I had to take the window seat.

At the first glance he looked a very humble kind of a person. He greeted me with a smile and soon the journey began. I am a very talkative person, so I was the one who started the conversation with him. First, I asked him about his hometown and to my surprise, he was living in the same colony in which I put up.

I was shocked as I had never seen him there. But he told me that he shifted recently from Delhi and was going there for the same purpose. He was going to Delhi to clear his dues and to bring anything that was left there.

When I asked him the reason of his shifting, he stated that he originally belongs to Chandigarh, but he was living in Delhi for the past five years as his father was posted there in a government department.

After that I told him about my background and family. We conversed a lot about our hobbies and other things.

Our tuning was matching from the first conversation as he was also the same age as mine. Our hobbies and interests were also very similar.

We exchanged phone numbers and remained in contact with each other after that day. These days he is a good friend of mine, and we share a decent relationship. He was a stranger to me when we met first time in the train but now, we are good friends.

A city or town you visited

What is special about that town or city?
What did you do there?
How did you feel after visiting that town or city?

I have visited many places in my life. My father loves to explore new places, due to that we get lots of opportunities to travel along with him. The town I visited recently is Manali, which is a hill station. We went there to visit a famous temple which was nearby Manali.

Well, the beauty of the city is breathtaking. Throughout our journey, I was constantly gazing outside the window and admiring the beauty of the nature. The lush green mountains and the fresh air was what impressed me the most about the city. Manali is a beautiful hill station which has small population. Hundreds and thousands of tourists come to Manali to enjoy nature every year. The fresh air and mesmerizing views we got in Manali are impossible to find anywhere in other parts of our country. The people of the city are very friendly and polite. Since it was a new place for us to explore, we were not aware about the routes of the city, but the local inhabitants guided us humbly.

I believe that if the locals of any tourist destination are amicable, it becomes easy to travel around the place. With the support of locals and using the limited signboards, we were able to roam around the hills comfortably. The city holds multiple markets that are embedded with different types of fashion outlets, souvenirs shops, and many other commodities.

We moved from one place to another through public transport and we were really satisfied with the taxi services there. All the tourist attractions in the city were spectacular. You can enjoy the snowy mountains and do various activities like bungy jumping, ice skating, white river rafting and many more. It was a full adventurous trip for us. If I get a chance, I would love to travel again to Manali as my experience was quite fantastic.

A website that is useful

For what purpose do you use that website?
Did you learn anything from this website?
At what time of the day do you use website?

I usually browse many websites on my mobile phone or sometimes on my laptop. I spend at least a couple of hours searching on the internet for new things. Since I am a social person, I love to spend two to three hours every day on various social sites.

But of all, Facebook is a useful website that I like to browse on a regular basis. It is my favorite one because you get to interact with so many people through this platform. This website is so useful in establishing contact with old friends. This site has really shortened the distance between people, which is the most enticing feature of it.

Also, we can share our photographs, videos and many other thoughts that come to our mind. It is a very engaging site. I have liked several pages on this site which are useful to me in my personal life. I can watch the videos and latest updates posted by those pages. In fact, I am also the manager of one Facebook page which has around a thousand likes and followers.

This page is about the youth of our country. I post latest content every day on my page and in return I get likes and some people also share the post with others. Not only this, but I have also made several new friends on this site who belong to other countries and cultures. This website is extremely useful in making friends from all over the world. In fact, one of my Facebook friends from another city has visited my home last year and it was a great experience living with him.

Apart from making friends, people can also do great business over this website. I have seen many companies advertising their products on Facebook. They can reach millions of people through this website as people from all over the world are connected through it. So, I feel that Facebook is one of the most useful websites around the globe.

A place where you like to listen to music

Where do you listen to music?
What device do you use for listening to music?
How do you feel when you listen to music?

Music is one of the most essential parts of everyone's life nowadays because it takes us away from the stress and depressing situations for some time. Listening to music is my favorite leisure activity. I love to listen to the music of various genres. I have typical playlist of my favorite songs that I like to repeat again and again. I can listen to music anywhere, anytime. But my favorite place to listen to music is in my bedroom.

My bedroom is the place where I can make myself most comfortable on my couch and feel the spirit of the songs. No one usually disturbs me in my room. My room is located at the back end of our house so there is no disturbance from any external sound.

Whenever I get bored, I listen to music. It helps me to get into a particular mood even if I feel low on that day. In my childhood days, I was fond of listening to songs, but I would listen to any song played on the TV. These days I have become very particular about my choices, and I listen to the songs listed in my playlist only.

Sometimes, I love to clean all the mess in my room while listening to music. This completes all my work without making me realize the time taken to complete that work. Music not only helps me to do all my tasks comfortably, but it also helps me in rejuvenating my mood.

Since I am fond of music, I have connected high-quality speakers in my room with my mobile phone through Bluetooth, and I love to listen to my favorite records. I can also connect them with my mobile phone through the cable to the speakers and then just play the music. Whenever I am listening to music in my room, I love to gaze at the beautiful garden near my house that is completely visible from the windowpane of my room. The mesmerizing view and the serene music make a perfect environment for my relaxation.

I listen to songs at numerous places, but my bedroom is the apt place for me to listen to my favorite songs.

A happy memory from childhood

What was the memory?
When did it happened?
Did you learn something from that memory?

My childhood was a memorable one as I enjoyed a lot in my school life with my friends. Even my parents were so encouraging that they supported me for every activity in my school time. There are numerous memories of my childhood that I still remember and cherish them. But the happiest memory from my childhood is from my school race competition. I was in class 5th when this competition was being held. It was conducted on the state level and few students were selected from the top schools of my city. I was one of the students from my school selected for that competition. The competition was held at Tagore Academy in my city. There were around 10 schools that participated in the competition. There were three rounds based on which finalists were to be chosen. In each round, the winning candidates were taken to the next round and the last ones were eliminated. Till the last round, all the students from my school were eliminated and I was the only hope left for my school. Every year, my school wins the competition. So, there were huge expectations on my shoulders. Finally, the last round started, and I was running like a professional athlete in the race and suddenly I felt a massive pain in my ankle. It felt like my ankle has been damaged severely. My foot twisted due to the unevenness of the track. For a second, I slowed down in the race but then the encouraging words of my coach stuck my mind and I forgot everything and stayed focused on the finish line. Finally, I came second in the race. I did not expect such a huge success from myself as my foot was in severe pain and I slowed down a bit. The injury was so bad that I was not even able to walk after the race. It was unbelievable for me to secure second position in the competition with such discomfort. If I would have not stopped for those few seconds midway, I may have won the race. I was awarded prize money as a reward for scoring 2nd position in the competition. I did not win the race, but it was one of the happiest moments from my childhood.

A time you moved home

Was it easy or difficult?
Did you lose anything in the process?
How did you do it?

Shifting is undoubtedly a daunting task as it involves so much work and time to do all the packing and then unpacking things. Adjusting to a new place is not as easy as it seems. Two years ago, we had shifted our home to a new place as the last one was not so spacious. The process of shifting was so tiring. Instead of hiring a movers and packers, we did all the packing and shifting of the household things on our own. The reason we did not hire a professional is that we were living in a rented accommodation, and we did not have many things to move. But I still remember I used to pack all the household stuff and carry it along every day till late nights. We packed all the things safely in different packaging boxes and sealed them properly so that no item gets damaged or lost. At the time of packing, we did not realize that it is so difficult to move all the items of a house. Apart from this, leaving the place where you have lived for so long is also very difficult. We were so attached to our neighbors that it was such an emotional moment for all of us. After shifting to the new place, we recalled our old house many times in the day. But as we were so busy in setting the new house, we forgot everything in a few days and settled at our new place. We were too excited to get into a newer, more spacious house where all of us were having our own rooms. Even here the neighbors are so good and there are much better facilities than we had in our locality earlier. We all were really satisfied after moving to the new place.

A time you moved school

When did that happened?
Did you like the new school?
Were there any problems at the start?

I have studied in two different schools. I left my first school at the age of eleven. I remember that I was in fifth standard when my parents decided to shift me to a bigger and better school. I used to study in a decent school, but the infrastructure lacked a bit. Although all my teachers were amazing, but there was lack of activities that led to this decision. My mother always wanted me to study in a big school. So, they bought admission forms and applied for the enrolment. I had to clear five exams and based on the result; I was admitted by the authorities. I was shifting to one of the best schools in our city. The name of the school is Shivalik public school. I was quite nervous on the first day as I knew none of my new classmates.

when I reached the school on the first day, I was welcomed by everyone, and my class teacher helped me a lot in adjusting to the new environment. I had never seen such a huge school in my life. I was helped by my classmates to a great extent. They took me to the canteen in the lunch time and showed me every nook and corner of the school.

There were so many new things that I saw for the first time in a school. This new school had auditoriums, football ground, basketball courts, gymnasium hall and many more facilities.

After that, my classmates also took my introduction. I felt so contented with the treatment of the school staff and classmates. I had so many confusions and questions in my mind before entering the gate of the school. But after the completion of the first day, I believed my parents made a great choice.

Your favorite TV program you watch

What is the format of the program?
How often do you watch it?
At what time the show is run on TV?

Whenever I am free, I love to watch TV as there is a wide variety of choice in terms of channels nowadays. The options are abundant so people of every age group can find something of their interest. I usually spend 1-2 hours watching TV daily. There are many programs that I like but my favorite program is "Kaun Banega Crorepati" on Sony TV. This program is the Hindi version of the show, "who wants to be a Millionaire".

It is my best pick because it is a very knowledgeable quiz show. The best part of the show is that the host of the show is my favorite personality, Amitabh Bachan, one of the finest actors of Bollywood. His voice and personality say it all. Many people view this show just because they want to see more of Amitabh Bachan. There are several contestants who take part in a group round. They must answer a question and the person who takes the least time to answer that question, wins that round.

The winner of the first round is selected to play this game and gets a chance to become a millionaire. This show involves a huge amount of prize money on each question you answer correctly. This show is my favorite one not because it gives me ample of knowledge for various questions asked in each round but also it is a good source of entertainment. In between the question rounds, there are few humorous chats between the host and the candidate.

Not only this, from the past few episodes of the show, there is an opportunity for the TV viewers to participate in the competition from their homes to win the prize money. In every episode, one question is asked to the TV viewers and the answers to that must be sent through a message. The one selected with right answer wins 2 lakh rupees. So, one can win money while watching the show.

The show is telecasted on every Saturday and Sunday in the evening time, so I get glued to my TV screen every weekend for this show.

A time when you felt embarrassed

When did this happen?
what happened?
How did you feel?

There are numerous moments in life that leaves a long-lasting impression on us. There have been some awkward moments in my life too but the one which I am going to tell you about is the most embarrassing moment of my life.

This happened quite a few years back when I was in 10th class. I had invited a few friends for my birthday party. I told everyone to come at NCA mall in the food court area for the party. When we assembled at the restaurant, we ordered plentiful cuisines.

We had a great time together. I cut the cake in the end and asked for the bill from the hotel staff. When I was about to pay the bill, I realized that I had no wallet in my pocket. I searched it thoroughly in all my pockets but could not find it.

I felt so embarrassed at that time. I was in shock for a few seconds. My friends were concerned and asked me about the issue. I told them that I was not able to find my wallet. I thought that I must have either left it at home or lost it on the way.

My friends consoled me and told me not to worry. One of my friends told everyone about the situation. So, all unanimously decided to pay the bill by splitting the amount among everyone.

I was so glad at that time and felt lucky that I have such great friends. I thanked everyone and assured them to return their money the next day. I kept my promise and retuned the money to each friend and thanked them personally.

Fortunately, I searched my room and found my wallet. I was so happy to find my wallet as I had more money in that than usual days. Despite the help by my friends, I felt very embarrassed. From that day onwards I always check my pockets for purse before leaving home.

A time when you felt nervous / anxious / frightened

What happened?
How did you tackle the situation?
Was it the first time when you got nervous?

There are several moments in our lives when we get nervous or anxious. But we learn something from every moment or situation that we encounter in our life. But what matters the most is how we tackle with such circumstances and what action we take at that critical time.

I would like to discuss a recent situation when I was very frightened. Couple of months back I was travelling in a bus. I was going to my friend's house who lives in Shimla. I had planned this visit as I was having a long weekend due to a local festival.

My friend called me and invited to his house for a couple of days. I was very excited about my trip as I was about to meet my old school friend after two years. I booked the bus from an online website and departed at 6 AM. The bus takes around four hours to reach Shimla. The highway to Shimla is under construction and drivers were cautious of the obstacles on the road.

I went in the rainy season and saw lots of small pieces of rocks lying on the road. These rocks were disintegrated from the hills due to heavy downpour from last week's rain. The frightening moment came when our bus suddenly stopped and skid sideways due to the heavy brakes applied by the driver. Many passengers fell in the bus as they were standing. On the other hand, my head hit the front seat and I got bruised. Everyone in the bus was stunned and asked the driver about the situation. The driver asked everyone to leave the bus immediately and take a safe cover. There was a huge landslide that had happened just in front of our bus. A huge part of the mountain fell on the buses and cars that were moving ahead of us.

We were so lucky that we were not the victims of that. Despite this, I was so nervous and frightened that I could not continue the journey. This happened at the halfway of our destination. I called my parents and they tried to calm me down and told me not to worry. My father came there along with my brother and took me back to home. Although we were saved by the driver's presence of mind, but I felt frightened for the whole week due to this incident.

Describe a person you think is a good parent

What is your relationship with that person?
How do you think he/she is a good parent?
What sort of relationship this person has with his/her kids?

Parents are always their child's best well-wisher. They can never think of anything that can harm their children. Even my parents are very caring and helpful to me in every situation. They are always ready to sacrifice their desires to fulfill my needs. But today I would like to discuss a parent who I think is the best example of a great parent, my elder sister. She is undoubtedly the best mother and a great woman too. She is very supportive of her kids. She has sacrificed a lot of things while raising her children.

She was working in a reputed company at a senior post. But her husband got transferred to a different state because of professional work, so she realized that her kids are not getting proper attention and they miss their father too. So, she decided to resign from her job and give her kids more time. And it was very fruitful, her extra care and involvement with kids made them quite happy.

Not only this, but she has also given great upbringing to her kids. My niece and nephew are very intelligent kids. They have learned good lessons from their mother and know well how to behave with elders, their friends, and relatives. She gives them space in their lives but punishes them for their mistakes too. She has maintained a great balance in her kids' life and allowed them to do every activity in their daily lives.

She has a huge influence on her kids as she has given them education about their culture, rituals, and religion. Many parents are not able to teach their kids about their customs these days. But she has provided her kids with every possible knowledge and views.

In the end, I will say that these kids are blessed to have such a mother in their life who is so caring, generous. I hope in future her kids will also treat her with same generosity and love.

Describe a piece of furniture at your home

For what purpose do you use it?
When did you buy it?
Describe that piece of furniture in detail

All the furniture placed at my home is bought with great sentiments by my family. Every piece of furniture in our house has a special purpose. But the one I love the most is the study table of my room. It is made from top quality wood. This furniture is very special to me because of many reasons. Firstly, I bought this from my own pocket money. Whatever money I used to get on my birthdays or any other occasion from my parents, I collected it in a savings account. When I had enough amount, I bought the study table of my room. This is not merely a study table but a beautiful piece of art that has been carved by the experts. I bought this table when I was in my school.
The table is of ideal height and width. It has two drawers on the left side and big rack on the other side, where I keep all my books and reference papers securely. There is one slider beneath the table that helps in keeping some useful papers.
The study table is entirely made up of wood. It is polished in the walnut color and has a natural wooden finish. I bought this table around five years back and it is still in excellent condition. I feel very comfortable whenever I use this table to study or do any other activity in my daily life.
I also love to read books on this study table. In fact, it provides a great storage capacity to keep all my books and stationery in it.
Also, it is portable, so I can shift it to any room in future. There is an LED bulb that is attached to the top of the table. It is extremely useful as it gives proper lighting whenever I am studying without affecting my eyes in any way. Hence, this is the piece of furniture that I like the most.

Describe a way to stay healthy

What is the importance of health?
What is the best way to stay healthy?
How do you keep yourself healthy?

Staying healthy is the most significant thing in our life. If one is not healthy, he or she will not be able to accomplish the dreams of their lives. Good health can make you rejoice your success in life. Not only this, but it also helps you to live happily and keeps you fresh and active in your day-to-day activities.
For me, eating home cooked food is the best way to stay healthy. What matters the most to our health is what we eat throughout the day. Most of the times, I eat homemade food. That really helps me to stay healthy and save a decent amount of money.
Today, most people prefer junk food, which has multiple side-effects on our body. Junk food increases the amount of extra fat in the body that can also lead to obesity in some cases.
Moreover, outside food contains a lot of oil and gluten, which can be detrimental for our health. Many problems like heart disease, diabetes, back pain, knee joints pain and many more are caused by eating excess junk food.
Whereas home-cooked food is nutritious and helps in maintaining body balance. It keeps you fit and active. The oil and spices we use at our home are not harmful to our body while in outside food, various artificial preservatives, colors, and ingredients are used that affects our body in a negative way.

It also disturbs our digestive system thus producing ulcers in the stomach, which can even lead to stomach cancer in some cases. Most people in my country like to carry their tiffin along with them which is packed with healthy and hygienic home-cooked food.

They do this because they know the importance of this type of food. Having junk food occasionally will certainly not harm your body but eating it quite often will make you inch towards major health issues in future. I can say in the end that eating homemade food is the best way to keep yourself healthy.

An expensive thing you want to buy in future

What will you buy?
Have you saved money for it?
When will you buy it?

Dreaming is everyone's birthright. We can dream of buying everything and anything in our life. There are many expensive things that I am not able to buy right now but will surely buy them in the future when I will be earning enough on my own.

Well, I am very fond of watches. I would like to buy a Rolex watch in my life whenever I get a chance. Having a Rolex watch is like a dream for me. As they are extremely expensive, and not so easily available in every store.

The Rolex brand is the most valuable watch brand in the world. The watch is super expensive, but the built quality is commendable. Rolex makes hundreds of different style watches, but I would like to buy the one in black and silver. It is an evergreen colours and goes with all kinds of occasions.

It is quite a prestigious watch because of the high-quality material which is used in its fabrication. It is made up of 904L steel which is the highest-grade steel in the world. The company owns its in-house science lab that works day and night to produce fantastic watches.

Every minor aspect is checked in the labs and error free watches are being manufactured by the company. One of the best things about these watches is that they are not made by robotic technology. Even now, the machines are managed by humans which involves supervision at each step of the manufacturing.

Wearing this watch is itself a prestigious and worthy experience. I know this watch is very expensive, but I am in love with this brand. So, whenever I get a chance to buy something expensive, I will buy a Rolex watch.

A time when you gave suggestion in a survey

Where did you participate in the survey?
What suggestion did you give?
Did you like participating in the survey?

Nowadays, people like to get feedback from the masses so that they can get a review. The reaction from the public makes them generate an enhanced product. We can easily see many surveys on the internet nowadays as we scroll through various sites.

There are different methods to conduct surveys. Some companies do it on the internet and some like to take the feedback from people in person. The survey in which I participated was held in a mall. Recently I went to a renowned mall in my city, and I saw few officials asking questions from random people wandering in the mall. They had all the questions written in a form and were asking people to fill it.

One of those officials asked me to partake in that survey. They told me that the 10 best feedback forms will be given assured prizes. I had a lot of time with me on that day, so I decided to give answers in the survey.

The form had questions about the mall's services and security, hygiene in the washrooms and many other things related to the mall. I gave all the answers as per my opinion with honesty. I go to that mall frequently, so I know the different aspects of the mall very well.

The form was a review-based survey in which we had to give 0 to 10 points on the different facets of the mall. At the end of the form, I was asked to write at least five lines about the mall or any suggestion that I want to give which was not covered in the questions. So, I wrote a suggestion to reduce the car parking fee of the mall as it was too high for my liking.

I wanted to give this suggestion because the mall was losing business due to the overpriced parking fee. The price for 2-hour parking is 200 rupees which is quite high as compared to rest of the malls in that area. I hope that they will take my suggestion seriously and do something about it.

At the end, they asked me to fill in my details such as name, age, sex, and phone number so that they could contact me in case I win the prize. However, I did not get any call regarding it, but I honestly filled the survey form and gave my suggestion in that. I really enjoyed participating in that survey.

Your favourite singer

Why do you like him/her?
What are his/her favourite songs?
How has his music influenced people?

Listening to songs is my favorite part-time activity as this not only makes me feel good but also takes away my stress during hectic schedule. Whenever I get time, I love to listen to songs of various singers.

But my favourite singer is Michael Jackson. The songs sung by him are very different and no one else can sing and dance like him. All his moves and vocals are just incomparable. He was a real legend.

He was a very well-known international American pop singer and was known as the "KING OF POP". His music records are just brilliant and no one till date has been able to break his sales records.

When this legendary singer took his last breath in 2009, everyone in the world was in mourn. He was not only known for his singing style and stardom but also for the lifestyle he was living. It was just so different and odd for some people.

The most famous blockbuster album of Michael Jackson is 'Thriller' which got sales of around 33 million worldwide. No one has been able to break such record till date for such a famous streak in the music industry.

He was famous for his various moves but the one which was a delight to everyone was Moonwalk as named by him, which I personally like very much. His other albums are Off the Wall, Bad, Dangerous, and lastly The Invincible. All his songs are my favorite and make me come out of my thoughts and dance to the tunes of it.

He was always in news for one or the other reasons and many people criticized him for his surgeries and other facial changes. Due to his ill health and aftereffects from many surgeries, he died at a young age of 50, but he is still there in the hearts of his devoted fans and will hold a special place in their hearts forever.

Visit to a strange place

Where is it located?
Why is it strange?
How often do you visit that place?

I am the kind of a person who loves to travel a lot. I have seen a lot of strange places in my life but the one which I would like to tell you is in Dubai. Last year, I went to Dubai with my family. There are many places in Dubai that are worth visiting like Burj khalifa, museums, beaches and many more. One of the strange places that I visited there is the Dubai Mall. It is a well-known mall in that country.
Well, this mall is the biggest mall in the world, and it is like a maze for some people. I went there with my parents and brother. We were all wandering in different directions and decided to meet at a certain point after two hours. When the time passed, I started looking for that landmark. It was located on the first floor, but the mall is so big that it has many different sections and locations at a single floor. It took me more than 30 mins to reach the meeting point.
There are multiple exits and entries to the mall that one cannot identify at a single gaze. For the first time visitors, the mall is like a puzzle that is very difficult to solve. But the mall was really pleasing to our eyes as it was decorated so nicely for one of their local festivals and there were many offers and discounts on all the brands. You can find any local or international brand in this mall but tracing any location in the mall was the most complicated task. Practically, it will take around two days for a person to explore the entire mall. I find that mall strange as it is such a humungous place that one cannot imagine.

Describe a piece of good news that you heard from someone

When did you receive the news?
What was it about?
How did you react to the news?

I have received several good news from people over the past few years. The one that comes to my mind right now is when I was selected for a quiz competition to represent my school at a national level.
That time I was studying in my 10th class and a team from a renowned quiz contest came to our school to select few students that will represent our school in the competition. This contest is telecasted on the national television and participating in it was a great deal for me.
There was a team of three people who were carrying a lot of documents with them. Our teachers introduced them to us and told us to follow whatever they say. Then, the team started distributing those papers to us.
All the students were asked to fill in the answers to the given questions on the paper. Those papers contained general knowledge related questions in objective type pattern. We had to just tick the right answer on the sheet. There were 100 questions in total, and we were given two hours to solve the paper. Based on the results, five contestants from each school were to be selected. I finished the paper in the given time and was very confident for a good result. I knew answers to most of the questions and I was hoping that I would be selected for the live quiz contest. The result was scheduled to declared after a week, so I was very excited for that. I could not sleep for six days as I was expecting a good result.
The result did not disappoint me. My class teacher broke this great news to me in the morning that I was selected along with four other students to participate in the quiz show. I was on cloud nine when I heard this news. I was congratulated by our principal, and she told me to prepare hard for the competition.

So, this is the news that I heard from my class teacher, and it made me happy.

A club that you have joined

How often do you go to that club?
What activities do you do there?
What is included in the club area?

There are many clubs near my place, but the one I have joined is the PCA club. This is the most famous club in my city as various international cricket matches are held in this stadium every season. Very few people have the opportunity to join this club and I am one of them.

The club is very well maintained by the management. I usually go there to learn swimming and play table tennis. They ponder highly upon the hygiene of the activity areas. They have a gym area, a sports area that includes various sports infrastructure such as table tennis, badminton, football and basketball

They have a very well-organized swimming pool area too that also has expert trainers who train the members in swimming class. Last year, my younger brother took swimming classes at our club and now he is a good swimmer.

There are numerous parties and events in the club that are organized on occasions like New year, Christmas, Diwali. I always participate in all the parties and activities as it gives me a chance to meet new people.

The security of the club is efficient as no one can enter the club without a membership card. Non-members are not allowed to use the facilities at the club. There is a huge restaurant area in the club where we usually party at special occasions. The food served at their restaurant is delicious and of supreme quality.

Since, the club is a part of the international cricket stadium, we can get a sight of players in the restaurant or other club areas during match days. I have met many cricket players at that time and taken their autographs.

I got the membership because of my father. He is the main member, and we are the dependent ones. So, we have our own card which we can use to enter the club and avail the activities. I go to that club at least once a week.

Tell about a subject you disliked in school

Which subjects do you disliked?
Why did you dislike this subject?
What type of subjects are interesting?

I liked most of the subjects in my school time but there were a few that I found to be a waste of time. Sometimes the curriculum has subjects which have little value when it comes to the practical life.

A subject that I disliked the most is history subject. I found it very boring to study in my school time. I think it is one of the most useless subjects that are taught in the society. I am not a big admirer of studying past dates and events. I believe that what has happened has happened. There is no point of remembering the dates and events as we have storage devices for that. We can save all the data in computers.

Instead, kids should be taught more aesthetic and dynamic subjects like math's and geography. They can learn more in these subjects and can also utilize these subject's knowledge in their day-to-day life. In the life of a common man, historical dates do not have much importance.

In our country's text books, the history subject contains the same information that was taught fifty years back. Nothing has changed and I think that information in the history textbooks is completely out of date and there are number of changes that are needed to be made to raise the standard of this subject.

According to my notion, present history is more interesting. So instead of having historical dates from hundreds of years back, the textbooks should include history from the past ten years only. This kind of history is more interesting to read and memorize.

I remember that I used to find history subject so boring that I could not study it more than fifteen minutes. I disliked it so much that I never opened history books in my study time at home.

I could not learn all the dates and names of the prominent personalities from the past. I simply could not remember the events and happenings. So, history was the subject that I disliked the most in my school time.

An interesting old person you know well

How do you know him/her?
What is interesting in him/her?
Is there any interesting thing that you can learn?

I am the kind of a person who loves to know different people. I know a lot of young as well as old people. If I could make a list, then I certainly know a lot of old people in my life. In this topic, I would like to speak about my grandfather as he is an old person, I know the best. He is the most interesting and intelligent person I have ever known. One can judge his knowledge and experience by just having a conversation with him. Since my childhood, I have idolized him as the person I want to become. His story is very interesting as he has earned a niche for himself.

He was brought up in a poor family but with his dedication towards work and honesty helped him to reach the pinnacle of success. He is a retired chief executive engineer from Delhi. He reached the top position in his department in a mere ten-year period. He achieved a lot of accolades during his service.

His age is around 80 years, but still, he is so active and energetic in whatever he does. He wakes up early in the morning and does his routine exercise. He is extremely fit and good at health as he is very diet conscious and exercises for an hour every day. He is fond of watching movies and using modern electronic gadgets. He has successfully adapted to the contemporary lifestyle. I am highly inspired by him in my life, and I follow him wholeheartedly in my personal as well as professional life. There is so much that I can learn from him. Whatever he teaches me on a general basis is of great help to me and I implement them everywhere to achieve success.

One interesting thing that I would like to learn from him is that how he wakes up early in the morning every day and follows his routine. He is the old person who is very interesting, and I know him very well.

A time when you felt angry

Do you often get angry?
What was the incident?
What did you do when you got angry?

Emotions are part of one's life. Different types of emotions come out in different situations of life. Sometimes, conditions are so compelling that it becomes impossible to control our emotions and temperament. Anger is also such an emotion that is ousted in people with very short temperament.

Sometimes, even calm, and easygoing people lose their cool in certain situations of their lives. I am such a person who does not get angry very often, but there can be some circumstances that can make me angry.

I still remember the incident that happened with me a few weeks back. I was driving back to my home late at night from my friend's birthday party. Since it was quite late, I was driving slowly.

I was on the highway and suddenly a child came in front of my car from nowhere. I quickly steered the car to the left and applied the brakes abruptly. I received a jerk, and my car was about to hit the pavement. But thankfully that did not happen and luckily the car did not hit the kid. For a moment, I went in a state of slight tremor. After a few seconds when I revived to my senses I got out of the car and inquired the child about her parents. Then I saw her mother coming across the road busy on her mobile phone talking with someone.

I got so angry looking at her mom as she was not at all concerned for her child and was busy on her phone. I really do not understand how parents could do this to their kids. It was such a careless act that is intolerable for anyone. The young kid was extremely scared and crying badly, so I did not say anything to her. But I really screamed at her mother and asked about her carelessness and ignorance.

She was guilty of the mistake of not taking care of her child and leaving her alone on the road, especially on the highway.

I am so grateful to God that I was driving slowly which saved the child. I hope people of our country will understand the value of using these gadgets at the right time, but not at the stake of the life of their kids.

Talk about an important photograph

On what occasion the photograph was taken?
Who is there in the photo?
Why is it important?

Photographs are an important part of our lives. Good cameras capture beautiful moments of our lives in a single click. Whenever we look at our old photographs, we revive various memories made with several people and places. I am having a huge collection of photographs with me since my childhood days. But the one that is my favorite is the family photograph of me with all my family members taken 5 years back. The photograph was taken at my cousin's wedding.

That photograph includes all my uncles, aunts, and cousins from both my maternal and paternal side. The photograph was taken at the end of the wedding party when everyone one was called upon by my grandfather for a family photo session. The reason that this photo is important is that this photo can never be taken again. Because two of the eldest members have passed away and some of my cousins are now settled abroad. Some are married and some of them have kids as well.

I remember that this photo was taken near the entry gate of the venue. As there were around forty people in the photo, it took a lot of clicks to get a perfect shot. The photographer was patient enough to deal with all of us. I was a young kid back then, so I sat in the front row with my cousins and the other members were arranged according to their seniority.

It is impossible for us to get clicked for such a photograph again. So, it increases its importance. I approached the photographer and ordered him to make a framed portrait of four feet wide and three feet tall. It is a massive photo that hangs majestically on the wall of our living room. That photo attracts every visitor's eyes. I love all my family members and whenever I miss them, I simply gaze at the photograph.

Describe an old thing

What is the importance of old things?
Is it important to you?
Have you kept that thing with you?

I like to collect things especially when they are given by a loved one. I have set aside a lot of old things with me that reminds me of my past. I think that old things hold a great importance in our life as we can learn from them. I have kept few of my childhood toys and games with me. The old thing that I want to describe in this topic is a retro watch that was gifted to me by my grandfather. My grandfather is no more with me, so I always keep this token of love with me as his remembrance. Whenever I look at this watch, I recall moments spent with him and how he used to play with me in my childhood. I remember he used to over pamper me and always save from my parent's scolding. The watch that I have is of gold colour with a leather strap. The strap is of brown colour that compliments beautifully with the watch. The watch is 24 carat gold plated. It is of Titan brand, which is one of the renowned brands of watches worldwide. The best part is that the watch is still in working condition. However, I had to get its battery replaced last year. I have kept that watch in a special watch box in my almirah safely. I specially ordered this elegant watch box from the internet. My grandfather gave me this watch when he realized that his end was near. I was around 7 and he called me to his room and told me to always value time and made me understand the importance of time in our life by gifting me this watch. His words still reverberate in my ears. Whatever I am today is just because of his lessons and teachings. I always keep that watch in my almirah and never allow anyone to wear it as it is so dearer to me.

First day at school/college/university

What happened that day?
How did you feel?
Did you find it interesting or boring?

I have studied in a couple of different schools. I would like to describe about my first day at higher secondary school. I read in a different school till my class tenth, but I changed my school after that. I do not remember anything about my first day at school in kindergarten that is why I will explain the first day at my senior secondary school. I was new to the school like most of my other classmates. Students from different schools enrolled in this school for their higher education. I found this school to be very different form my previous one. The new school was enormous with a lot of facilities in it. The first day when I entered the school, I was surprised to see the huge premises of the school. We were told to gather in the assembly area where the morning prayers took place. I felt very positive after reciting those prayers.
Then we were introduced to the principal of the school. He gave us a motivating lecture and told us about the legacy of the institute. We all were amazed to know about the facts related to the school. Then our class teacher took charge and gave us a small tour of the school. She showed us the different parts of the building and the play area and canteen. Then we were taken to the auditorium where we were shown the accolades achieved by the schools. Then we were explained the rules and regulations that we need to follow at the school. There was not a much of study that day as it was purely an orientation day. That day I was really impressed by the school's infrastructure and staff. I remember each moment of the first day at this school.

An activity you do to maintain good health

OR

An activity you find interesting

Did you do that activity?
How has that activity helped you or someone?
Why do you find this activity interesting?

There are many activities that I find interesting. The one that I will discuss with you today is yoga. Yoga is basically an array of physical, mental, and spiritual disciplines which initiated in ancient India. I find yoga interesting due to several reasons.

Various diseases can be cured through yoga exercises. People can remain fit physically and mentally with regular practice of yoga. Yoga contains hundreds of body postures that are involved to align the body with the nature.

This type of exercise developed around sixth century BCE. Nowadays most of the people in our country follow this practice every day. I am not a regular practitioner of yoga but whenever I get time, I do it in the morning time.

Every year on 21st June, Yoga Day is celebrated all over the world and especially in India with a lot of excitement. I always participate in celebrating yoga day as our colony organizes a mass yoga gathering every year. In this assembly, a trained yoga teacher is hired who teaches different exercises and postures for maintaining good health.

I did not believe in yoga earlier, but I saw some amazing results and started trusting it. I would like to share an example with you. From the past few years, my mother was suffering from heavy breathing and uneasiness in lifting weights. She was told by her friend to do yoga on a regular basis to get rid of this problem. She started practicing yoga for an hour every day and soon she got rid of all her issues. It hardly took her a month to get relief from her problems.

I find this activity stimulating as you do not need to lift a lot of weight or need to run for kilometers. Yoga is all about making right body postures and inhaling and exhaling in a particular manner. This is not as simple as it looks. But once a person is trained, it becomes easy to perform.

In my perception, I find yoga to be one of the most interesting activities.

Speak about a room in which you spent a lot of time

OR

Speak about your room

Why do you spend so much time there?
Do you like being indoors?
How do you spend your time there?

I am such a person that I like to spend most of my time indoors as the weather in my city is hot for most part of the year. I live in a joint family and we dwell in a big house which has five rooms. I am fortunate to have a personal room at the second floor of my house.

I spend most of my time in my bedroom. I go for my classes in the morning and come back by afternoon. After that I am pretty much in my room for the whole day. Sometimes I go out in the evening but for majority of days I like to be there.

My room is 10x15 foot in size and is equipped with all the latest amenities. An air conditioner is installed to keep my room cool and the room is painted in light blue color. I like this color very much so that's why I got it painted in blue color. I have a double bed in my room. Moreover, a study table is placed against the front wall across the bed where I keep all my books. I love to use my study table for writing and reading. My study table is quite big and can hold a great number of books and other items.

The front wall is painted in a dark blue color and rest of the three walls are in light blue. The dark wall has a few things on it. There is a painting that is hanged on that wall. I bought that painting from an exhibition last year. There is also a music system in my room which I play in my leisure time. I like to dance on loud music when I feel bored. I also spend time with my friends in my room. I remember when I used to study along with a couple of my friends in the exam days.

At the back side of the room, there is a huge window that can be opened easily when required. In the evenings when I feel that I am being too much indoors, I just open the window to get fresh air in the room. Sometimes I also like to gaze at the park that is right behind my house. My room is very special to me, and I spend most of the time in my room.

Speak about an adventurous person you know

How do you know that person?
Why do you think he/she is adventurous?
Do you like adventure?

I am more of a peace-loving person. I am not at all an adventurous person, but I know quite a few of them. I have a big friend circle and know some people who are very adventurous. An adventurous person whom I know well is one of my best friends, Amit.

He lives near my home, and we are friends since 2012. He is of same age as mine and we share a lot of interests but an unusual hobby that he follows is doing adventurous activities. I do not like to participate in such activities, but Amit is one of those who never backs off from adventurous activities.

He is a very cool minded person and is always ready to do anything. He is very energetic and enthusiastic. He loves to travel to new places and do uncommon activities. In his everyday life, he is always making plans to do one or the other adventurous activity.

I remember last year we went to Manali in the summer holidays. He was excited about the white river rafting that is famous there. When we reached Manali, the first thing he did was the river rafting. He did not waste any time and straightaway went to the bank of the river and asked the operators about getting on to the raft.

I decided to not go for rafting and rather wait for him. When he came back after an hour, he was so glad that he did that activity. He said he did it with ease and enjoyed it to the fullest.

When we became friends a few years back, he told me that he has a long bucket list of doing adventurous activities like bungee jumping and sky diving. Today, he has done all those activities and seeks for more adventure.

He is a real adventurous person and loves to do adventure whenever he gets time. This habit of his has a positive effect on his nature. I have seen that he is fearless and this attitude comes from doing adventurous activities that requires taking risks.

A meal you enjoyed at a restaurant

OR

Talk about your favorite restaurant

Where is it located?
What do you like the most about that restaurant?
How often do you go to that restaurant?

Usually, I prefer home-cooked food as it is not only good for our health but is also very hygienic. Although it does not mean that I do not like eating out. I love to go to new restaurants at least once in a week.

The restaurant I like the most is the Taj Restaurant. This restaurant is in Chandigarh. This is a buffet style restaurant and does not cater for a la carte customers. This restaurant is in the heart of the city and huge number of people flock to this place especially on weekends.

I love this restaurant for a few factors. The first one is the variety of food they offer. I am a vegetarian, and they have a great assortment of vegetable snacks in their menu. They serve around eight snacks along with salads, main course, and desserts.

In the main course, there are more than ten items that you can choose. All the snacks and main course items are mouthwatering. Once you are finished with your main course, they offer an abundance of desserts. I am fond of eating sweet items and like their chocolate brownie the most.

Apart from the variety they serve, they also take care of the quality of food they are serving to their customers. The menu includes different types of cuisines like Chinese, Mughlai, and continental. The best part is that you get free drinks with their buffet lunch and dinner. I always order virgin mojito as it is their most refreshing drink.

The ambience of the restaurant is top notch. The seats are comfortable, and the lighting is a bit dim that compliments the setting very well. Moreover, their staff is well behaved and always smiling.

This is a newly opened restaurants so the price for the buffet is also not that high. I love going to this restaurant again and again.

Describe an important decision you made

OR

Decision you made with the help of someone

What was the decision?
How important was it?
Who helped you in your decision making?

There are many decisions that I have taken in my life. A right decision can do wonders, whereas a bad decision in life can cost you a fortune. The one that I will discuss with you today is the decision that I took few days back (or after I cleared my twelfth class/graduation) with the help of my elder sister.

Till now, most of the decisions in my life are taken by my parents. They are the well-wishers and have always taken right decisions for me. Even I always consult my parents and elder sister regarding any important decision that I want to take.

After completing my twelfth class, I was in a lot of confusion. I could not make a choice between studying in India or abroad. I thought that it would be good for me if I pursue my higher studies in India but looking at the competition here, I had a fear of failure. On the other hand, studying from a foreign university or college requires a lot of funds. I did not want to bother my parents about this.

I have never been so jumbled in my whole life. I was not able to make any decision about my future and after some days I started feeling irritated. One day I decided to talk to all my family members regarding my frustration.

My sister understood my situation and calmed me down. She explained me the benefits of studying abroad. She also pointed out that the course I want to pursue will be better suited if I studied from a foreign university. She told me not to worry about the funds as she will talk to the parents regarding this.

My parents agreed and then my sister advised me to take the IELTS test. This decision cleared the air and confusion in my mind. Now I am really focused and have planned to apply in a university in Canada. This decision was crucial for me as my whole career was hanging in a balance. I want to thank my sister for helping me to take this important decision.

Speak about someone who is a good cook

How do you know him/her?
Why he/she is a good cook?
What type of dishes he/she can make?

I have come across many people whom I find to be good cooks. But the one I would like to talk about is my mother. She is a wonderful cook and makes stunning dishes. The reason that she is a good cook is because she likes to cook.

Cooking food is her biggest hobby. In her free time, she likes to watch videos of famous chefs and enjoys copying those recipes. She makes mouthwatering cuisine with minimal efforts. I have no hesitation in saying that she is the best cook I have seen in my entire life.

The reason that makes her a good cook is that she has patience. I think this is one of the qualities that is needed in good cooks. She tries different dishes every day and perfects most of them in a couple of attempts because she is never afraid of failures. Even if the dish is not made according to her wishes, she keeps on trying it again and again till she achieves the perfect consistency.

She is expert in making savory dishes. She likes to cook Chinese, continental, and north Indian food the most. I like noodles with chilly chicken in Chinese and butter chicken in north Indian category. I get so many different varieties of dishes every day. I never get bored eating food made by my mother.

She has a never-ending desire for making variety of dishes. She does it with great sense of ease and versatility. I like to eat everything that she makes. Apart from making food delicious, she is expert in plating the cuisines as well.

She has a diary in which she notes down all the recipes she makes. One day I was stunned to see her diary. She told me that she has written around one hundred unique recipes in that. I have suggested my mother to publish a food recipe book soon. So, in the end I would like to say that my mother is a great cook.

Describe a stressful day at school/college/university

What made your day stressful?
How did you manage the stress?
How do you deal with stressful situations?

Some days of our lives are so traumatic that they leave an imprint on our brain for the whole life. I was in my school when such an incident happened in front of me. I was roaming around with my friends in the school ground as it was the lunch break.

Suddenly, we heard a scream from the opposite side of the building, and we saw one boy lying on the floor. He fell from the second floor and was hurt very badly. All the students and other staff members immediately gathered around him. The scene was frightening for everyone as he was screaming in pain and lying in a pool of blood. I was terrified to see him as he was my friend Amit.

The medical staff arrived on the scene and gave him first aid. Then they took him to a nearby hospital. The injuries seemed to be severe as he fell on the floor from about twenty feet height. There was pin drop silence in the school after this incident happened. Everyone was praying for his speedy recovery. I was so tensed and did not go to my house. Instead, I went to the hospital along with some other students and staff members.

In these kinds of situations, I like to pray. When I perform prayers, it gives me peace of mind and strength. I was waiting outside the hospital and kept on roaming here and there. I was in constant anxiety, and it was one of the most stressful days for me at the school.

The sigh of relief came to us when we were informed that Amit was fine and out of danger. After some time, we were allowed to meet Amit where he claimed that it was just an accident, and nobody was at fault.

That day was a very stressful one for me as Amit was one of my good friends and I was constantly worried about his life.

A place where you like to read books

OR

A place indoor or outdoor where you can study

Why indoor/outdoor?
Is outdoor a better place to study?
Mention the place in detail

Everyone likes to study in a different environment. Personally, I like to study at a place where no one can disturb me. So, the place where I can concentrate more on my studies is my personal room.

I have kept one study table in my room, where I usually study. It is the most comfortable place for me to study as I can focus more on my work rather than things that distract me. The study table is quite big and can store a lot of books and stationery. The study table is made of Teak wood which is one of the finest types found in India. It is polished in a tan color. There is a luxurious seat with the table that adds to the comfort of studying on it.

The lighting in my room is also on the brighter side which makes reading books easy. The curtains in my room can be pulled up for more natural light in the room. There is a balcony attached to my room so whenever I need a short break, I can stroll there for a few minutes and recharge myself.

My room is at the backside of our house, so luckily there is negligible outside noise or distraction in my study room. There are all the amenities like air conditioner, mini fridge and computer in my room which makes it easier for me to study for long hours.

If I feel tired studying on the study table, I can sit in a relaxed posture on my bed and continue my study. I am a fan of studying indoor as outdoor noise and activities divert my attention a lot. So, my personal room is the place where I like to study / read books.

A movie or TV show that made you laugh

Describe the show/movie
Speak about the actors
How this movie or show is funny?

I am fond of watching movies and TV serials as they deliver great entertainment. I usually do not get a lot of time to watch TV on the weekdays. So, the only day left for me is Sunday. On Sunday, one of the most famous shows is telecasted on TV, The Kapil Sharma show.

I love humorous shows that can make me laugh and give me some stress-free time. Nowadays, I am watching this show regularly. It is a hilarious show that involves various comedians and celebrities that visits the sets of Kapil Sharma, the host.

This serial is broadcasted only on weekends for one-hour in the evening and is hosted by a well-known comedian Kapil Sharma. The host of the show is famous in our country and is famed for his funny satires. His excellent standup comedy makes him different from all other comedians.

The show is accompanied by various other famous comedians like Ali Asgar, Upasana Singh, Sunil Grover, Kiku Sharda, Chandan Prabhakar, Sumona Chakraborty. All the actors in this show are super funny and makes everyone laugh hard.

This show is witnessed by a huge number of people who are invited to be the audience at the show. Every weekend, some famous personalities visit their show, and they do a lot of hilarious stuff with them. This show is a one-hour dose of stress-free time. It is one of the highly viewed shows of all time in our country.

I eagerly wait for this show every weekend. I finish all my work before the show is about to start and I am glued to my TV screen until the show ends. I even love to watch the repeat telecast of this show on weekdays.

So, I feel that this is the show that makes me laugh every week.

Talk about a dish you know how to cook

Can you cook many dishes?
Do you often cook it?
How is that dish made?

I am not a cook, but I can make a few dishes. I believe that cooking is an activity that everyone should know irrespective of their genders. Mostly in our country, men are not associated with cooking, but I think they should also know a bit of cooking so that they can survive in every situation.

I can mostly make Indian dishes. The one that I like to make is rice with kidney beans. This is one of the most popular dishes in the part of the county where I live. This is also known as the royal dish. Most people make this dish to please the guests.

I eat it every week especially on weekends. I love to make this dish and serve it to all my family members. My friends are also fond of eating this dish when made by me. This is a simple, yet it takes a bit of time to prepare.

To make this, red kidney beans must be washed and soaked in water overnight. This process helps them to cook faster and brings the best taste. For preparation, add two tablespoons of oil or ghee in a pan. In that, put ground onions and tomatoes. Then add salt and red chilies to taste.

Heat the mixture until it is cooked properly. Then pour the soaked kidney beans and this mixture in a pressure cooker. Add a couple of glasses of water for desired consistency. Let it cook for thirty minutes. On the other hand, soak some rice for ten minutes and then boil it in a pan and serve hot with kidney beans.

This is a dish that has a lot of spicy curry in it. It is best served hot. I am in love with this dish, and I always love to cook it when I am in joyous mood.

A time when someone did not tell you the whole truth

When did this happen?
What was the truth that was not revealed?
How did you feel when you came to know about the truth?

There are many instances in my life when I was not told the whole truth. This happened when we went to a private bank to open a bank account. I had to open a savings bank account, so I went there as it is one of the renowned banks in our country. I went there along with my father.

I inquired about the opening of the account at the reception. I was escorted by the receptionist to the counter where new customers are directed. I was asked about my age and was given a form to fill. I filled all the details in the form and submitted it to the employee at the counter.

The lady behind the table asked me to tick mark the type of account I would like to open. There were three types of savings accounts that came with different benefits. The first one was free of charge and had no condition of maintaining a minimum balance in it. Other types of accounts were expensive to maintain but had many benefits.

Since I am a student and there can be times when my account will not have much balance, my father suggested me to open the simple account with zero balance. I told the bank employee to open a normal savings account. They told us to wait for fifteen minutes and asked us to deposit a small amount of money to activate the account. I deposited five thousand rupees that day.

After a few days I received a message that some money was deducted from my account. I had made no transactions, so I became suspicious about it. I went to the bank immediately and asked them about the deducted money.

They told that the charges were subtracted due to low balance in the account. They deducted one thousand rupees from my account. I argued that this was a zero-balance account and asked how they can charge me for low balance. I was angry and complained this issue to the manager of the bank.

Then the manager told me that it is mandatory to keep at least ten thousand for a month when you open a new account. I told the manager that I was not provided with this information at the time of opening account and demanded for a refund. But my efforts went into vain as they did not give me a refund.

I felt betrayed by the bank staff as they did not tell me the whole truth and conditions of opening a bank account. I felt dejected and learned a lesson that day to check all the terms and conditions in detail.

Talk about something you taught to a teenager

OR

Talk about something you taught to someone

What did you teach?
How much time it took?
Did the person learn that thing?

There are a few things in my life that I have been able to teach to teenagers. One thing that I would like to tell you is when I taught something to my cousin. My cousin is only fourteen and he wanted to learn to send and receive emails.

He called me one day and asked me if I was available and could teach him this skill. I told him to come over to my place someday. After a couple of days, he came to my house to learn that skill. I started teaching him the different aspects of email.

First, I told him about the different websites that offer to create free email id. We picked one and made a new account on that. I told him to choose an identity and a unique password for further use. He chose the id and created a new password.

Then we opened the email homepage and I trained him to compose different kinds of emails. I also taught him to send attachments with the email. I could notice that he was curious when I was telling him all these things. Then he asked me about creating new emails faster. Then I showed him the template section where we can store different templates for different occasions.

After that I told him to open the emails received by him and how he should draft the reply. I also taught him the method to save email list and how he can use shortcut buttons to perform different functions to save time. I told him everything about emails that I know. Then I asked him to send me some emails so that he could perfect this art. He spent around three hours with me and learned most of the things that I taught.

At the end, he thanked me and told that it was an urgent need for him to learn how to send and reply to the emails. He was extremely happy that day as he had learnt a new skill set that will help him in future as well.

When you found something that someone lost

What did you find?
How and where did you find that thing?
Did you return that?

I have seen a couple of people in my life who find a lot of lost things. I think I am not that lucky but one day I found something that I could have never imagined in my life.

Last year I went to a theater to watch a movie. During the movie I opened my shoes and placed it below the seat. After the movie was over, I noticed that my shoes were pushed deep under the seat. So, I had to bent down and look for my shoes.

I got the shoes but to my surprise I also found something lying on the floor. I quickly pulled it and noticed that someone had left his wallet accidently over there. It was a men's leather wallet. It was swollen like a ball and when I opened it, I was shocked to see that it was stuffed with a lot of money.

I inspected further and found some ATM and credit cards as well. I quickly put it in my pocket and brought it home. I had no idea what to do with it. I told my parents about this and showed them the purse. My father told me to check the wallet thoroughly and see if I could find the owner. Otherwise, he suggested to return the wallet to the mall authority.

In the side pocket I found some fancy looking visiting cards that suggested a name along with phone number. There was no address on those cards, only name and a mobile number. I called on that number, but no one picked the call. After some time, I received a call from the same number, and I asked that person if his wallet was lost.

He acknowledged instantly and told me about the color and belongings of the wallet. I told him my address and asked him to pick up the wallet as soon as he gets time. He came to our house the next day and thanked me for finding his wallet. He said that he never expected to find his wallet as there was a huge amount of cash in it.

He was glad and kept on thanking me for the gesture. He then gave me two thousand rupees note as a token of appreciation, but I refused saying that it is all your money, and you deserve all of it. He thanked again and insisted me to keep that. I kept that note but later donated it to a private charity.

So that was the thing that someone lost, and I found it.

Describe a beautiful home you have seen

Who owns the house?
Describe the house in detail
Why do you think that house is beautiful?

Recently my friend shifted to a new house. He invited me to visit him on a Sunday. I went there in the morning and what I saw there was nothing short of a great experience.

My friend's new house is like a king's palace. It is built in a total area of four thousand square feet. It is a huge area that has a house in the center and the surrounding area of the premise is a courtyard. There is a huge entry gate at the front that leads to a parking area. The exterior of the house is painted in white colour.

The main door of the house is magnificent. The carving on the wooden door looks elegant. The main door opens in a common area that has sofas, a table and stairs leading to the upper floor. As soon as one enters the house, you get a luxury feeling. The lighting on the roof is of warm white colour which perfectly complements the white marble on the floor.

The floor is pure white but reflects a golden tinge with the lights on. There are five bedrooms on the ground floor. I went to my friend's bedroom and asked him to show all the corners of his house. His room was painted white in colour with beautiful design on one wall. The floor was the same as in common room. The room was glittering and was looking fantastic.

I also saw the other rooms in which the colours were a bit different, but the floor was same all over. All the things were chosen according to the taste of the individuals in the family. The roof of the house has a down ceiling. The ceiling has gorgeous led lights that adds to the overall beauty of the house.

Most of the walls of the house on the ground floor are painted in white but the walls in the drawing room were colourful and vibrant. The drawing room is big with a seating capacity of twenty. The drawing room is decorated superbly. There is a huge chandelier that hangs in the center of the drawing room.

Then we went on the upper floor where I saw only one room. That room was huge and had all the sports related equipment and a ping pong table. I was so excited to see it and played a couple of games with my friend. The upper floor also had a big terrace garden. I saw such a beautiful terrace garden for the first time in my life.

I felt so good after visiting this house. My friend's house is the most beautiful house that I have seen in my entire life.

A subject you did not like but now you find interesting

How did you develop interest in that subject?
Why did you not like it earlier?
Do you still read that subject?

I did not like most of the subjects in my school time. I thought that mathematics, chemistry, physics and especially history are useless subjects. I was always inclined towards practical subjects like biology, physical education, and computers.

I hated history as a subject when I was at school. I could never remember all the dates and events of the past. I never scored good in this subject and found the history class to be the most boring one. But after all these years I have started to find my curiosity in history.

I found my interest in history when I read a book written by Mahatma Gandhi. The name of the book is 'My experiments with truth'. When I read the book, I was impressed to find the history in it. Our history is so rich that we must preserve it and encourage kids to read it as well. This book taught me about the struggles that our past leaders have made to achieve freedom for our country.

I have gained a lot of interest in the history subject from the past few years and have read several books on it. Apart from reading My experiments with truth, I also read about the autobiography of the former president of the republic of South Africa, Mr. Nelson Mandela. The name of the book is long walk to freedom. From this book I came to know that Nelson Mandela spent almost thirty years in jail and still came out to become the first black President of South Africa.

History teaches us a lot of things that we can follow to take right decisions in the future. Reading history inspires us to achieve greatness in our lives. I have now made a habit of reading about history every day. I spend around 30 minutes in reading something about the past. I feel that history subject has attracted me a lot in the recent times.

Something you bought but did not use

Do you like shopping?
What was the product and why you did not use it?
Do you regret buying it?

I love shopping and whenever I get chance I like to shop. Sometimes I shop unnecessarily and repent afterwards. One thing I remember that I bought and did not use is a perfume.

I bought this perfume from my trip to Dubai, but I did not even use it once. I went to Dubai last year with my family and was excited about the trip. We saw myriad attractions over there and went to a lot of shopping malls.

There we came to know that Dubai is famous for its Oudh. Oudh is basically essential oil that has long lasting fragrance. People of Emirates use Oudh in their daily life. This can be called as perfume because Oudh is not known in the outer world by many. This perfume comes in an endless variety of fragrances and colours.

Someone at our hotel suggested us to visit Meena Bazaar which is a local market in Dubai to buy that perfume. We went there immediately and started looking for shops that were selling perfumes. We got notice of a huge multistoried shop and its facade was designed in a perfume bottle shape. We all were attracted to it and went inside the shop to buy the perfume.

I am not a huge admirer of perfumes, but I use them on certain occasions. So, I thought of buying one as a souvenir from Dubai. The Oudh perfume is packed in a traditional glass flask. It is not sprayed but applied gently to the neck and other body parts directly.

The salesperson told us to gently rub a small drop of this oil and then apply it to clothes or wherever necessary.

I bought a fancy bottle that contained 50ml perfume. I tried the fragrance on the neck and liked it pretty much. The fragrance was pungent and stayed on the body for most part of the day. After some time, I could not bear the smell and had allergic reaction on my body.

It was a non-returnable product so I could not return it. The bottle is kept with me in my dressing almirah, but I have not used it even once. I have no regret of buying that perfume as I have kept it as a souvenir.

Time when you had to change your plan

What was the original plan?
Why did you change the plan?
Was it easy to change plan or you faced any difficulty?

I generally do not change my plans. I like to stick to my plans and follow them strictly. But there was an instance when I had to change my plan. This happened last month when we were planning to visit Goa.

We had planned this trip a lot of days in advance. I took the responsibility of booking the flights, hotels, and the tour. We were planning this trip with my other relatives. In total we were eight persons, and I was excited for that trip. We booked our flights and hotels from a renowned travel website. I had paid all the amount for the tour in advance, so I started preparing for the trip a week before. I packed all the necessary clothes and items.

My other family members also did all the preparations for the trip. We had to leave on Sunday for Delhi as we had to catch the flight from there. Unfortunately, on Saturday my cousin got seriously ill. He was diagnosed with acute fever and viral infection. We were so worried about his health, and I thought that trip would be cancelled as we had to depart for the trip next day. I was also concerned about the bookings that we had made. The doctor advised him to take rest for at least five days and suggested not to go on the trip. For this reason, we had to change all our plans. We all decided to postpone the trip. Fortunately, our tickets and hotel bookings were refundable. So, we were able to change the dates of our travel. I contacted the travel website and got the response swiftly. They modified our bookings and gave us new tickets and vouchers. We postponed the trip ten days ahead so that my cousin could recover properly because we did not want to go without him. So, this is the time when I had to change my plans.

A person you wanted to be like

Who is that person and what does he do?
Why you want to be like him/her?
Have you become like him/her?

OR

A sportsperson you admire the most

I admired a lot of people in my childhood. There were many heroes that I followed because I always wanted to be like them. There was one person whom I wanted to be like. He is my all-time favourite cricketer, Sachin Tendulkar. I am a great follower of this game. In my childhood I used to watch cricket matches whenever I had free time. I remember that most of my friends were interested in watching cartoon programs, but I was always indulged in cricket matches. Most of the youngsters in our country who play cricket are inspired by Sachin Tendulkar. He earns a great respect around the world from cricket lovers. He is known to be the greatest cricketer to have graced the cricket field till now. He holds countless records in the game and some of the records set by him looks so unbelievable. Most of the people reckon that no one will be able to achieve those records. I was a huge fan of Sachin Tendulkar and always wanted to become like him. I used to imitate his style of batting and, I would do certain gestures that he did while playing. I had a huge poster of Sachin on the wall of my bedroom. I always looked at his poster and imagine becoming like him and play this game for my country. He has great qualities in him. He is extremely calm in nature and understands the situations and tackle the difficulties in a mature way. He used to play with calmness and has won crunch matches for our country. This is the quality that I surely wanted to borrow from him. Not only me, most of the youngsters in that era wanted to become like him. In the playing days he had that charisma which was admired by everyone. I wanted to be like Sachin Tendulkar in every aspect of life. Although I could not become like him, but he is such person whom I admired the most in the past and I still do.

OR

There are many people in my life whom I want to be like. The person whom I want to be like is Harmanpreet Kaur. She is an Indian cricketer and plays an allrounder for the Indian women's cricket team. Recently she was awarded with one of the most prestigious awards, Arjuna Award for cricket by the ministry of youth affairs and sports. She was born in 1989 in Moga, Punjab. Her nick name is Harman. She is a top order bat and bowls right arm slow. She made her debut for the country in 2009. She has set many records on this field. She became first women cricketer to score 100 runs in a twenty over match in 2018. She went through a lot of struggles in life before becoming a settled player in the Indian team. She was awarded the captaincy of the team in 2018. While she is playing the game, she looks very aggressive. She has an attacking style of play and is famous for hitting the ball long. I like her playing style and most of the young girls follow her and take inspiration from her to become cricketers. Women in our country were not interested in playing cricket previously. Their thinking changed after they realized that cricketers like Harmanpreet Kaur can earn such a great name and fame by playing this game. I am following her from many years, and I am a huge fan of her game. I have always wanted to become like her and create a niche for myself. She is such an inspiration for all the girls who look to take up this sport. I was very impressed with her and always wanted to become like her.

An occasion when you bought/made a special cake

Why did you buy the cake?
Why is it special?
Give details of the cake

I must have bought numerous cakes in my life as there are special occasions every year. Generally, I buy cakes on my friends or family member's birthday. But the time when I bought a special cake was the wedding reception of my brother. This cake was extremely special due to many reasons. The first reason is that it was my brother's wedding, and I was really pleased on that day. Also, it was going to be the biggest cake that I have seen or bought in my life.

My father put the responsibility of buying the cake on me. So, I went to a bakery where I generally go. It is one of the renowned bakeries in our hometown. I went there a week before the function. I asked the manager of the bakery about the special cakes for wedding functions. He handed me over a cake book in which thousands of designs were printed. He told me to choose one for the occasion. I was so confused as there were so many cakes in that book. My preferred type of cake is chocolate based. So, I told my requirement to the manager and then he suggested me to buy chocolate mud cake. He told that the cake is made from hundred percent chocolate topped with more chocolate on the outside of the cake. I finalized that cake but did not tell anyone about the design and type of cake. I made full payment in advance, and they assured that our cake will be delivered on time. Another reason that it was a special cake is that I had never seen such a huge cake in my entire life. The cake was designed for two hundred people. When they delivered the cake at the wedding venue, everyone was surprised to see the huge size of it.

They carefully unwrapped the cake and placed it on the table where the cake was to be cut. The cake was made in several parts, and they assembled each part on the table. The height of the cake was around four feet. I had never seen such a wonderful cake in my life. After the cake was cut, everyone praised it. The taste was fantastic, and the presentation was equally good. Undoubtedly it was the most special cake of my life.

An aspect of modern society that you dislike

Which aspect do you dislike?
Why do you dislike it?
Is modern society better than the older one?

Change is the unchanging law of nature. This line is true in every aspect of the world. I have seen a lot of changes in the perception, customs, and culture over the years. But the biggest change has happened in the lifestyle of people, and I do not like it at all.

People are now becoming lethargic and dependent on technology for most of their chores. I dislike the intervention of technology in our life. Technology is useful for us but only up to a certain extent. After that it becomes a menace.

These days I see most of the people hooked to their phones. Nowadays people are using internet more than ever and the usage continues to grow in the future as well. This is a dangerous trend as we are disconnected from the real world. People are living in a virtual social world where they interact with people and their friends through social networking sites. But there is no physical contact and emotions.

Apart from this, today's children are staying indoors as compared to the past. They do not like to go out and play. Instead, they are stuck in either mobile phones or video games. It is a terrible inclination towards such activities. I do not like when I see kids sitting at home and watching cartoons instead of playing outdoors.

There has been a hazardous invasion of technology in our lives. People in the past used to walk a lot but today people use vehicles to travel short distances. This habit has made people lazy and weak. Due to such lifestyle, immune systems are getting weak as well.

In my area, I have come across many people who are facing the deficiency of vitamin D. The major reason behind this problem is that people like to stay indoors whereas vitamin D is absorbed from sunlight exposure. In the end I would like to say that I do not like the overdependence on technology in the modern society.

Describe a famous scientist/inventor you know about

How did you know about him?
What has he achieved?
What made him famous?

Scientists have brought the revolution in our world. They are the ones who have given us some of the best things in our life. They have invented so many things on our planet that have made our lives easier. I adore many scientists of our country, but whom I admire the most is Dr. APJ Abdul Kalam. He was born in the small coastal town of Rameswaram.

I came to know about this great man when I was in school. I read many articles describing his achievements and his autobiography as well.

He has given his expert ideas in the aeronautical field. Not only this, but his contribution to the Defense area of our country is also remarkable. He is widely known as the "Missile Man of India" as he was one of the biggest contributors in the launch vehicle technology in space and missile development program.

He launched India's first missile vehicle in the space in the 1990s, named SLV-III Project after joining the ISRO. He deployed the Rohini satellite in space in 1980. His work was so brilliant that he got immediate approval from the Indian government to proceed with his work for the Indian satellite launch vehicles. Being the Director of the satellite program, he hired more engineers for his assistance and launched many satellites successfully over a period of three decades.

Many missile programs were initiated in 1980 under his leadership to develop ballistic missiles for the defense of our country. He was also involved in a few manned and unmanned space programs. His contribution to our country not only ends here, but he also served as the President of our country from 2002 to 2007. I think he was still unknown to a lot of people until he became the president of our country. He was also known as the People's President for his humble nature and his knack of meeting people casually in public.

I am not only inspired by his excellent work in the technology but from his personal life too. He came from a humble background. Despite this he was able to study hard and became one of the most eminent scientists that India has produced. Apart from this, he has written myriad books. His autobiography has been read by millions of people across the world. The name of that book is Wings of Fire.

He has received various prestigious awards in his lifetime like Padma Bhushan, Padma Vibhushan, Bharat Ratna and many honorary doctorate awards for his excellence in the aeronautical industry. I admire him as one of the greatest inventors of our country.

Describe a school you have studied in

What was the name of your school?
Explain the details of the school area
Did you like the school?

I went to one of the famous schools in my city. I read in Woodstock School. It is a public school and is still one of the renowned schools in my city. The school was situated three kilometers from my house. I used to ride my cycle to the school. Our school was built in a huge area and had all the modern amenities in it.
I will start with entrance. There was a huge gate at the front which is painted in yellow and burgundy colour. These are the theme colours of our school. There was a reception area right at the entrance of the school on the right-hand side. It led to a huge parking area where school buses were parked.
There are several buildings in the school premises. The first one was known as A-Block. This block had classes 10th, 11th, and 12th. The principal's office was also located in this block. This block was the most disciplined wing of the school at that time.
Behind the A-Block, there was a smaller building known as B-Block. In that block, classes 5th to 9th were placed. In front of the block A and B, a huge 100 by 100-meter playground. That ground was mainly used for hockey and football practice. Adjacent to the ground was a big canteen area and two basketball courts.
On the other side of the playground which was the largest building in the school campus. This building was known as block – C. This building houses a boy's hostel and primary classes. The hostel area is not that big, but it is very neat and clean.
Adjacent to the hostel area, there was a big dining hall where hostel students used to have their meals. Opposite to the dining area, there was a huge auditorium was where we regularly watched educational movies and documentaries.
Right in the center of the school, there is a huge assembly area where all the students used to gather in the morning and do prayers. I really enjoyed my time at the school. I was blessed to study in such school where all the conveniences were offered accompanied with world class infrastructure.

Expensive clothing you have bought lately

Why did you buy that expensive piece of clothing?
Tell about the dress
Do you wear that dress quite often?

I generally do not buy expensive clothing but there are some occasions in life when one needs to buy fashionable and expensive clothes. I remember when I had to buy an expensive attire for my brother's marriage. The marriage party was to be held in the evening, so I decided to buy dark coloured three-piece suit. This was the first time when I had to buy such dress. I went to the market and started looking for a perfect dress for the occasion.
I explored all the branded shops and tried a lot of suits there. But somewhere down the line I was not satisfied. Some suits were perfect in fit but the colour was not attractive. On the other hand, some had attractive colours but did not fit well. So, I decided to get my suit stitched from a tailor. I found a renowned tailor in the town and told him my requirements. He showed me a couple of books containing hundreds of clothing designs. He also recommended me to buy a particular type of cloth for the suit. Hence, I bought a black-coloured cloth and took it to the tailor. The piece of cloth costed me around ten thousand rupees. I was not impressed with the design that tailor showed me. So, I browsed the internet and took out a three-

piece suit design from there. I showed it to the tailor, and he assured me that he would imitate that design to perfection. He did a couple of modifications to that design so that it would suit my body type. The stitching cost of the suit was five thousand rupees. Then I had to buy a matching shirt with the suit. That shirt was of white colour and costed me around two thousand rupees. I do not wear this dress often as it only suits on parties and special occasions. I had never got such an expensive clothing for myself but when I wore that suit, I felt that it was worth every penny.

OR

I am not very fond of expensive clothing. I always set a budget before purchasing anything new. But there has been a time where I shopped limitlessly which was on my brother's wedding. In the Indian culture, a lot of importance is given to all the rituals which are performed in a wedding and getting decked up for them is the most favourite part of all the girls. I was extremely excited for the wedding and wanted to look the best, so I bought a Lehenga which is a traditional form of an Indian Gown. It is a Gown designed by one of the renowned designers in our country, Sabyasachi. The dress was looking stunning but was expensive. So, I decided to look for more shops.

Then I went to other shops and saw hundreds of designs, but nothing could match the dress I had seen earlier. So, I went back to the shop I had gone previously and ordered the dress. It was an expensive dress and I had to pay twenty-five thousand for it.

The dress was royal looking with a combination of vibrant colours. The main colour of the dress was bottle green along with yellow scattered all through. The detailing and design of the dress was mesmerizing. The tailor at the shop took my measurements and altered the dress according to my size. I wore that dress on the wedding reception of my brother and everyone at the wedding venue gave me flattering remarks and told me that I was looking like a princess. I had never bought such an expensive dress before this occasion.

Time when you had to take care of a baby

Who was the baby?
Why had you to take care of him/her?
How did you feel about the situation?

I like to play with small kids and babies. But it is not an easy task for an inexperienced person to take care of a baby. It may seem an easy task but from my personal experience I can tell you that it takes a lot of courage and experience to oversee a baby.

There was an instance in the past when I had to take care of a baby for a couple of hours. My sister's baby is one-year old whose name is Amy. He is very adorable and do not cry too much like other kids.

He still does not walk properly so there must be someone to look after him all the time.

Earlier my sister had applied for a job in a multinational company. She received an interview call, and the company was in the city where we lived. She called me and asked if anyone was at home to take care of Amy.

I told her that everyone had gone out for one or the other work and I was the only person who was present at home. She told me about the situation and rushed to our home and asked me to baby sit Amy for a couple of hours.

I was reluctant at first, but finally agreed to take the responsibility. She bought a bag full of Amy's toys along with spare clothes and baby food. She quickly explained me how to make baby food and how to feed him when required. I told her not to worry and leave Amy with me. My sister hurried for the interview, and I was left alone with him.

I started playing with him as soon as my sister left because I did not want him to notice that his mother is not there. I made funny faces to make him laugh. After a while he was feeling hungry and started crying for food and made gestures indicating that he was hungry. I quickly made the baby food by adding boiled water in the oats pack. I fed him all the food and it made him extremely happy. We continued playing with toys and I spend a wonderful time with my nephew.

After some time, my sister came and thanked me for babysitting him. I told my sister that I had a wonderful time with Amy, and she could drop him anytime with me. So this was the time when I had to take care of a baby.

Something that you borrowed from your friend or family

Why did you borrow?
Is borrowing a good habit?
Did you return the thing?

I do not usually borrow things from others as I consider it a bad activity, but I think borrowing from a good friend or family member is not a bad idea. I have borrowed few things from my friends and family in the past. But I remember once I needed a digital DSLR camera for my school trip to a wildlife sanctuary. I did not buy a DSLR camera as it is very expensive. I am extremely fond of clicking wildlife photographs and the camera that I own is old and do not click clear pictures.

So instead of buying that thing I called one of my best friends who had this camera. My friend got ready to give me the camera on the first call. He told me to collect the camera from his home and he would also teach me certain functions of the camera that I do not know.

I reached his home and he handed me the camera along with its accessories and safety gear. He explained me how to use the accessories and the different modes to get the best picture. Then he packed the camera and equipment in a bag and wished me luck.

I wanted this camera badly as one does not get a chance every day to visit wildlife sanctuary and click wildlife photographs. I thanked my friend and promised him to return his camera in the same condition.

I took that camera on my trip and clicked hundreds of pictures. I felt amazing while clicking the pictures. The camera also had an extra lens attached to it which helped in to zoom the far away animals and places.

My other colleagues were really impressed with the camera and my photography skills. Some of my mates wanted to borrow the camera from me but I told them it is not mine. When I came back, I saved all the pictures in a laptop and handed over the camera to my friend with a big thanks.

Describe a noisy place you have been to

Do you live in a noisy environment?
Why was the place noisy?
Did you get uncomfortable?

It is not difficult to find noisy places in our country. We have the world's second largest population and there are countless vehicles commuting on the roads. In this topic, I would like to explain my visit to PCA stadium which is situated in Mohali. I went there to witness a T20 match between India and Australia.

This was a world cup match and was held in 2016. I had never felt such a huge noise before in my life. The match began at 7 PM and ended at 11 PM. It was one of the noisiest places that I had ever been to.
As soon as I entered the stadium, I saw the stadium packed with people cheering for their respective teams. The match was held in our country so most of the spectators were supporting India. Even before entering the stadium, the noise of the crowd could be heard from outside.
It was a crucial match so there were an estimated forty thousand people in the stadium. I had never seen such a huge crowd at one place before. When the match started, people were less noisy. But when the Australian wickets started to tumble, people began to shout loud in ecstasy. People generally create noise to lift the morale of their supporting team. India batted in the second innings. The match was a close encounter but a great batting performance from Virat Kohli ensured that India won the match. With every shot Indian player were playing, people were celebrating it like a festival. Some were blowing whistles and others were smashing empty water bottles to create sound.
I was surprised to see that some people had brought blow pipes and other musical instruments to create a noisy environment. I had never heard such noise continuously for four hours. However, I enjoyed my day as India won the match.

Describe a social networking website/platform you use

Do you use social networking sites often?
Which is your favourite one?
Why do you like it?

These days, most of the youngsters are engaged in social networking websites. Youngsters use it for the most part of the day to connect to new people and to see what is happening in their friend's life. I use social networking sites every day. My favourite one is Facebook. I have been using this website from a couple of years and have made many new friends within country and abroad. I have also connected with my old friends with whom I lost touch. I use this website for more than an hour every day.
There are many reasons to like Facebook. The biggest reason is that you stay connected to your friends 24x7. You can post your photographs and you can let people know what is happening in your life. similarly, you can check what your friends are up to these days.
Apart from this, I have found a lot of my old friends on Facebook. Now, I regularly chat with them and get the updates about their life. Moreover, one can like different pages on this website to get information regarding that page. For example, if you like cars, you can like pages related to cars. They will show you videos and updates related to latest cars in the market.
One can also watch news and latest trends in the world. You can also connect with people who are living in foreign countries. Not only this, but you can also promote your business on Facebook. One of the other advantages of using this site is that you can even sell or buy new and used products. I am extremely fond of using this website for making friends in foreign countries.
In total I have made around hundred new friends in foreign countries. I chat with them and try to learn about their culture and lifestyle. I also do video calling with my friends and relatives who are living in foreign countries. All in all, it is a wonderful social networking website.

Describe the politest person you have come across in your life

How do you know that person?
Why do you think that he/she is polite?
Share your experience with that person

I have come across some polite people in my life, but I would like to speak about a person who is my relative and I think that he is the politest person I know in my entire life.

I am talking about my uncle who lives in Himachal Pardesh. His hometown is Bilaspur, and I often visit him in my holidays. I love to go there as it is a neat and clean place with fresh environment. Himachal Pradesh is one of the greenest places in our country.

I would like to share something about my uncle's personality. His name is Rakesh, and he runs a bakery. He is running this business from the past twenty years, and he is doing well in it. I have never seen such a polite person in my entire life. He is not only polite to his friends and family, but he speaks in the same way to everyone.

He is never in an angry mood, and I have never seen him shouting at anyone. His speech is polite and direct. He is a man of few words and only speaks when it is required. He is always gracious to his customers, and I have seen people praising him for his well-mannered speech and behavior.

I can recall an instance when me and my uncle were riding through a market and suddenly, we got hit by a speeding car. Luckily, we did not get injured. There were some minor bruises. Suddenly huge number of people gathered and started criticizing the car driver who hit us. Immediately my uncle told the crowd to not shout at him and let him go as it was not his fault and it was just a judgement of error on the road. My uncle politely solved the situation, and we came back home. That day I learned a great lesson from my uncle that one should remain polite and humble in every situation of life.

A polluted city you have visited

OR

Describe a place you visited that has been affected by pollution

Why did you visit that city?
What sort of problems were there?
Is government doing anything to solve this issue?

India is a country that is rapidly developing in a lot of areas. Due to that, there have been many industries opening up that contributes to pollution. I also think the demand of vehicles has increased drastically which has led to extreme pollution in some cities.

The most polluted city that I have visited in my life is Delhi, the capital of India. Although it is one of the most developed cities across India, but it is also the most polluted one. The main reason of Delhi's pollution is its population. Delhi is one of the densely populated cities in India. People move there from all parts of the country in search of jobs and business opportunities.

I have visited Delhi a lot of times as my relatives live there. I face some pollution related problems whenever I visit there. I face difficulty in breathing and stomachache when I visit Delhi. I came to know from an article that 30% of people living in Delhi are suffering from respiratory problems. When you enter Delhi, you can see a huge pile of waste on the left-hand side of the National Highway. That indicates that not many active steps are taken to manage the waste. There is also the problem of clean drinking water in Delhi. Many residents do not get access to clean drinking water. Many parts of the city are highly developed, but some are extremely dirty. I have seen many people wearing face masks as a precaution against polluted air. Last time when I went to Delhi, I had difficulty in breathing. I had to take medicines for five days to get back to normal. I saw millions of vehicles on the roads that continuously create noise and air pollution. There were some steps taken in the past to curb the pollution in the city. Electric trains and busses that run on clean fuel were introduced that run on clean fuel. Despite those efforts, the pollution keeps on growing in the city.

A talkative person

Tell about that person
Why does he/she talk too much?
How do you feel about him/her?

I know a few people who are talkative in nature, but I have never seen anyone more talkative than my sister Pamela. She simply loves to talk and talk. She is elder to me and works in a multinational company as a website developer. She is tall and has sharp features with fair colour. She looks extremely beautiful in traditional attire.

No one can get bored when they are in the company of my sister. She can make anyone talk to her. I think that's why she has a lot of friends. She can make friends easily. Whenever I see my sister, I always see her talking to someone on phone or in person. I have asked her about the reason behind this. She replied that talking is a therapy for her. She feels relaxed while talking. She always shares her feelings with the family members and bares a jolly nature. I think the reason behind her nature is that she shares all her problems and does not keep it to herself. If she is in a worry, she always tells me. She also encourages other people to speak up.

I remember when she was in school, our parents used to receive a lot of complaints from her teachers. All the complaints were regarding the excess talkativeness in the class. Although she was a brilliant student academically, I have never seen anybody talk like her. Even if she is not well health wise, she cannot stop talking. I always advise her to talk less to save energy, but God knows from where she gets all the strength to talk nonstop.

Interesting news you read in a newspaper OR An article you read in Newspapaer

What was the news?
Where did you read it?
Was the news helpful to you?

I have little interest in reading newspapers. I get my news mostly from the internet. But sometimes I pick up a newspaper on weekends and read the main headlines.

I borrowed a newspaper from my sister as she reads it regularly. I generally read the main headlines and skip some of the pages. However, on that day I decided to read the newspaper thoroughly. I took Hindustan Times newspaper from my sister. I came across one column of a page that I found interesting, and I would like to share that news article with you. That news article was given by the government of our country, and it was an announcement of a scheme that was initiated by the prime minister.

The name of the scheme is 'Pradhan Mantri Awaas Yojna'. Under this scheme the government announced that people of our country will now get quality housing at low cost. In that article, the government announced that the scheme will be available to every Indian who qualifies for it.

In that news, the prices of two-bedroom apartment were also given. The prices were unbelievable as it was a government backed scheme. The price was around twenty lacs for a two-bedroom apartment whereas a normal apartment in a private colony would cost double.

In the news, the site of the project was also mentioned. They also provided the details of the banks that would be approved for the finance of the apartments. The government opened the applications for the apartments and mentioned the last date of application for the scheme. I was so impressed with the news article that I showed it to my whole family. So that was the interesting news article that I read recently.

Talk about an instance when you invited a friend for a meal in a restaurant or at home.

Why did you invite him/her?
Where did you invite him/her?
What sort of meal you had?

I have invited many friends to my home and restaurant for meals. One instance I would like to share with you is when I invited an old friend of mine to a restaurant.

Few days back I met one of my childhood and school friend on a social networking website. I got his number from there and called him immediately. I came to know that he has now shifted to a different city. I had discussion with him after a long time, so I invited him to visit the city someday.

After a few days I received a call from him, and he told me that he is coming to our city the next day. My parents had gone out for a couple of days for some work and there was no one to prepare meals at home. So, I decided to call my friend to a famous restaurant of our city.

Next day I reached at the restaurant and reserved a table. He came there after ten minutes. We shook hands and gave each other a tight hug. I was a bit emotional that time as he used to be one of my best friends. Soon we ordered some snacks to eat. We talked all the time about the things we did at school and gossiped about our old friends. After the snacks we ordered the main course. I ordered Chinese because my friend likes it very much. We ordered noodles along with vegetable Manchurian. The meal was served hot and fresh. This restaurant is famous for authentic Chinese food. We had fantastic time talking and the meal was also wonderful. After that I insisted him to stay at our home for a night, but he had to go back.

Describe a meeting or discussion about fake news

What was the news about?
What did you discuss about it?
Was the news fake or real?

Due to globalization, it has become easy to access information on the go. Most of the times the news that we receive is correct but there can be times when we receive fake news, and we believe in it blindly.

Three years back, a fake news circulated on the TV and the internet. The news was that the new currency notes in our country contains nano GPS chips. Even the big media houses and most of the news channels in our country spread this rumour.

I was at a party with my friends and suddenly this news popped out on the TV. Soon it was all over the internet. Everyone started believing in that news without realizing that this kind of a thing is not possible. The news channels were showing that the Nano chip has been embedded inside the 2000 rupee note to detect the location of it. The news anchors stated the reason that government has done is to track black money and raid people who store huge amounts of notes illegally. This news was shown on all the TV channels and people were posting about it on the social media.

There was an intense discussion between me and my friends about the news. Some of my friends were backing me and supported the idea that it was a fake news. Others believed what they saw on TV. They argued that there must be some truth about the news that's why all the news channels are showing it.

One of my friends also explained that a nano chip is not so small and thin that it can fit a currency note. He told that it is impossible to inject such chips in millions of notes as it would drastically increase the production cost. At the end, we all decided to wait and see if the news was true. After some days some news channels revealed that it was a fake news and apologized to people for that.

Talk about a job one of your grandparents did

What type of job it was?
Did he/she enjoy it?
Would you do the same job?

I was extremely close to my grandfather, and I have taken a lot of inspiration from him in all aspects of life. He has always guided me to the right path. Right now, my grandfather enjoys a retired life but still does voluntary work to pass his leisure time. My grandfather is a well-qualified man and has a master's degree in literature. He worked as a head Librarian in a public library for more than thirty years. He did his job with utmost sincerity and never complained about anything.

He retired ten years ago but he misses his job. He still goes to the same library to read books and relive his working days. He spends around two to three hours in the library whenever he goes there. He told me that he used to work from 8AM to 4PM.

He was the head librarian, so his responsibilities included taking care of the condition of library and to maintain records of the book in the library. He was also responsible for the preservation of the old books. My grandfather tells me that he had to work hard to get this job. He had to clear an entrance exam and there were only seven posts, but the number of candidates was in thousands. He got the job and immediately liked it.

My grandfather reads a lot of books, and he tells me that he developed this habit while working at the library. He started as a librarian but after some time he was promoted to the post of head librarian. He is still sincere towards his work. He enjoyed every bit of his work as a librarian.

Describe a family business you know

Why do you think it is a family business?
What sort of business do they do?
Are you inspired by them?

One of the biggest business family in India is the Ambani family. Their family business is named reliance industries. The reason it is a family business is that all their family members are involved in some sort of business responsibilities. They are multi-millionaires and run hundreds of industries across India. The Reliance Industries was founded by Dhiru Bhai Ambani. Then he handed over the business to his two sons Mukesh Ambani and Anil Ambani. Both brothers parted their ways a few years back and now run their independent industries. Mukesh Ambani is married to Nita Ambani and they both have two sons and a daughter. All five members are in business, and they manage it superbly. Reliance industries is dealing in hundreds of products across the world. Their main business boomed due to the success of their Petro chemical industry. On the other hand, Nita Ambani owns a cricket team franchise, Mumbai Indians. She manages everything related to that team and is also seen motivating players throughout the matches. Recently the reliance industries launched a telecom company by the name of JIO. This company has taken over millions of people. Most of the people are now using this company's mobile connection rather than other brands. This company is managed by Mukesh Ambani's sons. This family works together very well, and I hope they keep growing like this in the future as well. I am so inspired by all of them, and I aspire to follow the footsteps of Mukesh Ambani and would like to become a successful businessman in future.

Talk about your favorite movie star

What type of personality is he/she?
Has he/she influenced you in your life?
Do you feel actors can make good role models?

Indian film industry has produced many film stars who have earned name and fame throughout the world. But for me one name stands out and that is Akshay Kumar. He is also famous by a nick name, Akki. His real name is Rajiv Hari Om Bhatia, but he changed his name when he came into film industry 30 years ago. He belongs to India, but he is now a permanent resident of Canada. He has appeared in more than 100 movies and has won myriad awards, including the National Film Award for the best actor along with a couple of Filmfare awards as well. He is married to another famous actress Twinkle Khanna.
He is one of the most successful actors in the Bollywood film industry. Most of his films are on the top of charts and inevitably does great business. I like him personally due to the kind of films he has done over the past few years. He has portrayed incredible history and sacrifice made by our Army men in the films like Kesari, Holiday, and Baby. He also makes films on social problems so that he can inspire people to change for better. His recent movies like Toilet and Padman earned him a great respect from every corner of the world for raising social issues that are still prevalent in our country. Not only this, but he is also a super fit actor and does most of his action stunts himself. He always inspires people to remain physically fit. He makes videos and post them regularly on the social media sites regarding the importance of being healthy and fit. He knows martial arts and practices yoga in the morning. I have taken a lot of inspiration from him regarding the importance of health and fitness in our lives. I think that actors can be great role models. The reason is that people watch them in movies, and they follow them from heart. So, actors can easily inspire people to do well in life and they can be great role models as well.

A person who has encouraged you recently

Who is that person?
How has he/she encouraged you?
Do you feel that we should have role models in life?

There have been many people in my life from whom I have taken inspiration to do well. Recently I was encouraged by a person named Amit. He is my neighbor and a good friend of mine. He is six years older than me, and he is one of my well-wishers. He lives down the lane and we often hang out together. He is working in a Bank as a manager. I learn a lot of things in his company. We often go for evening walks in the local area. Recently I discussed something with him about my career. I told him that I was looking to study in one of the renowned institutes in Delhi. To which he politely disagreed and suggested me to get my degree from a foreign university instead of studying in India. I asked him about the reason, and he explained that universities and colleges in India these days are charging almost the same fee as the universities and colleges in Canada and Australia. So, it is better if you study abroad as you will get more exposure to different environment and culture.

Further, he suggested that the study pattern in Canada or Australia is more practical that here in India. He also told me that those countries are also offering students to work part-time along with studies. He continued that working along with studies will make me industrious and intelligent. He explained me at length about the other benefits of studying abroad.

That day I felt really encouraged and took the matter of pursuing my further studies in Canada. That's why I am taking the IELTS exam. I think that it is important to have role models in our lives. Instead of looking for inspiration from celebrities one should find role models in people around me. Like I found mine in my friend. So, Amit is the person who has encouraged me in a great way in recent times.

Talk about a practical skill you have learned OR Talk about a practical skill you have

Which skills do you have?
Explain one practical skill you have learned
Is it important to be skillful?

I have a few practical skills that I have learned over the past few years. I can swim and I can drive a car as well. I think that practical skills are crucial to learn as these skills are necessary for your growth in life. One skill that I think everyone should know is the computer skills and how to operate all the functions of a computer.

I learned this skill when I was in my school. I learned most of the practical skills of computers from my teachers at school, but I also took computer classes in my summer breaks for two consecutive years. I think this skill is one of the most critical skills to learn in life these days. Most of the work is done using computers and integration of computers in every field is inevitable. We cannot imagine an office work that is done without computers.

From mailing important data to the companies from receiving and downloading important files, computers have come a long way. We can maintain records of millions of people in a small computer. We can even control machinery through computers.

Most of the industries these days are dependent on computers and robots to perform mechanical tasks. I know a lot of things about computer. I can send and receive emails and I can also maintain data using Microsoft excel software. I know how to use power point software and create slides and business presentations. I can also use editing software for altering pictures and videos. It is not that difficult to learn all this. I learned all of this in four months.

I think it is essential to be skillful as it separates you from others. Even in the job interviews these days mark sheets do not matter. They look for people with more practical skills and prefer offering jobs to them.

Describe an unusual vacation you went to

Do you like vacations?
Why was the vacation unusual?
Did you enjoy it?

I am the kind of a person who loves to go on vacations from time to time. I plan vacations after every six months. One day, I was surprised by my father when he announced to all the family members that he is taking us to a vacation this summer holidays.

That holiday was unusual in many ways. The first reason was that I had never been to a beach area. I had never seen a seashore in my life before. Due to that reason, I was extremely excited for the trip.

There were many types of landscapes and things that I found very unusual. I am talking about the time when I went to Phuket. I found that place extremely beautiful but very unusual as well. Phuket is an island that is a part of the republic of Thailand. It is situated in the southern part of the country. Phuket is surrounded by sea, and I was surprised to know that weather remains constant all year round. I live at a place that has ever changing weather and variating temperatures. I live in a land locked state where sea is far away.

I saw ocean and hills everywhere in Phuket. The landscape and trees there were very different from the place where I live. The other unusual part of the holiday was food. We could not find Indian food easily. The food there was dissimilar from what we eat back home. There was more sea food and other items that were unfamiliar to us.

People there were different looking, and their body language was quite unusual as well. But they were extremely friendly in nature. There were many noticeable things that differed from the things in my hometown and country. We did a lot of activities there that are not easy to find in our country. I think the reason I found that holiday unusual was that I visited a foreign country for the first time. I saw things that I had never seen before.

I absolutely loved that vacation and would like to go there again if I get a chance.

Describe a surprise party you organized for your friend

Why did you arrange the party?
How did you plan the party?
What was your friend's reaction?

I have been a part of many parties and I love to surprise my loved ones by throwing parties for them. I have a very special friend in my life, and we always celebrate our birthdays together. I am talking about Amit who is my childhood friend as well as my neighbour. Few days back, I told Amit that I will not be able to party with him this year. He was upset and asked the reason. I told him that I had to go to one of my relative's marriage party out of the town, so I would not be able to celebrate his birthday with him.

That was my plan to surprise him with a birthday bash. I deceived him by making an excuse as I wanted to surprise him this year with a grand birthday party. The reason I planned the surprise was that one of our common friends Anuj was also coming from America to visit the country. So, I planned the surprise party along with Anuj. First, I had to make sure that Amit was present in the town and would not go anywhere else otherwise the surprise would have been of no use. I booked a party hall in a restaurant for twenty people and made all the selections of food and drinks. I also selected a special cake for him.

On the birthday, we all gathered in the hall and one of my friends went to Amit's house to pick him up. As soon as Amit reached the hall, we all surprised him with a loud greeting and hugs. He was shocked and expressed his happiness by thanking us all for making his day wonderful.

He was also surprised to see Anuj who had come from America. We all enjoyed the party, and the memories of that day are still fresh in my mind.

Describe people who raise awareness about the environment

Who they are?
How do they create awareness?
Do you feel they are effective?

I came to know about this group of people who raise awareness about the environment a couple of years ago. But now I follow them actively on social media and I know a couple of members personally. The group is working in our city from the past four years.

The name of the group is Go Green. People in that group are mostly environmentalist and they care about the environment seriously. They arrange a few awareness programs and events to make people aware about the environment. They make sure that people living in our city take care of the environment. They arrange cycle rallies on Sundays and raise slogans against the production and usage of single use plastic bags. Recently, they gathered hundreds of people from all walks of life and swept the roads and other dirty parts of the town. They also publish a newsletter and leaflets to alert people about the necessity to maintain environment. They also focus on saving drinking water. Last year they had organized a big event that highlighted the need to save precious drinking water. In that event they told how people can save water by using sustainable methods. Not only this, but this organization has also raised slogans against the excessive use of vehicles in the city. More vehicles contribute to pollution so they suggested that people should focus more on carpooling methods or using cycles for commuting. They emphasized that this will not only save the environment but will also save your hard-earned money. Yes, they are extremely effective as they get so many comments from people on their social media posts. A lot of people comment on their social media posts and express their appreciation and offer help to the organization.

They do a lot of work locally and has gained popularity over time. Many people especially youngsters have joined them in this campaign, and I am also thinking of joining them soon.

Describe an experience when children made you laugh

What was the situation?
How the children made you laugh?
Is laughing a good activity?

I can recall one instance from my memory when some children made me laugh out so loud that I was not in my control. This happened when I was strolling in a park and saw some kids making a lot of noise.

There were around twenty kids who were aged between six and ten. When I went near, I noticed that someone was guiding them to act. When I spend some time there, I came to know that they were rehearsing a comic skit for their school's annual function.

I sat on a nearby bench and started observing their performance. Slowly other people gathered and soon there were around twenty people who were watching the practice. The kids were looking well trained and followed every instruction of their coach.

They were speaking dialogues that were very funny and complex. They were divided in two groups and one by one each member of the group would taunt each other by using a funny line or conversation. It was an extremely hilarious act that made me laugh.

They spoke their discourses in such a way that they were sounding extremely humorous. They were addressing each other in a very funny manner. They practiced that skit for about thirty minutes, and I found it hysterical. Those children made me laugh out loud with their every act and dialogues. I could not believe how they managed to speak in such a way despite their young age.

I feel laughing is a great activity. Some doctors also suggest that laughing loud can cure cardiac issues and it also contributes to increasing the blood flow of the body. I have seen that people do not laugh whole heartedly. They should do this activity more often to maintain happiness in life.

Talk about a situation when you complained about something and got good results

Why did you complain?
How much time was taken to get the thing resolved?
Do you often complain about things?

I have complained to a few governments as well as private departments over the past years. This time it was a serious issue that needed to be addressed to the local authorities for prompt action.

Generally, governments in our country do not act quickly over complaints so at first, I was reluctant to speak about the problem but when it got over the head, I wrote several letters to the local authority about the situation.

I live in a colony, and it is well maintained in most of the aspects. But the condition of roads and footpaths is terrible. There are large potholes in the roads everywhere. Recently the potholes had become worse and become a cause of concern for safety. A couple of accidents happened due to these potholes. Few days back, a biker slipped due to the potholes and sustained serious injuries.

Many people in the past have complained about this situation but no one has looked upon it yet. Then I realized that I must do something about it. So, I wrote several letters to the municipal council and District Commissioner's office about the issue. I sent an email containing the photographs regarding the condition of the roads. I was hopeful that my complaints would bring some results.

To my surprise, they acted in a weeks' time and the maintenance team arrived at the spot to analyze the issue. The team met the people of our colony and promised to act soon. After a week all the roads were laid again, and footpaths were repaired. I was so pleased to see government taking the action in such a short time and resolving the problem.

No, I do not complain about things too much but whenever I see something wrong happening, I always complain about it. I think if your complaint can solve problems then complaining is a good thing.

Talk about a job that helps make the world a better place

Explain that job
Why do you think so?
How has that job changed the world?

There are many jobs that make people's life better. Those jobs make the world a better place to live. I think that doctors and teachers are the professions that are crucial in developing the world. But I reckon that people working as scientists are the ones who are making the world a better place to live.

In my perception, scientists work constantly in improving our lives. There have been millions of inventions in the recent past that have led to improvements in the life of people. Scientists have contributed immensely to making our lives better.

Right from the invention of the light bulb to the discovery of an LED light. We have seen so many new things coming in the market every other day because of the hard-working scientists. They are constantly occupied in improving the existing technology and developing the new one.

Scientists have been instrumental in developing new drugs for diseases that were incurable in the past. As a result of developments in the field of medicines, the life span of humans has also increased.

There have been several scientists who made a mark on the society. Scientists such as Nikola Tesla, Thomas Alva Edison, Einstein and APJ Abdul Kalam have made this globe a better place to live. I have utmost respect for the scientists living around the world. They sacrifice their personal time for improving people's lives.

I think this job has made the world a better place to live. The inventions made by the scientists have made people's work easier. Scientists do not often get the credit for putting their efforts in the field of science. This job is one of the most thankless jobs in the world.

Describe a person you know who likes to help people in free time

Who is the person?
How does he/she help people?
Why does he/she help people?

I know one person who lives in my neighborhood. His name is Vishal Sharma, and he is around 60 years old. He recently retired from a government post. He is the one who helps people living in our colony in every possible way.

He is very active despite his age. He is always seen doing something in our area. If anyone needs any kind of help in the colony, they go to him. He like to listen to the issues of public and help them in solution. He once told me that he has earned a lot in life and now wants to give something back to the society. He lives in a big house and has also made an office on the ground floor.

There he meets people and listen to their problems. Then he explains them how they can get their work done. If they are unable to do that, then he provides them assistance and he does not even charge the fee for it.

Recently Mr. Sharma formed a committee that would look after the cleanliness and maintenance of the colony. Now the committee collects one thousand rupees each month from all the households to save the funds for the maintenance.

He is always available whenever someone needs him. He keeps an eye on things that needs improvement. He never cares if it is day or night, he looks after the work tirelessly. He always asks people to keep the surroundings neat and clean. He is an environmentalist and is seen growing plants and trees every weekend.

Recently there was a problem regarding the roads in our colony, but the local authorities were not looking to solve the issue soon. Mr. Sharma took the job in his hand and visited the government offices regularly to convince the authorities and got the work done.

He is so inspiring, and I wish there could be more humans like him everywhere.

Describe a person who speaks foreign language very well

How do you know that person?
How can that person speak that foreign language well?
From where he/she learned it?

I know a lot of people on Facebook who are from another country and speak different languages. But I would like to speak about my uncle who is living in Spain from the last ten years. He is working as an electrical engineer there.

His family is also living there with him, and he visits India every year and lives with us for 15-20 days. He is an intelligent person and talks sensibly. His both sons were born in Spain hence they do not speak a work of Hindi. They either speak Spanish or a bit of English.

He could not speak Spanish fluently earlier as he was still learning the language. But from the past three or four years he speaks that language like natives. When he comes to India, he talks to my cousins in Spanish. I do not understand a word of it, but I like to listen to their talk. I try to understand their conversation, but I can only recognize a few things and that too, from their gestures.

When he recently stayed with us, I asked him to speak the language and teach me some words and phrases. He taught me some common phrases and some greeting words in Spanish. For example, Hola is hello and adios is bye. I also learnt that gracias is thank you.

My uncle told me that he took the basics of Spanish classes in Spain and gradually learned the language. He told that it is important to live in a foreign country to learn their native language. It took him five years to learn the language properly.

I found this language to be interesting, and I have planned to learn Spanish in future. Spanish is also one of the most popular languages all over the world.

A time when you had to wait in a traffic jam

When did it happened and how did you manage it?
What was the reason behind the jam?
Are traffic jams common in your country/city?

Last month I got stuck in a traffic jam when I was going to my home. I was driving a car and suddenly I saw a lot of cars blocked on the road. I thought it to be a regular jam, but I was about to witness something that I had never seen before. I stopped the car and noticed that the vehicles were not even moving an inch. Even after thirty minutes there was no movement. So, I decided to play songs to get rid of my boredom. I was surprised to see that the jam was growing with every passing minute and there was no way out.

Everyone came out of their vehicles and were looking at each other in frustration. I was trying to find out the cause of the jam. One person coming from the other side of the road told us that an accident that happened half an hour ago was the main cause of the jam. After waiting for another hour, the traffic started moving slowly and soon the jam was cleared. After moving ahead, I noticed two big busses lying sideways. This was the reason for the jam. It was horrifying to see the accident site. There was some blood spilt on the road. A lot of glass was scattered as well. I was praying for the victims of the accident. Next day I read in the newspaper that three people were killed in the accident and rest of them sustained minor injuries. I was relieved to read that only three people died because one would assume from the magnitude of the accident that many people would have deceased. Traffic jams are quite prevalent in our country. Most of the traffic is found in the cities of our country than towns and villages. Most of the cities are overcrowded that leads to a lot of traffic on roads. Other reason of traffic on road is poor driving habits. Government is making efforts to reduce the traffic, but no results are seen.

Describe an important year in your life

Why that year was important?
Did you achieve anything that year?
What did you do well in that year?

I always consider every year important in my life, but I feel that the year I completed my 12th class was the most important year from a lot of perspectives. Many events happened that years and because of it I consider that year to be the most important year of my life. In that year I completed my most anticipated milestone of life. I got good results in my 12th class examinations. The year was also crucial because I had to decide about my future. I was confused between studying in India or to go to a foreign university for my further studies. My father helped me in making right decision at that moment.

After receiving the 12th result, I was looking for career counselling. One of my uncles suggested me to appear for the IELTS exam and apply a study visa to the foreign university. He told me about the benefits of studying abroad. He emphasized that one gets great exposure while studying in a foreign country.

At that moment I was inspired by my uncle and started researching about foreign institutions. I found that it would be better for me if I study in Canada. From that day I decided to pass my graduation from a foreign university. The moment made that year great for me as I had the aim for my future now. Another important event happened in the same year that changed my life. My elder sister got married. I share a great relation with her. Although I miss her very much, but we remain in regular contact with each other. She is a great friend of mine and I share everything with her. She lives happily with her husband, so I feel that made my year great. I achieved many things that year but what makes that year important for me is the marriage of my sister and the decision of my career.

Describe your favorite way to relax

Why are people under stress these days?
Describe your favourite way to relax
Do you get stressed?

Recent studies have shown that more than 30% of people working in private sector are suffering from stress related problems. There are numerous factors that cause stress. The main reason I think is the high expectation that people carry and if they are not able to meet their expectations, they get stressed. Sometimes I get stressed, but I get out of it quickly. There are many ways through which I keep myself relaxed. The first one is listening to songs. I also like to play some outdoor games to get out of anxiety. I like to go out and do shopping in this kind of a situation. But my favourite way to relax is to go out with my friends and spend time with them. When I meet my friends, I forget all my worries and tensions. Whenever I am with my near and dear ones, I feel great. I have many friends who are always available when I need them.

I generally go out with my friends in the evenings. I also like to spend night outs at my best friends' house. I have been extremely fortunate to have such friends in my life. One of my friends live near to my house who is always present with me when I am in trouble. I remember once I was going through a rough time and feeling low. I could not share anything with anyone, but my friends came to my rescue and lifted my spirits. They helped me to get out of that situation by supporting me. I am lucky to have such friends in life.

Yes, I get stressed when I am not able to complete anything on time. I get anxious sometimes when I am confronted by a problem in my life. But every time I manage the stress in some way or the other.

Your favorite means of transport

Do you use public or private transport?
Speak about your favourite means of transport
Why do you like it?

I use both kinds of transport in my day-to-day life. I use public transport like bus and train when I need to go for a long journey. On the other hand, I use my private car/bike in my daily routine. Both have their own advantages and disadvantages.

I also like to board planes as they are fast and convenient. But in regular routine I think that car is my favourite means of transport. Whether I use my own car, or I hire a taxi, car is undoubtedly my preferred mode of transport. Car has several advantages over other means of transport. It is one of the most luxurious ways to travel short and long distances. One can easily travel for long periods of time by taking regular stops. Cars are generally quite efficient. It is a weatherproof vehicle, and you can travel nonstop in any kind of weather.

Hot weather can be tackled by the air conditioner and cold weather can be suppressed by the heater in the car. In a single car four to five people can travel together. There is also boot space to keep your luggage in most cases. Moreover, cars can travel on most of the terrains.

I have a car which I use in my daily life. It is my dad's car, but I can use it whenever I want. I go out with my friends in the car. I enjoy long drives with my friends on weekends. Cars do not require much maintenance. One can get it serviced after every six months. It is the most reliable vehicle of our times.

I have been to many trips on a private car. The best part is that we can stop anywhere and get the feel of the surroundings. I would like to conclude the topic by saying that out of the other modes of transport, car is my favourite one.

PART – 2

FOLLOW-UP QUESTIONS AND ANSWERS

Sports

Do you like sports?
Yes, I love playing sports. I used to play cricket in my school time. Nowadays I like watching cricket matches and play it whenever I get time.

Which sports is the most famous in your country?
Our country invented hockey but the most followed sports is cricket. People follow cricket as a religion in our country. They get very emotional during the crucial matches. Most of the kids also like to play cricket in their free time in my country.

What are the advantages of playing sports?
Playing sports is a great activity as it involves us physically as well as mentally. There are many advantages of playing sports. It teaches us teamwork and keeps us fit. One can also opt sports as his/her career.

Is there any disadvantage of playing sports?
I do not think that there is any disadvantage of playing any sports. However, if one doesn't play it with proper safety equipment then it can be harmful. Also, there can be serious injuries while playing sports. This is the only disadvantage I can think of.

Which sports are generally preferred by women?
I think these days women are playing all sports. There is no sport that women are not playing. Even recently, women were seen playing cricket matches at international level which is a great sign of equality.

Do you think sports bring people together?
In a country there can be a lot of different opinions among people when it comes to politics and other things. But when it comes to sports, everyone supports one team and I think sports do bring people together.

Plant

Which plant do you like the most?
I like basil. It's a wonderful plant and has numerous qualities. A lot of people believe that the leaves of basil can relieve fever if consumed directly or in tea. Some people in our country consider the basil plant as sacred and often worship it.

Which is the most common plant found in your country?
Rose plant as it can be seen everywhere in my country. I think it is because that this plant doesn't require a lot of watering and sunlight. And it also gives beautiful flowers. That's why people like to grow this plant.

What are the benefits of growing plants at home?
I think the first advantage is that it purifies air. Some plants have natural scent which suppresses foul smell nearby. I think that plants look beautiful regardless of their variety. These are the major benefits of growing plants at home.

Do you like gardening?
To be honest, I am not very fond of gardening as it requires certain skills that I don't have. You need to have a lot of patience and resolve to do gardening. My father is fond of this activity, but I never developed any interest in it.

Do you think everyone should grow plants?

I think at least once in a lifetime; everyone should grow a plant. It's a noble cause, moreover growing plants have a lot of advantages so I think that everyone should grow plants.

Food
Speak about your favorite cuisine.
I love Chinese. It's delicious as well as healthy. Most of the Chinese dishes are either stir fried or steamed. I like steamed food as it has less calories. Whenever I get a chance to eat outside, I prefer Chinese.

Which is your favourite dish?
Vegetarian haka noodles are my all-time favourite. I can eat this dish 10 times a week. I can't resist myself wherever I see Chinese food.

Which is the traditional food of your country?
I live in the northern part of the country so the staple food here is wheat. So, anything made of wheat is the traditional food in the north side. If we move towards the east and south regions of our country, then rice is the traditional and the most common food.

Any dish that you like to cook?
I like to cook vegetable fried rice. It is an easy dish to cook. We need to take some vegetables and mix them with boiled rice and add some spices and sauces to make it. It hardly takes 30 minutes to prepare this dish.

Do you like fast food?
As the name suggests this food is cooked fast. I like to eat it occasionally as it is delicious and cheap. But mostly I prefer homemade and traditional food as it has all the nutrients and essential minerals needed to sustain good health.

Education
Do you like the education system of your country?
Yes, I feel that education system of my country covers almost all the basis but there is one area where we can improve a lot and that is curriculum. The syllabus is old and needs immediate restructuring. Most of the students are learning certain things that are out of date and things that are not at all practical.

What changes do you want to make in the education system of your country?
I would like to make a couple of changes to the system. The first one is to make the education more practical rather than cramming theory books. The second change will be in the curriculum. It needs to be diverse and should develop a student holistically.

How many hours a student should read books apart from his studies?
I think it is unfair to them. They are under a burden of so many books already. But reading is a great habit. If students can take out some time to read about great leaders or personalities, then I think it is a good idea. Students should spend around three hours a week on reading material apart from their curriculum.

Which was your favourite subject in school time?
My favourite subject was science. I liked the diversity in science when I studied the different aspects such as physics, chemistry, and biology. I used to be active during my science class as we would learn new things every day.

Any subject that you didn't like?
I never liked mathematics. I used to get confused when I saw all the questions and equations. That was the subject that I never understood completely and not once scored well. I got a lot of headaches while solving the problems in math's.

Which type of education is better, distance learning or regular schooling?

In my opinion, both types of education have their advantages. If a person is in a job or a business, then distance education is a boon. But if the student has ample time to study then he or she should go for the regular education.

Leisure activities
What do you like to do in leisure time?
I generally play music and surf the internet. I like searching for new places around the world and new songs that release every week. I also like watching cricket matches whenever I get time.
What kind of leisure activities do the women do in your country?
Women generally prefer to watch sitcoms and movies. These days a lot of females are involved in watching fashion related shows and documentaries. Most women have feminine choice when it comes to free time activities.
What kind of leisure activities do the children have in your country?
Children in our country like games and sports. Cricket is the most popular sport, so children watch it and play it with their friends. Video games are also popular among kids.
Do you feel that one should read books in leisure time?
Why not? I think it's a great habit to have. I like to read books and I think people should read them too. It gives us knowledge as well as understanding of life.
Who has more leisure time in your country, men, or women? Why?
I think if the women are home maker, then women have more leisure time than men. On the other hand, if a woman is working then it's the other way around.

Wealth
What is more important, health or wealth?
I think both are integral part of life. Health comes first because a healthy person can enjoy all the stages of life. Wealth is also one of the most important aspects in human's life as well. So, I feel that health and wealth are not equally important, health comes first and then wealth.
How will you spend 10 million?
If I am given this much money, I would like to make my dreams true. First, I will donate ten percent of the money to charity. Then I will buy a small house for myself. With the remaining money, I will travel the world.
Why do you think wealth is important?
I think wealth is the only thing that can make our dreams true. If we want good education, great medical care or want to travel the world, wealth is required. Wealth fulfills most things in life.
What are the advantages and disadvantages of being wealthy?
There are many advantages such as one can travel the world, can buy whatever he or she wants. Wealth can let you buy big houses and cars. But I don't think that there is any disadvantage of being wealthy.

Weather
How is the weather like in your country?
Weather is quite diverse in my country. India is a big land, and all parts have different climate. In north, you will find summers and winters. In eastern side, you will find more rains than any other part of the country. In the south, weather is almost same throughout the year as its mostly the coastal area with tropical climate.
Which is your favourite weather?

I like summers because you can wear light clothes. Moreover, you can have loads of ice creams and cold drinks. The best thing about summers is that one can enjoy long days. Summers gives us an opportunity to visit swimming pools and amusement parks. This fun can only be enjoyed in summers.

Do you dislike any weather?
I don't like rainy season. There are two major reasons for that. One, it gets wet everywhere and people without cars and private transport struggle a lot in our country. Secondly, it gets humid after the rain stops. I don't like to sweat a lot, so I don't like humid and rainy season.

Do you feel that weather affects the mood of a person?
When weather is nice and dry, I like it very much and if it is rainy then I feel depressed. Similarly, if a person doesn't like summers or hot weather, he or she might not feel great in that kind of weather. So, I feel that weather can affect a person's mood.

What kind of weather is good for the crops in your country?
I think it depends on the kind of crops one grows. Mostly dry weather is good for staple crops like wheat. On the other hand, rice requires a considerable amount of water. It depends on crop to crop.

Travelling
Do you like travelling?
I absolutely love travelling as it breaks the monotony. I like to go out whenever I get time. It relaxes me and recharge me for the days to come. I go out with my friends on weekends and especially in the month of December.

How does travelling makes you feel?
It makes me feel wonderful because I learn so many things while travelling. I come to know about different cultures, places, and food when I travel. I feel complete when I am travelling.

What are the benefits of travelling?
There are many benefits of travelling. The first one is that a traveler learns behavior pattern of people from different societies. Moreover, it gives them a chance to visit new places and eat different types of cuisines.

Is travelling costly in your country?
No, I think travelling in my country is not that expensive. If you travel by air, then it can be a bit costly but if you chose to travel by bus or train then I think you can travel at low cost. Our country is well connected by rail so I believe that it will be the best and cheapest option.

What are the things that a solo traveler should keep in mind before travelling?
Before travelling solo, I think there are couple of things that the traveler should keep in mind. Firstly, he or she should carry all the first aid medicines and should have enough funds in case of an emergency.

Animals
Which animal do you like the most?
I like cow. It is one of the sacred animals in our country and is worshiped by a lot of people. Cow gives us milk and its dung can also be used as a fuel in traditional homes.

Should animals be kept as pets?
Animals should be kept as pets as they are our true friends. Animals such as dogs are widely regarded as the best pets across the world. Millions of people keep dog as a pet due to its loyalty and vigilance traits.

Should we eat animals?
I think this is a debatable topic. In my personal view I reckon that it is up to an individual whether to eat animals or not. Across the world, billions of people eat animals and there are many who don't. it's a personal choice of public.

Do you feel that animal products such as leather shoes and bags should be banned?
Yes, I think there should be a complete ban on the killing of animals for making leather products. Our science is so advanced that we have already invented alternatives. So, I don't think that there is a need to kill animals to produce such products.

Which is the most common animal that can be found in your country?
India is such a big country, and we can see all types of animals here. The most common ones are cows and dogs. A lot of people in rural area keep a lot of cows as pets. Moreover, dogs are also kept as pets by many people in my country.

Happiness
Is it important to remain happy?
Yes, it is crucial to be happy as it can treat several problems as well as can elevate your mood. Being happy is one of the biggest challenges these days. I think a person who's happy is always healthy.

What are the factors that influence happiness?
There can be a few factors that influence happiness. It depends upon an individual as to what makes him or her happy. Some people are elated by earning more money and some simply feel happiness while travelling.

How can a person remain happy?
A person should never try to manage things that are beyond control. Also, one should try to wake up early in the morning and practice a bit of meditation. You should also try to watch comedy movies or accomplish small tasks on time to remain happy.

Do you think happiness is linked to good health?
I totally believe that our health is linked to happiness. I have seen a lot of people who are not happy, and they tend to be mentally disturbed than people who are always in a joyous mood. Happiness has a direct impact on our health physically as well as mentally.

Law
Describe a law in your country.
I would like to speak about the child labor law. No child under the age of fourteen years can do paid work in our country. If someone is found engaging a kid who is under fourteen, then he or she might be put behind bars or imposed with a heavy fine.

Do you feel laws are strong enough in your country?
I think the laws are stringent in my country. If anyone breaks the law, then he stands for a strict punishment by the penal system. The laws can be improved in certain areas but most of them are fine.

Is it important to follow all the laws?
Yes, the laws are made for the betterment of all the citizens of a country. It's essential to follow the laws as it keeps the running of the social machinery smooth.

Is there any law that you want to introduce in your country?
Yes, I want to make a law under which it would be compulsory for every citizen of the country to get education up to senior secondary. Under this law the government will provide the funds required for the education of people.

School
What type of school did you go to as a child?
I went to an English medium school which was located near my house. The school had all the facilities that are needed for the overall development of the students.

Which type of schools are better, government or private? Why?
I think in my country most people prefer to enroll their kids in the private schools because they are more concerned about student's progress. They also focus on the co-curricular activities. Moreover, private schools have the right sort of infrastructure and environment of study.

Do you feel schools should be allowed to charge tuition fee according to their standards?
No, I think government should make a law as these days private schools are charging huge amounts of fee to enroll the kids. Under this law the no school should charge more fee than a maximum limit set by the government.

How do you think government schools can be improved?
According to my notion, government should take the initiative and responsibility to take care of the quality of the government schools. The government should hire professionals that can revive the condition of the government schools in our country. They can add more facilities and infrastructure with low fees to attract more people.

Do you feel that school plays a major role in the development of a person's life?
Unquestionably, schools are like temples and students worship the books and their teachers. Schools teach us a lot of things in life. We make our first friends at the school. We come to know about the etiquettes we need to have in different situations. It plays the biggest role in the development of a child.

Dance
Do you like to dance?
Yes, I like to dance. I like to do bhangra and I also dance on the Bollywood songs. I like to do free style dance as I am not a professional dancer. I generally dance in the weddings and celebrations with my friends and family.

What type of dance is popular in your country?
We have so many types of dances in our country. Kuchi pudi, Bharat Natyam, Bhangra are one of the most popular dances forms across the country. Different regions have different styles of dancing.

Why do people dance?
I think dance is a way of expressing one's feelings. Just like music and writing, people like to dance to express themselves. I mostly dance when I am happy. In our tradition, people dance on weddings and other celebrations.

Is dance different for men and women?
There is a subtle difference in the expressions of dance for both the genders. Although the dance type will be the same, but the steps and hand moments will be different for men and women.

Wedding
What is the wedding like in your country?
As India is a big nation, we have several styles of weddings in our country. Most of the people in our country like to celebrate weddings with great enthusiasm and excitement. They like to buy expensive jewelry and lots of dresses.

Have you ever been to a large-scale wedding?
Recently I went to the wedding of my friend's brother. It was the best wedding celebrations that I have seen in my entire life. There were unlimited cuisines, and the wedding venue was decorated like heaven. The bride and groom were wearing expensive dresses and there were all the things that you can expect from a big fat wedding.

What is the importance of marriage in our life?
I think marriage is an association between the couple and their families. Marriage enlarges the family, and you know that you have more people in your life who will be there in your thick and thin.

Do you feel marriages in the past were better organized than today's marriages?

I learnt from my elders that the marriages in the past were long and simple. There used to be a couple of dishes to eat, and relatives would gather at the home of the groom and bride and be there for more than a month to celebrate the wedding. So, I think that marriages in the present are better as no one has enough time and the events are also managed in a better way.

What changes will you see in the marriage celebration after 20 years?
I reckon that there will be a lot of changes in the celebrations in the coming 20 years. People have now become more conscious of the spending they do on organizing the functions. There will be less show-off in the marriages and people would rather spend more money on buying the assets than organizing big functions.

Sleep
How many hours do you sleep every day?
I sleep for 7 – 8 hours every day. I get to bed by 11 and wake up at 6 AM. I feel that I need at least 7 hours of sleep to get my body back to full potential. On weekends, I take a nap in the afternoon sometimes.

Do you like to sleep?
Everyone likes to sleep, so do I. I like my sleep very much. Whenever I am feeling tired or frustrated, I go to sleep. If I am not feeling well, I prefer to sleep more. In a way, sleep is like a medicine if used in a proper manner.

Do you dream?
I usually don't dream while I sleep. But occasionally, I get unusual dreams at night. I get dreams of meeting my idols, achieving my goals and some wired ones as well. Once I had a dream in which I was falling from a building.

Do the people in your country discuss their dreams?
I have never shared any of my dreams with anyone. Neither any person has shared his or her dream with me. I think this is a personal thing, so people feel hesitant to share their dreams with others.

What are the disadvantages of sleeping long hours?
In my opinion, it's very dangerous to sleep for more hours than usual. First, it destroys your productive time, and it is not good for the health of a person. More sleep leads to obesity and obesity leads to several diseases.

Family
What type of family do you live in?
I live in a joint family. I think I enjoy living in a joint family as we have more members who can be there for us when we need them. There is more harmony when you live in a big family. I have 9 members in my family. I like every one of them.

What are the advantages of living in a nuclear family?
I think the only advantage that you have while living in a nuclear family is that you don't have a lot of interference. There are a smaller number of members, so it gives you freedom to do whatever you want.

What are the disadvantages of living in a nuclear family?
I think the only disadvantage of living in a nuclear family is that a person has very few people to go to when he/she feels troubled or depressed. A person can sometimes feel lonely in a nuclear family.

Do you feel that families are disintegrating day by day?
Yes, the families in my country are disintegrating as a result of some factors. These days people don't like interference from others and like to live in their own way. That's why this situation has occurred.

If given a chance, would you like to live in a nuclear family?

I don't think that I can live in a small family. I like to have people around me as I am a talkative person. I think we learn a lot of things from people around us. Moreover, I am the kind of a person who likes to live in a joint family.

Friends
Do you have one or two or many best friends?
I have only two friends who can be called as best friends. I can share every part of my life with them. I think it's never good to have too many friends. One or two good friends are enough.

Do you feel that there are advantages of having a lot of friends?
I think that few friends are enough. You don't need to have a lot of friends in order to fulfil your social needs. Having a lot of friends can lead to trouble sometimes. If you have a greater number of friends, then you must give them time. That means you have very less time for yourself.

What do you do in case you have a misunderstanding with a friend?
I always call my friend up and try to talk to him or her. That's the best way to approach if you have any misunderstanding between friends. I will share my point and will listen to his or her point as well and try to find a way out.

What can be risky among friends?
I think there can be one thing that can be very risky. We share a lot of secrets between friends and sometimes we trust a person who's not worth trusting. The secrets can get leaked which can lead to a lot of problems.

Do you feel that we should invite our friends to family functions?
I think it's important to invite our friends to the family functions as they are also like family. Friends know everything and they are the part of our lives. So, it becomes important to call them to our family functions.

Hometown
Tell something about the place where you live.
I live in Mohali. It is a neat and clean city. There is no scarcity of greenery in my hometown. There are numerous gardens and parks which are made for the public. Infrastructure is great and all the facilities like education, shopping complex and hospitals are in abundance.

Is there anything you would like to change about your hometown?
I would like to change a couple of things about my hometown. The first thing that I would love to have is increased frequency of public transport. Ours is a developed city but lacks public transportation. Secondly, I would like to see more cycling tracks around the city.

Is there anything that makes your hometown special?
Yes, greenery makes my hometown special. It is one of the greenest and cleanest cities in my country. This is also a planned city, so everything is well lined up and easily accessible.

Which place in your hometown is special to you?
I like going to the PCA cricket stadium. It is an international stadium situated in the heart of the city. It has a club, and I am a member of it and I like to go there for swimming.

Is there any famous personality that lives in your hometown?
There are many famous personalities that live in Mohali. Many Punjabi singers live in my hometown, and I have come across many of them while roaming around the city. Some famous sports personalities are also dwelling in my hometown.

Colours
Which is your favorite colour?

I like blue the most. It is a symbol of calmness and keeping cool. I like this colour as its sooths my eyes whenever I look at it. I also look good in blue-coloured clothes. I like blue so much that I got the walls of my room painted in this colour.

Do you feel that a colour can change a person's mood?
Yes, colours can change a person's mood. If someone is feeling down and out, then I think they should wear bright or vibrant colors as it will elevate the mood. On the other hand, looking at dull colours can depress the mood.

Do the colours have religious importance?
In our culture, colour has a lot of significance in religion. For example, at the time of worship, red is sacred. While in some communities, white is a sign of purity.

Is there any colour that you don't like?
There is no colour that I don't like but I can say that I don't like light or dull shades. I am an optimistic person; hence I like vibrant colours. Dull colors make me feel annoyed.

Which colour is mostly preferred by women in your country?
From my few interactions with women, I conclude that most of them like pink or red colour. I think it's because of the reason that pink colour gives a feminine look, that's why women like it.

T.V
Do you watch TV?
Yes, I watch TV in my leisure time. I like discovery channel and music programs. I like to listen to the latest songs, so I always tune into such TV shows and channels. Watching discovery is like studying in a university as it gives an abundance of knowledge.

For how many hours do you watch TV?
I watch TV for around one and a half to two hours. I love watching TV as it gives me a lot of knowledge and it is also like a stress buster for a lot of people.

What are the bad effects of watching TV?
There are several bad effects of watching TV. I think a person can get addicted to it and may watch it for long hours. This can affect eyes as well as the overall health of a person.

How many hours should the children watch TV?
I feel that children under the age of two should not watch TV at all. And children above the age of two should be allowed to watch TV for not more than two hours per day.

Do you watch News on TV?
I only watch news when there is something interesting or any incident that has happened. Otherwise, I generally don't watch news channels.

Culture
Is it important to preserve our culture?
Its indispensable to preserve our culture as it reflects our past and history. If we are unable to preserve our culture, then the upcoming generations will not be able to learn the traditions and values from the past. Preserving culture should be the main priority of people these days.

Is the culture in your country different from other cultures?
Our culture is very different from the rest of the world especially the western countries. I reckon that the culture in my country is like some neighboring countries, but I still feel that every country has its own culture.

Is there any culture that you like the most?

In our country, the culture of celebrating festivals is the best culture and I like it the most. The reason is that when we celebrate the festivals together, it increases harmony and respect between people of different cultures and religions. Diwali is such festival which is celebrated across all religions and regions.

Do you feel that people should change their culture when they move to a foreign country?
I don't think that's a good idea to change the culture after moving to a new country. One should never forget his or her own ethics, practices, and customs. I think they should try to adopt the new culture without forgetting their own.

Do you feel that there has been a cultural mix in some countries?
Yes, there has been a lot of cultural mix in some countries across the world due to globalization. This is not a bad thing at all. I believe that it brings people from different castes, races and regions together.

Business and jobs
Would you prefer to do job or a business?
If given a chance, I would like to get a job first. After taking experience of four to five years, I will plan to start a business of my own. I feel that before starting a business one should do job.

If given a chance, what kind of business you would like to start?
If I am given a chance, I would like to start a business related to import and export of certain products. I like travelling so that's the best possible business which can offer me more travelling.

Is there any job that you dream of doing?
I dream of working in the parliament of India or in a big politician's office. I am very curious to know how the life of big politicians is and how they work for the country. I would also like to contribute to the country's development through this kind of job.

What kinds of jobs do women prefer in your country?
Women generally prefer to do white collar jobs in my country. Most women are highly educated, so they prefer to do managerial jobs. They also like teaching jobs so that they can spare out time for the families.

Globalization
What are the positive effects of globalization?
Due to globalization, more and more people are connecting with each other. There have been great improvements in terms of transportation and communication. It has brought a lot of positive changes in the world.

What are the negative effects of globalization?
Globalization has proved to be beneficial for humans, but it has also created some chaos. Due to globalization, many people have lost their jobs to technology and internet as most of the work is now done by robots and computers.

How has globalization changed your life?
It has impacted my life in a positive manner. I have now access to my friends who are living in abroad. I can make a video call to them in a blink of an eye. This has been possible only through globalization.

Speak about the biggest advantage of globalization?
I think improvements in the transportation has been the biggest advantage of globalization. Nowadays we can travel in fast trains and aero planes, and we can reach our destination in a relatively short time and more comfortably.

How can globalization change the future?
I think globalization will change the future quickly. We can already see a lot of developments in the field of transport, medicine, and technology. In future, the focus is on the communication and to take it to the remotest of the areas due to which more people will connect in a better way.

Magazines

Do you read magazines?
I don't read magazines regularly, but I have read a magazine recently. The name of the magazine is Autocar. This magazine has an abundance of knowledge regarding the recently launched cars and about the best cars in market. It also has customer's reviews for selected cars. I liked this magazine very much.

What type of magazines are popular among women in your country?
In my perception, women like to read fashion related magazines. These kinds of magazines are helpful for them to get updates regarding the latest fashion in clothes and accessories. I often see my sister reading this type of magazine.

Do you feel that men read more magazines than women?
I think women tend to read more magazines than men as there is more variety of magazines for women rather than men. Moreover, I have read a survey in a newspaper, and it suggested that in our country more women prefer to do reading than men.

Do you feel magazines can teach us something?
Yes, magazines teach us a lot of things. We can learn from magazines if we absorb the knowledge given in it. There are some magazines such as Competition Success Review which is read by thousands of students across India. Students learn the latest trends in competitive examinations and education.

Are the magazines better than newspapers?
I think magazines and newspapers are very different from each other hence should not be compared. Magazines are better in terms of visuality and printing quality. On the other hand, newspapers are best for current news.

Newspapers

Which is your favourite newspaper?
I love reading Hindustan Times. It is one of the oldest newspapers in our country. Its pages are well laid out and different news items are divided into different sections. There are a couple of supplement newspapers in it as well.

Do you read newspaper every day?
No, I don't get this much time, but I feel that one should have a habit of reading newspaper every day. This is an excellent habit as it keeps you updated about the happenings. I read it mostly on the weekends.

Do we learn anything from the newspaper?
Yes, we learn a lot of things from it. People mostly learn a lot of new words and latest news. We also learn how to arrange such huge amount of information in such a compact way.

Is there any page of newspaper that you like the most?
I like reading the sports section of any newspaper. In my favourite newspaper, the sports page is always the second last page. I get a lot of knowledge about different sports events and about sportspersons.

Do you feel that newspapers print fake news?
I don't think that newspapers print fake news as they have a huge responsibility on their shoulders. Although some news editors try to print exaggerated or spicy news to attract more readership. But most newspapers have genuine news.

Library

Have you ever been to a library?
Yes, I have been to many libraries. The one which I liked the most is the British library, which is situated in Industrial area, Chandigarh. It is one of the most modern libraries in the city. It holds a large collection of books for its members.

Should there be an entry fee to the library?

No, I think that entry to the library should be free for the public. This encourages more and more people to come and get themselves educated. This will also inspire the habit of reading which is diminishing day by day.

Do you feel books should be given on loan for free?
No that's not a good idea. I think that there should always be a minimal fee for the book lending. If the library lends books for free, then there can be a loss to the finances. In order to maintain the running costs and books, reasonable fee should be charged.

Do you feel introduction of computers in the libraries is a good idea?
I feel that computers have changed the way people live. They are also helpful in libraries as computers can store huge number of electronic books and volumes which are rare, or which are in bad physical condition. People can simply open the readable file in the computer rather than reading from a physical copy.

Do you feel number of libraries should be escalated across the country?
The count of libraries should be increased everywhere in the world. In my perception book reading is the best way to pass the leisure time and to get knowledge. If the number of libraries is risen, then more people will begin to show interest in reading books which will be great for the mankind.

Zoos
Have you ever been to a zoo?
Yes, I have gone to Chat Bir Zoo which is located near to my hometown. I have visited this zoo more than ten times. It's a big zoo and has a variety of animals. The entry ticket to the zoo is reasonable and is worth visiting.

Which is the best time to visit zoos?
One of the care takers at the zoo told me that the best time to visit zoo is March and April in summers and November and December in winters. At this time of year, most of the animals are active and playful so it makes it the best time for visitors to see the real character of animals.

Have you seen any strange animal in the zoo?
I have seen a lot of animals in the zoo over the years but the strangest animal that I have seen is the Alligator. It is very lazy in nature. I have seen them from close quarters, they remain in the same position for hours and don't even move an inch. But when they are hungry and are ready to be fed, they are very active.

Should there be an entry fee to the zoo?
I think there should be a decent amount of entry fee to the zoo. There are several expenses that the zoos bear to take care of the animals. They feed the animals, pay the salary of the staff and other miscellaneous expenses.

Do you feel zoos are the best place for animals?
I think zoos take care of the animals in every possible way, but it is not the best place for them. I feel that forest is the best habitat for animals. Forest is the natural and more accommodating habitat for them. They can roam freely, and they can hunt and eat on their own. Forests provide more resources to animals than zoos.

Museums
What is the importance of museums in life?
Museums are an integral part of life. From museums we can gain so much knowledge about the past events and society. It's always good to visit a museum as it reflects the past of ours and inspires us to take the legacy forward.

Have you ever been to a museum?
Yes, I have seen two museums in my life. The first one I saw was the government museum which has primarily textiles and tools from the past, the second one is the Ripley's Museum in which I saw strange collections from all over the world.

Have you seen anything interesting in the museum?
Indeed, once I saw the skeleton of a whale fish. I never thought that I would be able to see such thing in my life. The structure was massive, and each part of the skeleton was explained nicely. I think it was really an interesting thing to see.

Do you feel museums are boring?
Not at all, I think museums are one of the most interesting places to visit. One can learn so many things from museums. These kinds of places have abundance of knowledge and I feel that information is never boring.

Do you feel that children should also visit museums?
Absolutely, I feel that it is a great place for children to visit. There are many museums which are solely dedicated to kids and the learning there has been made simple especially for kids. I think it's a great idea to take children to museums.

Vegetarianism

Do you eat non-veg?
No, I am a vegetarian. I used to eat non-veg but from the past 6 years I have given it up. I think that eating non-veg food can be unhealthy sometimes. That's why I left eating it.

What are the benefits of being vegetarian?
There are a few benefits of being vegetarian. The first one is that your digestive system remains neat and clean. Vegetables improve the metabolism of the body. It also fulfills the nutrition and essential vitamins required in the body.

Do you feel meat consumption should be banned?
No, I don't think that meat consumption should be banned. I strictly think that it is up to an individual's choice whether to eat meat or not. There are numerous people who depend on the meat industry. So, I think it's not a good idea to ban the consumption of meat.

Do you feel meat eating is not good?
I left eating meat a few years back as I thought it is not good for health. Moreover, I believe that killing animals for consumption is cruel. So, I think meat eating is not good.

What are the drawbacks of being vegetarian?
There are no such drawbacks of being a vegetarian. But in some cases, vegetarians can find it very difficult to survive in western countries where vegetarian dishes are hard to find. Other than that, I don't think there is any disadvantage of being a vegetarian.

Computers

How have computers helped us?
Computers have helped us in every possible way. Nowadays, computers are used in every field whether it is medical or engineering. Computers have overtaken numerous operations in big industries. They have also helped us in our daily chores and needs.

Is there any negative side of computers?
Indeed, computers have taken over manual labor in most of the fields. Computers have killed a lot of jobs in certain areas. It has made us lethargic and dependent on them for every small tasks.

Do you use computer in your daily routine?

Yes, I use computer every day. From searching latest news or anything on the internet, I use computers. I also use computers to play video games and watch movies. It's a helpful device in daily routine.

Have we become slaves of computers?
Certainly, we have become slaves of computers and it has become our master. We look forward to computer for most of our needs. We are fully dependent in most of the tasks whether it is related to work or leisure.

Do you know someone who does not use computer at all?
Yes, my grandfather does not use computer at all. Although he uses mobile phones, but he never uses computer. He is smart and knows everything about latest gadgets, but I have never seen him using a computer.

Internet
What are the advantages of internet?
Internet holds abundance of knowledge, and we can access it anywhere but for that you need a data pack or an internet connection. The biggest advantage of internet is that we can talk to our near and dear ones who live thousands of kilometers far away from us.

Do you often use internet?
Yes, I use internet every day for two to three hours. I use it for getting updates on latest news and to talk to my friends and relatives living in foreign countries. Sometimes I use internet to operate my e-mails.

Do you feel kids should also be allowed to use internet?
I think kids should be allowed to use internet for their schoolwork and leisure time. One important thing is that parents should set a time limit for the use, and they should also install a browser that is compatible for kids which does not show adult content.

What are the changes that have been instrumental due to the innovation of internet?
The biggest change due to the internet is the way we can connect with people from all over the world and the other one is the internet browsers from where we can get knowledge of anything within a blink of an eye.

Do you feel that government should provide the internet for free?
I think internet is no longer a luxury but a requirement in today's world. If it can be under the budget of the government comfortably then why not? In some countries, the governments are already providing internet for free.

Sky
Do you see sky?
Yes, I see sky. I generally see the sky briefly when I go out of my home for the first time in the morning. The first thing I do is to see the sky.

At what time of the day do you see sky?
I generally see the sky in the morning as well as at night when the stars are shining. In the daytime, it's too bright to look at the sky. So, I feel that early morning and evening is the best time to observe sky.

Have you learned anything after seeing the sky?
I have learned that we are so small, and nature is so big. When I see the sky, it looks unlimited. It appears never ending just like God. I think seeing the sky makes us humble and thankful.

How do you feel when you see sky?
It feels extraordinary. I just admire the beauty of sky and I also praise the lord for wonderful things that he has given us. I feel energetic when I see sky.

Do you also see stars?

Yes, quite often I see stars. Whenever I stroll in the evening or at night, I see the stars. I try to find the constellations of stars that we studied during school time. I see that all the stars have different level of brightness, and they look pretty among the Moon.

Cars
Which is your favourite car?
My favourite car is Toyota Fortuner. It is an SUV car. SUV stands for sports utility vehicle. This means that this kind of car can be run on any terrain without breaking a sweat. I love this car as it is powerful and big as well as looks amazing.

What is the importance of having a car in life?
It is indispensable to own a car these days. A car can accommodate four or five members of the family and it doesn't matter whether it is raining, or the sun is burning hot, you can travel in the car comfortably and safely.

Do you feel number of cars is increasing on the roads rapidly?
Absolutely, the number of the cars are escalating with each passing day. I think easy payment options have made possible for people to buy cars. Now almost everyone can afford a car, that's the main reason behind the growth in the traffic.

What should be the mandatory features in the car?
There should be a couple of compulsory features in the car. The first one is the airbags, and they should be standard across all variants. The second one is the advanced braking system which is helpful in emergency braking.

Have you ever seen a strange car?
Recently I saw Mahindra Eco for the first time. It was a beautiful looking car but the strange thing about that car was its size. It is a two-seater electronic vehicle that looks pretty unusual on road due to its small size.

Tourism
How has tourism evolved society?
Tourism has bridged the gap between cultures and languages. More people nowadays are learning new languages and eating new cuisines. The society has formed a mixed culture due to tourism and it has also increased the understanding among people.

Do you feel tourism generates income?
Tourism generates a lot of income for the people involved in it. When tourists go to a certain place, they rent a car, hotel, guide, and they also buy souvenirs and try local food. This is financially helpful for the people of that place.

Have you ever met a tourist?
Yes, I met one tourist last year when I went to Rajasthan. I saw a lot of tourists there especially from the foreign countries. I got a chance to talk to him. I shared a lot of information about my country, and he told many things about his own. I felt amazing after conversing with him.

Have you been to a tourist place?
Yes, I have gone to a few tourist places. I would like to tell you about Goa. It is a fabulous place for everyone. Goa's coastline is lined with wonderful beaches and restaurants. The food over there is delicious and people are super friendly.

Do you feel tourism has increased from the past time?
There has been a great increase in the number of tourists these days. This is primarily due to the ease in transportation. Many flights have been introduced because of which the price has reduced. Therefore, more people are encouraged to travel.

Crime
Why do you think crime is increasing day by day?
There are a few reasons behind the increase in the crime rates. The biggest reason I feel is the rising unemployment rates in our country. Due to unemployment, many youngsters are forced to sit idle, hence there is a tendency among youngsters to commit crime.

Do you feel there should be strict punishment for every crime?
No, I think punishment should be given according to the severity of crime. Some crimes are hardcore, and others are forgivable. Hardcore criminals should be treated with strictness whereas in case of a small crime, the criminal should be given counselling to bring changes to his/her behavior.

What are the most common crimes in your area?
There are very few crimes that are reported in my local area as there is a lot of strictness. But most of the crimes that are happening are related to snatching and robbery.

How can the government control crime?
Government can do anything; I think they can also eradicate crime from the society. Government should have harsh punishment and zero tolerance policy for dealing with crime so that the criminals would think twice before committing a crime.

Have you ever been affected by a crime?
Yes, unfortunately I was affected by crime last year when my phone was snatched from the roadside. I was walking on the pedestrian and suddenly a motorcycle came from behind at full speed and the pillion snatched it from me.

Health
How do you keep yourself fit?
I do light exercise in the morning like jogging and running. I think it is the best way to keep oneself fit. I also follow a stringent diet plan in which I have reduced my sugar intake to keep myself fit.

What is the importance of good health in our life?
I think there is a huge importance of good health in our life. A healthy person can enjoy all the facets of life. Good health enables a person to work and earn more. A healthy person is also mentally strong.

Do you feel that good diet leads to good health?
Without a doubt. I think when it comes to maintaining health, most experts say that its seventy percent diet and thirty percent exercise. Therefore, diet plays a bigger role in maintaining good health.

What is healthy food according to you?
Any food that covers all the essential nutrients, vitamins and minerals is a healthy food and food which does not have a lot of fat content but are full of proteins. Lentils, eggs, and green vegetables are the perfect example of healthy food.

Do you like healthy food?
Yes, mostly I prefer healthy food. Occasionally I also eat fast food or junk food but most of the times I eat cereals in breakfast and lentils in the dinner. I think these two food items are good for health.

Exercise
What kind of exercise do you do every day?
I like to do yoga and breathing exercises in the morning. If I do something rigorous, then I choose to do it in the evening. I think that morning is the best time to do exercise.

What type of exercise do the people do in your locality?
In my locality, I see people doing every kind of exercises. Youngsters like to do cycling and running, whereas most of the old people prefer yoga and light exercises.

Is there any exercise that we can do without any equipment?

Indeed, there are a few exercises that we can do without using any sort of equipment. Yoga is one and the second is running or jogging. People can also do breathing exercise without using any type of equipment.

Do you feel exercise can be harmful?
I don't think exercise can be harmful because. It can only be harmful if you are doing it without prior information and guidance.

How much exercise should everyone do in their daily routine?
According to me, everyone should spend at least thirty to forty-five minutes in doing exercise. WHO suggests every person to take a minimum of eight thousand steps in order to maintain good health.

Foreign language

Do you speak any foreign language apart from English?
No, I don't speak any foreign language apart from English. However, I am keen to learn Spanish as it is widely used throughout the world.

Why is it important to learn English?
It is essential to learn English as it bridges the gap between most of the people. English is the world's most widely spoken language. English opens a lot of opportunities as it enables a person to take his/her thoughts to millions of people around the world.

Is it good to learn the language of a country where you are travelling?
It's not mandatory to learn the language of the country where you are visiting but you should try to learn some important phrases as it can help you in desperate times. Some people learn the basics and main phrases because they like to indulge foreigners in conversation.

Do you feel regional languages are important?
We can never preserve our history if we don't preserve regional languages. It's essential to protect such languages and make our next generation learn it. It's good to learn foreign languages but regional languages are of huge importance.

Do you feel there should be only one language in the whole world?
I think it is not possible. There are numerous countries that don't speak the same language. There are remote places on Earth that don't have access to internet and outer world. So, it will not be easy to teach them a universal language. Although having single language in the whole world would be a huge advantage.

Space exploration

Do you feel governments around the world are spending unnecessary money on space exploration?
I feel sad when I see huge sums of money being wasted on space exploration. It's a real waste of precious money. I think instead of investing money on space exploration, governments should spend money to progress the undeveloped parts of our planet and make it a better place for people on Earth rather than finding other planets and aliens.

What are the benefits of space exploration programs?
I am strictly against these kinds of programs as I don't think it brings any kind of advantage. Its only wasting money on certain observations that may or may not exist.

If given a chance, would you like to travel to space?
If given a chance, I would love to go to space as it is a rare experience. I think very few people on Earth have been able to spend time in space, so I would not deny this opportunity.

What will you do when you will reach space?

The first thing that I would like to do when I reach space is to find my country on Earth. It would be great to see my home country from space. I will also try to locate other countries on Earth and test my geographical knowledge.

Is space tourism a good idea?
I feel space tourism will be a reality soon. I also perceive that it is definitely a good idea as it would be possible for masses to be in space. This type of tourism will still be rare as it will be extremely costly and perilous to life.

Future

Do you plan your future?
Yes, I do. It is crucial to plan the future events. I know that future is not in one's hand. But planning about the future certainly brings benefits.

Do you feel that future can be seen?
I never believe in such things, and I feel that it's foolish to think that one can see the future. It's all myth and should not be believed.

What things are you planning to buy in future?
I am planning to buy a house before I get married. I will also buy a big car and some property.

Where do you see yourself in the next ten years?
I want to see myself well settled in Canada / Australia ………… in the next ten years. I want to have a happy life for me and my family.

Are you too worried about your future?
No, I am never worried about my future. I always keep myself in present and leave the rest in hands of the almighty. So, this way I am never anxious about my future.

Hotel

Have you ever stayed at a big hotel?
Yes, I have stayed at a five-star hotel once when I went to Dubai. The name of the hotel is Taj Palace which is in Deira city center. It was a massive hotel with luxury rooms and extra ordinary interiors.

Which is your favourite hotel?
My favourite hotel is Taj Palace as it is nothing short of a wonder. There is a jacuzzi tub and a big swimming pool at the roof of the hotel. The rooms are spacious and luxurious with all the facilities that one can dream of having in a five-star hotel.

What type of hotels are there in your city?
In my city, there are all types of hotels, from one-star to five-star. The most prominent one's are JW Marriot, The Lalit, Hayat Regency and Mount View Hotel. These hotels raise the standard of the city.

Why do people stay at hotels?
There can be a few reasons behind this. The main reason is that if people go to another country or any city where they don't have a friend or a relative, in that case people book hotels. Apart from this people stay at the hotels when they go out for holidays.

Is staying in hotel costly in your country?
It completely depends on where people want to stay. If you stay at a decent three-star hotel then I think that India is a country where you will find cheap hotels. When it comes to five-star or luxury hotels then the prices are beyond most people's budget.

City and village

Which place is better to live, city or villages?

I think better place to live is city as it offers more things than living in a village. Most of the rural population is moving towards city these days as they vouch for more opportunities in education and employment.

What things you can improve in the city where you live?
I think there can be improvements in the transportation system of our city. There is hardly any public transport that one can find. People use their own vehicles which is a huge burden on their pocket.

Have you ever visited an important city/village?
Yes, I have visited many important places in my life. A city that is important in our country is Jaipur which is in Rajasthan state. It is important as it has preserved a lot of history and it is also a tourism hub of our country. It generates a lot of tourism revenue and employment for the locals.

Do you feel villages are better to live than cities?
I feel cities are always better than villages due to number of reasons but there are a couple of advantages of living in a village as well. People are more friendly and the environment is free from pollution and contamination.

Speak about a city that is very well developed.
In my viewpoint, Chandigarh is a very well-developed city in our country. It was the first planned city of our country. It is designed in a way that every part of the city is easily accessible from all four directions and the amenities such as education and hospitals are located nearby the residential area of every sector of the city.

Childhood
Share any fond memory from your childhood.
I certainly have a lot of childhood memories. The one which I remember is when I was selected as the most intelligent kid in a competition. I remember the event as I was five years old at that time and I still have the pictures of that event with me.

Is childhood the best stage of life?
Indeed, childhood is undoubtedly the best stage of life due to number of reasons. A kid is free from any burden whether it is of education, or of getting job and earnings for the family. Most of the kids are stress free and euphoric in nature during childhood.

Do you feel children have less burden than adults?
Children certainly have less burden than adults. Older people are under immense pressure these days. Whereas children have no responsibilities on their shoulders.

Do you feel that childhood is the best stage to learn things?
I fully agree that children have more ability to learn than adults. Their mind is fresh, and they have more time to practice things. Research shows that children catch things easily than adults and they take less time to adapt to anything.

How was your childhood?
My childhood was probably like most people's childhood, stress free, burden less and full of enjoyment. I feel that I am lucky to have parents who never stopped me from learning anything.

Jewelry
Do people like to wear jewelry in your country?
Yes, there is a custom and tradition in my country to wear jewelry. Mostly women adore the ornaments and jewelry around neck, ears, and wrists. Some men are also fond of wearing jewelry items.

What type of jewelry is popular among women?
I think every type of jewelry is liked by women. They mostly appreciate earrings and neck pieces. I have seen a lot of women wear anklets in my country. Basically, they relish every kind of jewelry.

Do you feel spending money on expensive jewelry is good?
In my perception, spending on expensive jewelry is not a bad idea. Most people in my country like to buy jewelry made of gold and diamonds. These materials have a great exchange value. Hence, jewelry can be exchanged for cash in crunch times.

Does jewelry have any religious importance in your country?
Yes, in my country there is a religious importance of wearing jewelry. Women in India wear Mangal Sutra, which is a necklace made of gold and other materials. It represents those women wearing it are married.

Do you wear jewelry?
No, I don't like to wear any jewelry item. I tried it once, but I don't like the feel as it interferes a lot in some body postures. So, I never thought of wearing any jewelry again.

Songs/music

Do you listen to songs?
I am very fond of listening to songs. My favourite singer is Sonu Nigam, and I hear all his songs in my leisure time. I generally listen to Hindi Bollywood, Punjabi, and English songs.

Which is your favourite song?
My favourite song is Heal the World song by Michael Jackson. This song became the best song soon after the release. The meaning and lyrics of the song are beautiful. The video is also great to watch.

Which type of music do you like?
I like Pop music the most. I also like to listen to Trance, Rock, Jazz and Classical. Every type of music is unique, but I feel that Pop songs are the best.

Who's your favourite musician?
My favorite musician is Shankar Mahadevan and he's a singer as well. His music is unique and fresh. He's one of the most respected musicians in our country. He also judges the popular show, Rising Star.

How do you feel when you listen to songs?
I feel tranquil and calm. Songs relaxes my mind and gives me energy to do more things. In a way, music inspires me to do well in life.

Art and craft

What is the importance of art and craft in our life?
Art and craft release the emotions in a beautiful way. It triggers our creative side and encourages us to do better. I think without art and craft, our life will be dull.

Have you ever participated in an art and craft competition?
I have participated in a lot of art and craft competitions in my school time. I remember how the staff of the school used to take us to the open parks where the competition would take place. Hundreds of students competed together.

Do you feel art and craft is dying out due to the developments in technology?
I don't deny the fact that art and craft is losing its importance with the advent of technology. These days art and crafts are also designed by computers. Human interference in this field is minimal. Today's youngsters are not patient enough to be interested in art and craft.

Do you think art and craft should be a compulsory subject in schools?
I am completely in favour of having art and craft as a compulsory subject in the school. This will enhance creative side of the students and widen their horizon.

Do you feel art and craft is a waste of time?
Not at all, art and craft are the way to go. Most people these days don't give importance to it, but the fact is that without art and craft, our traditions will die out.

Parks

Do you like visiting parks?

I love visiting parks very much. I feel close to the nature when I visit parks. I have a lot of parks near my home, and I generally go there early in the morning or late evening to enjoy the fresh environment.

Which is your favourite park?
My favourite park is the garden of silence which is in sector 1 of Chandigarh. It is a big park with lots of green areas. In the center of the park, there is a huge idol of Lord Buddha. I often go there to relax myself.

What kind of people go to parks?
I have seen every kind of people in the parks. I see kids playing with their friends. I see youngsters doing exercise and running. I also see old people there roaming from one end to the other.

What are the activities that people do in the parks?
People generally go to parks for walk and exercise. Some youngsters go to play different games and sports, but most people visit parks for leisure walks. I have also seen few people going there for reading books while sitting on the benches.

Should there be an entry fee to the parks?
No, there should never be an entry fee to the parks. This way less people would be encouraged to go there. I think it is the basic duty of the government to provide parks in every locality for free of cost.

Books

Do you read books?
Yes, I read books in my free time. I read at least three to four books every year. I feel we get a lot of knowledge regarding certain things from books that we don't get at school or college.

Which is your favourite book?
My all-time favourite book is long walk to freedom by Nelson Mandela. This book is his autobiography and was written by him after he came out of the prison.

Which genre of books do you like the most?
Mostly I like autobiographies and biographies of prominent leaders and celebrities. In this way I get to learn about their secrets to success.

What are the advantages of reading books?
There are many advantages of reading books. The first one is that it teaches you a lot of vocabulary. Secondly, it increases your knowledge and reading speed. Moreover, reading books is a great free time activity.

Is there any disadvantage of reading books?
I can't see any disadvantage of reading books. The only drawback is that it takes a lot of time to read books. For example, if you read a book of five hundred pages then it would take around a couple of months. Whereas a movie made on that book, or an audio version of it would be absorbed in three to four hours.

Festivals

Do you celebrate festivals?
I love celebrating all the festivals. India is a land of festivals as we have so many different religions in our country. I like to celebrate Diwali, Holi, Christmas, and all other prominent festivals. I believe celebrating festivals together with your friends and neighbours increases harmony in society.

Which festival do you celebrate every year?
I always wait for the Diwali festival. This day holds a great importance in the history of our country. On this day, Lord Rama returned to Ayodhya after fourteen years of exile. So, people on this day celebrate to commemorate the return of lord Rama.

What is the importance of celebrating festivals?

The biggest importance of celebrating festivals is that it promotes love, peace, and harmony among everyone in society. Celebrating festivals also keep us attached to our customs and traditions.

Is it important to spend huge amounts of money on celebrating festivals?
No, I think there is no need to spend huge sums of money on celebrating festivals. Celebrations can be simple yet enjoyable. Friends and family members can gather, and they can have a meal together.

Do you also celebrate festivals with your friends and neighbours?
I always celebrate all the festivals with my friends and neighbours. I remember, last year on Diwali our neighbours arranged a function in which everyone from locality and their relatives came. I can never forget that celebration.

Politics

Who's your favourite politician?
Girdhari Lal is my favourite politician. He was the AJP party's candidate in the 2014 elections and became the minister of our country. He has taken up a lot of issues in his own hands and ensured that our country moves in the right way.

Do you follow politics?
Yes, I follow politics but not every time. I like to listen to the debates of some of the prominent leaders of our country and I try to absorb as much information as I can.

Do you feel that being apolitical is good?
Being apolitical is not good for anyone. Humans are naturally political as it is our right to be political. For the betterment of any country, everyone needs to be political.

Do you think politics have changed over time?
Politics and politicians have changed a lot over the past few years. Previously, politics was not so commercialized but these days, politics is advertised, and politicians are much more dynamic and vocal in their opinions as compared to the past.

Have you ever met any politician?
No, I have never got a chance to meet any political leader in my life. If given a chance, I would love to meet the Prime minister of my country.

Superstitions

Do you follow superstitions?
No, I don't follow any kind of superstition. I feel it's not necessary in life as we are in the modern era and believe in science. I think there is no place for superstition in this world.

Speak about a superstitious person?
In my neighbourhood, there is a middle-aged woman. I find her very superstitious as she performs a lot of rituals. I always see her performing certain kinds of rituals that look unusual and impractical. She told me once that she doesn't wash her hair on Tuesdays and Thursdays as she considers it sinful. I find it very strange.

Do you feel that superstitions are a waste of time?
Absolutely, there's no doubt that superstitions are a complete waste of time and efforts. It keeps us confused and distracted throughout the day. I feel that one should stay away from superstitions.

Why do people follow superstitions?
There are a couple of reasons behind this. The first one is that they don't have confidence in their abilities and hence they rely on superstitions. Another one is that they are stressed and are not able to find solutions to the problems, in that case they are inclined towards such activities.

What are the common superstitions in your country?
I have seen some people not washing their hair on certain days and some like to eat curd before leaving their home. Some like to recite religious hymns, and some like to offer certain food items to animals and

birds in return for good luck. People also like to wear certain colors depending on occasions. There are endless superstitions that people do in our country.

Fashion
Do you follow fashion?
Yes, I follow fashion sometimes and like to be updated in terms of my clothing. I like to look for latest apparels and designs in the market.

Do you like to be aware of the latest trends?
As I told you that I keep myself aware of the latest trends in clothing, accessories, shoes, and other stuff. It gives me pleasure and joy in looking for new items.

Who is more inclined towards fashion, men or women?
I think if you would have asked me this question ten years back then my simple answer would have been women. However, these days men are not far behind as they indulge themselves into latest fashion more than women.

What type of fashion do people do?
People like to wear fancy dresses and shoes. Women are fond of different accessories whereas men mostly like to state fashion through shoes, belts, and watches.

Why do people follow fashion?
People follow fashion to make their presence felt in the crowd. Some people do fashion to conceal their insecurities. Also, some people look up to the celebrities and try to mimic their style.

Gifts
Have you received any gifts in life?
Yes, I have received a lot of gifts in my life. I generally get gifts on my birthday and special occasions. I love receiving gifts as it gives me a lot of happiness while opening it.

Speak about a special gift you have received?
I have received myriad gifts but the most special was the Samsung galaxy watch that I received from my sister. It's a smart watch which tells about the number of calories I have burnt in the whole day. It also gives me a lot of details about my current health and what needs to be done to get myself fit.

How do you feel when you receive gifts?
I feel on the top of the world when I receive gifts. I feel enthusiastic when I receive gifts from my near and dear ones.

What kind of gifts you give to other people?
I usually like to give gifts which can be kept by them for a long time. I give wall clocks, photo frames, pens and note diaries. It also depends on whom I am giving the gift. If it is a kid, then I like to give an educational toy.

Do you feel it is important to give gifts on weddings?
It's a great idea to give gifts to the wedding couple. They are about to begin a new life and I think that it is essential to give them gifts. We must gift them home appliances or stuff related to furniture so that it helps them in their new life.

Name
What is the difference between name and surname?
Name is the individual identity of a person whereas surname represents the family background. Surname in our country depicts the family or caste from where a person belongs.

What is the meaning of your name?
The meaning of my name is _____. I believe that my personality resembles my name.

Who gave you this name?

This name was given by my grandfather. I like my name very much and I think it is a blessing from him.

Would you like to change your name in future?

Not at all, I won't change my name in future. It is the name by which I have been identified over the past so many years. It is a huge part of my life.

Why do people change their names?

There can be a few reasons behind this. Some people have long names, so they cut short it to form a new name. Some people change their names when they move to a foreign country as their name is sometimes difficult to pronounce.

Bar-b-que

Do you like doing bar-b-que?

I love doing it in the winters. I generally call my friends and cousins at my home where we have a bar-b-que set up in the backyard.

Is bar-b-que a difficult thing to do?

You definitely require a lot of patience while cooking in this style as some meats can take long time to cook. Also, you need to have the skill of firing up the coal if you are using a traditional bar-b-que.

What do you usually cook on bar-b-que?

I usually cook different items like chicken, lamb, cottage cheese and some vegetables on the bar-b-que. Once I have also smoked fish, but it didn't go well.

Where do you generally do bar-b-que?

I have a set up at my house in the backyard but sometimes I also do it outdoors with my friends as I have one portable one as well.

is the food prepared on bar-b-que healthy?

Yes, most of the items that are prepared in the Indian style don't require oil. So, anything cooked on bar-b-que is healthier than frying.

Shoes

What sort of shoes do you like to wear?

I generally like to wear shoes that cover my foot well and are comfortable from the sole. Moreover, I like dark colour shoes.

From where do you generally buy your shoes?

I mostly buy my shoes from the local market or malls where branded variety of shoes is available. I also buy it from online shopping sites if I get a good price there.

Do people judge one's personality from shoes?

Yes, some people do judge a person's personality from shoes because they think that shoes depict choice, discipline, and standard of a person.

Do you wear same shoes every day?

No, I wear casual and comfortable shoes in my day-to-day life. However, on occasions, I wear formal and good-looking shoes.

Do you prefer branded or local made shoes?

I always choose branded shoes for two reasons. First, they are extremely durable and good looking. Second, they provide more comfort than local made shoes.

Web series

Do you watch any web series?
Yes, I have watched a couple of web series. Recently I watched Money Heist and Squid Game. Both these series were superbly made and were extremely popular around the world.

Do you feel the charm of cinema has lost due to web series?
Up to some extent, I agree that cinema's charm has taken a blow. Now some people prefer to sit at home and enjoy latest movies and web series as they are more intriguing and catchier.

Are web series a waste of time?
Yes, I feel they are a complete waste of time. Although they indulge you in a great manner but this is what makes it dangerous. People often procrastinate their important chores in lieu of watching these web series.

Would you recommend me to watch any web series?
Yes, I think you should watch squid game which launched recently. This is one of the most addictive web series that I have watched. The actors have acted wonderfully, and the sets and characters look surreal. It is the kind of web series that has never been made in the past.

Decorating

Do you like decorating your house?
Yes, I love decorating my house by using show pieces and paintings on the wall. I also decorate the exterior of my house using decorative plants in fancy pots.

Why do people like to decorate their houses?
People want their house to look beautiful and welcoming, so they like decorating their house. Also, many people are creative, so they put certain things in house that look good.

How do people generally decorate their houses?
People like to decorate their houses with flowers, some like to add a painting or wallpaper to a certain wall of the house. I have seen some people even keeping live decorative plants in their houses.

Do you feel decorating wastes money?
No, decorating enhances the ambience of a place. Putting money in making a place better looking is not a waste of money in my perception.

New Year

What do you generally do on New Year's Eve?
I am always excited about the new year to arrive on December 31st. I enjoy the night with my friends and family members at my house.

How and where do you celebrate the first day of new year?
I generally celebrate on the New Year's Eve. On the first day of a new year, I like to work and set new goals for my life.

Do you make any resolutions for the new year?
Yes, I do. I always write it on my personal diary and try to achieve as many resolutions as possible in that year. I always make plans at the start of a new year.

Is there any goal that you were not able to achieve in 2021?
Yes, I made a resolution with myself to cut down the intake of junk food, but I was not able to achieve that. I generally eat it every second day and want to get rid of this habit.

How do you think about working on the first day of the new year?
I think it is great idea to work on the first day of the year. It is one of the best feelings that someone can get. I think we should all work on the first day of the year to start our year in the positive way.

Nature

Do you love nature?
I think nature is only meant to be loved. I love every aspect of nature when it comes to the different landscapes. My favourite one is white sand beaches and warm ocean water.

Is there any threat to the nature these days?
There is a huge threat to nature in a lot of ways. The coral reefs of certain parts of the world are diminishing at an alarming rate due to water pollution and human activities. Also, there is a hazard to the eco system of some delicate parts of the world.

How can we solve the environmental problems?
I think we need to come together to solve the growing issue of environment. We should make people aware of the consequences and encourage them to spread this message and contribute towards the conservation of the environment. We must set an example for others by doing something in this regard.

Is nature kind or harsh?
Nature has both sides. Nature can be really kind sometimes whereas it can be life threatening as well. A good weather is a kind gesture of nature. On the other hand, earthquakes, typhoons, and other natural disasters are harsh. Nature is very unpredictable.

Do people often enjoy nature?
Yes, some people enjoy nature more than others. Some people do gardening, walk in the woods, or admire the beauty of a garden. However, some people these days are more inclined towards materialistic things and don't like to spend time with nature.

Shopping

Do you like to go out for shopping?
I love to do shopping whenever I get a chance. I buy clothes and shoes for myself. I also like to shop the accessories and other electronic items. I think shopping acts as a stress buster for me.

Who tends to shop more, men or women?
It's difficult to answer, I think both genders shop equally. The interests can be a bit different. Men like to shop electronic gadgets and shoes whereas women generally prefer clothes and make up kits.

What kind of shopping is popular in India?
People do all sorts of shopping. From buying vegetables and fruits for consumption to buying luxury cars and expensive jewelry. People buy according to their pockets. I have seen that most of the people in my country like to do shopping. Even some people relish window shopping.

What's the future of shopping?
I think people will continue to buy things in the future as well. One thing will surely change, and that is the way of shopping. People will prefer to shop online rather than going to the shops physically.

Technology

Do you feel technology has evolved humans?
Indeed, technology has evolved the beliefs and lifestyle of human beings. They have now become more prone to technology rather than practicing traditional beliefs. I feel it has brought both good as well as bad changes.

Is technology boon or bane?
It works both ways. Technology has advanced a lot in the recent times, and it has been a great boon for the mankind. On the contrary, it has brought a lot of disadvantages as well. It has made people lazy and dependent.

Speak about a recently invented technology?
I love smart watches. It is recently invented in the past few years. It's the best gadget to have. You just need to tie it to your wrist as you would tie a traditional watch. But the difference is that it will not only show you the time but will also tell you about your health and other notifications.

Is technology dangerous?

In some cases, technology can be dangerous. Artificial intelligence might be useful in some cases but things like data leak and overdependence on technology can be hazardous.
Do you feel we should limit the use of technology in our daily life?
I think there is a huge need to curb the amount of technology that we use every day. We should only use it when it is required. Needless use of technology is injurious for us.

Bicycle
Do you own a bicycle?
No, I don't own a bicycle, but I am planning to buy one. I feel it has numerous benefits. We can use it to commute from one place to the other without burning fuel and it also keeps us fit.
Is cycling good for health?
It is great for our health. When we cycle, we are not only going from one place to the other, but we are also using our body to pedal it. it's a great form of exercise.
Do you feel that we should observe a bicycle day every year?
I my perception, we should observe a bicycle day every year. I would rather say that it should be celebrated every month across the globe so that people can be aware about the rising pollution and can get inspiration to use cycles more often.
Can bicycles solve the traffic and pollution problems?
I am a firm believer that the use of bicycles can solve the traffic and pollution problems to a great extent. If more people start using bicycles, then others will also follow the precedent. This way there can be a lot more improvements in certain issues.
Are there any bicycle tracks in your hometown?
Yes, in my hometown most of the main roads and the leading roads have the facility of a separate bike lane. This encourages more people to ride bicycle. This also ensures safety for the riders.

Work
Do you feel work is worship?
I am a believer of smart work than hard work. I think that work should be considered as work and should not be mixed with worship. We work to earn bread and butter, but worship is done for the peace of mind.

What kind of work you do every day?
I do a lot of different works every day. I mainly study my textbooks and read books other than my syllabus. I also like to help my mother and father in the daily chores such as dish washing and cooking.
Do you feel working for more than eight hours is a bad idea?
As I told you earlier that I believe in smart work, and I usually don't prefer to work for long hours. I think an individual has a lot of other things to do as well except work. One should focus on work but for a limited period and then devote rest of his time to family, friends, and leisure activities.
How many hours do people work in your country?
Most of the people work eight to ten hours in a day. I have seen some people working more than that. According to me, working for 7 to 8 hours is an ideal scenario.
How many working days are there in your country?
Most of the people work from Monday to Friday. There are some private organizations that work on Saturdays as well. Some businesses even run seven days a week. There's no fixation to working hours.

Studies
Do you like studies?
I like studying very much. I study for around three hours a day in which I also study apart from my curriculum. I like to read material related to technology and science.

How should we plan our study?
We should plan our study according to the time we want to devote on studies, and we ought to plan in a way that we don't get tired of studying. I think the best way to plan studies is to study for an hour early in the morning, one hour in the day and one hour at night. This way we will not feel bored of studying.

Do you feel students often study trivial subjects at school?
Yes, we have a lot of subjects in school which are of little use in our real life. We should not be taught the difficult historical dates for the previous event; we have the computers for storing our data. More practical subjects should be taught in the schools.

Is it important to study hard?
Yes, it is necessary to study hard. Whatever time you can give to your studies, you should study with full concentration and efforts. You are only going to get good grades if you study hard. There are no shortcuts to it.

What is smart study?
Smart study means studying in a way that you learn everything in less time. There are an array of mobile applications and software that teach you in a practical way. This type of learning is much better and effective than theory learning.

Email

Do you write e-mails?
I write emails occasionally or when I want to accomplish any official work. Till now I think I have hardly sent any personal email to anyone. All the mails have been professional, and work related. Exchanging study material with friends or some important documents with someone.

Do you receive e-mails?
I receive a lot of emails because these days if you visit someone and you drop your email over there, then get ready to receive promotional emails every day. All the mails that I receive are mostly promotional and of very little use to me.

Have you ever received an important e-mail?
Yes, once I received an important email from a friend. He sent me the list of important questions for the final exams of my 10th class. I was excited to receive that email as it helped me prepare well for the exams.

Are e-mails helpful?
Emails are extremely helpful as we can send and receive important information and data. Email helps us to store our work and attachments electronically. We can open old mails and information anytime without breaking a sweat. We don't need to store documents and files anywhere as it can be easily retrieved from the emails.

Speak about a recent e-mail you sent.
I sent an email to my friend. In this email, I send him a lot of photographs that I clicked on our trip to Jaipur. I attached more than 50 pictures that I clicked and send him through email.

Smoking

Do you agree with the statement that smoking should be banned?
I agree that smoking should be banned completely at the public places as it harms public. Otherwise, the sale of cigarettes should not be barred as it is the right of a person whether to smoke or not.

What are the ill effects of smoking?
Smoking is harmful for the lungs. There is a caution sign on the pack of cigarettes that suggests, smoking is injurious to health. It also causes different types of mouth cancers. All in all, smoking is a deadly habit.

Should there be dedicated places for smoking?

Yes, government should try to make dedicated spaces for smokers so that the smoke does not affect the public. This way, smokers can enjoy smoking without disturbing anyone.

Are there any smoking chambers in your city?
Yes, there is one smoking chamber that I have seen in a mall. I went there recently and saw a small chamber where a couple of men were smoking.

Do you feel government should advertise heavily against smoking?
I think government is already advertising against smoking on a lot of platforms in our country. Whenever we go to watch a movie, there is always an advertisement regarding the negative effects of smoking. That advertisement reaches millions of people every day.

Your country
Speak about a specialty of your country?
The biggest specialty of my country is its diversity. In India, you can see all the religions and culture existing happily together. We have different types of landscapes that are found all around the world. We have all the seasons that can possibly occur.

Do you like your country?
I love my country very much. We have done impossible things as a country over the past few years. Our country is developing at a rapid speed. We are one of the most popular nations in the whole world due to our achievements.

Do you feel India is developing faster than ever?
I have no doubts in this statement. I think we are in the race to become a developed nation. Our country is witnessing the most rapid developments since previous years. I hope that we get the results soon.

Speak about a place where every foreigner should visit in your country.
There are numerous places where foreign tourists can visit in India. In the northern part of our country, we have the tallest mountain range, the Himalayas. It is untouched and serene. A lot of people from our country and foreign as well visit these mountains for relaxation and to observe the beauty of nature.

Does your country have strong ties with its neighbours?
Yes, my country is surrounded with a lot of neighboring countries like Pakistan, Myanmar, Sri Lanka China, Bhutan, Nepal, and Bangladesh. We can even enter Bhutan and Nepal without obtaining a visa. This shows how good the ties between India and these nations are.

Going out
Do you like going out in the evening?
I love going out in the evenings. I feel rejuvenated and relaxed at this time of the day. I like to go for a walk on my own or play cricket and football with my friends

Which is your favourite place to hang out in your city?
I like to go to Sukhna Lake most of the times. It's a beautiful lake lined with numerous varieties of plants and trees on one side. There is a seperate track for walking as well as jogging. One can view the Shivalik hills at the backdrop of the lake.

Do you like going out with your friends or family members?
I like going out with both, it depends upon the situation. If I am going for a party, then I like the company of my friends. If I am going for a picnic or holiday, then I prefer family.

Which places do you visit on weekends?
I mostly visit hill stations and lakes. I live in Chandigarh where Shivalik hills are only an hour drive from there. Whenever I feel jaded, I like to visit Kasauli hills.

At what time of the day you go out for fun?

I like to go out for fun at any time of the day. Mostly I go out in the evening and sometimes early in the morning as well. If I plan to enjoy the nature, then I go in the morning. If I want to enjoy parties, then I prefer evenings.

Clothes
What type of clothes do you wear in daily routine?
I generally wear casual clothes in my daily routine. If the situation demands, then I change to the formals. If I am at home, I like to wear comfortable clothes.
Do you like fashionable or comfortable clothes?
I prefer both depending on the occasion. If I need to look good, then I wear fashionable clothes whether they are comfortable or not. But generally, I am the kind of a person who prefers comfort over fashion.
What type of clothes do the people wear on weddings?
People in my country wear heavy clothes on wedding functions. They like to spend huge money on buying clothes for the wedding ceremonies. The colors they wear are vibrant and bright.
Do you prefer branded clothes?
I prefer branded over local clothes. There are two reasons behind that, first one is that the branded clothes last long and the second one is that the designing of brands is unique.
From where do you buy your clothes?
I usually buy my clothes from the brand outlet or in the shopping malls. I also order some of my clothes online from the trusted e-commerce websites.

Trains
Are trains a mode of transport in your country?
Yes, trains are widely used by almost all the people in my country. We have all kinds of trains ranging from cheapest to the most luxurious ones in the world. India is a big country; hence train travel is the most preferred one. India has a complex yet effective network of railways.
Have you ever travelled in a train?
I have travelled uncountable times on a train. I generally travel by Shatabadi and Rajdhani Express. These two are the fastest and the most convenient trains in our country.
Is travelling in trains safe in your country?
Travelling in train is very safe in my country. There are many security personnel that are deployed to ensure the safety of the passengers. Also, there are advanced CCTV cameras these days which also contributes to the security factor of the trains.

What are the advantages of travelling in a train?
There is a bundle of advantages of travelling in a train. The first one is that you can move freely as the trains are more spacious than a bus or a plane. Another one is that we have the option of sleeper class at very cheap rates in which people can travel first class without burning a hole in their pocket.
Do the trains get late in India?
It happens a lot in our country, and it can get frustrating sometimes. This aspect of the railway system is not yet improved. Once I got stuck at the station for about seven hours waiting for the train. Sometimes it can get even worse.

Time
What is the importance of punctuality in our life?
I think being punctual is one of the most important attributes to have in life. Being on time shows how dedicated you are towards something. Punctuality is a trait that all successful people have.
Do people value time?

No, I don't want to say this, but it is a harsh reality in our society that people usually don't value time. Most people are not true to their commitments and appointments. This shows that they don't value punctuality.

Do you make timetable for your future?
Yes, I tend to make timetable for my future. It allows me to plan my work accordingly and I mostly finish my tasks on planned time schedule. It is helpful for people who are not able to manage their time in a proper way.

Do you feel that we should value time?
It's crucial to value time in our lives otherwise the time will not value us. Once the time has passed, it never comes back. So, it's necessary to respect time.

Were people more punctual in past time?
I think yes, people were more loyal towards time in the past as compared to present. People nowadays are lazier due to the advent of technology.

Reading
Do you like reading?
I love reading very much. Most of the times I read self-help books and auto biographies of famous politicians and sportsperson. I read at least for one hour every day.

What kind of materials do you like reading?
I prefer reading all sorts of material. I pick random books to read. I just fall for the cover or title of the book, and I don't care what sort of book it is. I feel every book teaches you something.

Do you feel reading can be addictive?
Yes, it can be very addictive. I have seen people reading novels and books for hours and hours continuously. Reading books for too long can have negative effects, the most common is insomnia.

What are the benefits of reading?
There are numerous benefits of reading. We can enhance our vocabulary and learn new phrases. It also gives us huge amount of knowledge. Reading increases our memory and ability to debate on certain topics.

Have you seen anyone who's a good reader?
Yes, my elder brother is a wonderful reader. His reading speed is incredible, and he also remembers everything that he reads. He can complete a two-hundred-page book in four to five hours.

Restaurant
Describe your favourite restaurant.
My favourite restaurant is Bar-b-cue World. It's located at multiple locations in my city. It is a restaurant chain and only serves buffet lunch and dinner. I like going there as they have tremendous variety of food items to choose.

Do you often go there?
I go there once a month or if there is a special occasion. I like to celebrate my birthday with friends and family at this place.

Which dish do you generally order there?
I don't order anything as it is a buffet restaurant. It's up to us to choose the dish we want to eat. I like honey chili cauliflower and grilled mushrooms.

Is restaurant food good for health?
No, restaurant food is not good for health. We should avoid it as much as we can. On the other hand, it does not harm too much if we consume it occasionally.

Why do people visit restaurants in your area?
People visit restaurants when they celebrate an occasion with their family or friends. They also visit there sometimes when they are tired of eating homemade food and don't want to cook themselves.

Pollution
What are the causes of pollution?
There are several causes of pollution like garbage and, industrial waste, generation of electricity through coal and vehicles. These are the main sources that create pollution in the environment.

How can we overcome this issue?
We can overcome this issue by creating awareness among people about the ill-effects of pollution. Government can take several steps to create a neat and clean environment.

What can government do to control pollution?
Government can make strict rules against people who create unnecessary pollution. Heavy fines should be imposed and in severe cases, imprisonment should be given.

What are the major problems caused by pollution?
There can be serious issues that can be caused by pollution. Thousands of marine species are dying due to dumping of plastic into the ocean. More people than before are suffering with respiratory problems.

Which type of pollution is most common in your country or city?
In my city, the most common type of pollution is the air and noise pollution. These days, there are a huge number of vehicles running on the roads. The exhaust emissions have led to massive air pollution.

Population
Is population a problem in your country?
It's a big problem of my country. A lot of people in my county are unemployed because of the population explosion. Job creation is not there but the demand is increasing by leaps and bounds.

What are the causes behind the increase in population?
People are not educated enough to know the consequences of huge population. Illiteracy plays a part in the reason behind growing number of people.

Is one child policy the solution?
No, I think that it is not the right solution. China did it few years back, but it didn't work well. Initially they were able to control population but after some years, proportion of old people increased which led to numerous issues in healthcare and industry sector.

How can we curb population?
The best way to control population is to create awareness among people on public platforms. Government should encourage people to give birth to not more than two kids and give incentives to those who follow the instruction.

What are the disadvantages of an overpopulated country?
The biggest drawback of huge population in a country is that the unemployment rates shoot up. More people will struggle for one job position. Another problem is that the demand is more than the production, resulting in inflation.

Home

In what kind of a home do you live?
I live in a big house as I put up with all my cousins in a joint family. Our house consists of eight rooms, four at the ground floor and rest on the upper floor.

What type of homes are there in your locality?
We have similar kind of homes in our locality. It differs from size to size though. The width and length can be different, but the height and number of stories allowed are the same for everyone. People are not allowed to build more than a three-story house in my city.

Is it important to have a parking space at home?
Yes, I think it has now become a basic requirement of everyone. To have personal parking space in the house is a blessing. I think every house should have a dedicated parking space.

What is the difference between living in a house and an apartment?
A house comes with a lot of advantages. In house we can modify anything, we have more space, and we can add multiple floors to it. In apartment, security is there, and the cost is less. Both have their own merits.

What type of home do you prefer to live in?
I prefer to live in a big home that is an independent house. I like to have more space hence I don't like to live in apartments. I love to live in a house that is also big from inside and should have multiple floors.

Mobile phones

Do you use mobile phone?
Yes, I use mobile phones. I use a Samsung smart phone for a variety of purposes. I like to play games sometimes and also watch movies on it. I also like to read e-books in my free time. The main function that I use in mobile phone is calling and messaging.

Should school children be allowed to use mobile phones in schools?
School children should never be allowed to use mobile phones in schools. That is their time to study and being thoughtful whereas mobile phones are a distraction for kids.

How has mobiles changed our lives?
Mobiles have changed our lives in a lot of ways. Previously we used to have an alarm clock to wake up, a camera for clicking pictures, radio, and TV for entertainment. But, with the advent of mobiles, we don't need any of those devices. Everything is made possible by merely using a mobile these days.

What are the negative effects of mobile phones?
The biggest effect of mobile is on the health. People use mobiles for a longer period. We are always hooked up to mobiles for any task. It would not be wrong to say that we have become slaves of mobile phones.

Are mobile phones expensive in your country?
There are certain brands that are expensive in India but most of the mobiles are not expensive. One can get quality and feature loaded mobile smartphone at reasonable price.

Drinks
Which is your favourite drink?
I love mango shake. Every year I wait for the summer season to arrive as the availability of mangoes is in that season only. I drink mango shake every day in summers.
Can you make a drink?
Yes, I can make cold coffee. You just need to mix a teaspoon of coffee powder and some sugar according to taste in chilled milk. Then shake it intensely to get a frothy cold coffee. You can also add vanilla ice cream to enhance the experience.
What benefits do the cold drinks have?
There are not many benefits of cold drinks as they can cause cough or cold and are extremely sweet. But, at the time of extreme summers, one should drink soda or cold beverages to avoid heat stroke.
Do you also drink fruit juices?
Yes, I like all sorts of fruit juices. My favourite ones are the pomegranate and black current juice. I think fresh juice is great for the digestive system, and our skin.
Do you take hard drinks?
No, I don't take hard drinks.

Malls
How are malls better than shops?
I feel malls are spacious and have more variety under one roof. In summers, it's good to go to mall as the entire shopping complex is air conditioned. Malls have other activities to do as well.
Are there any malls in your hometown?
There are more than 7 or 8 malls in my hometown. I live in a modern city so there is no scarcity of malls. Some are of small and medium size, but Elante and VR are massive.
For what purpose do you visit malls?
I visit malls to shop for my clothes and I also go there to watch movies. I even go to malls to dine as there are numerous options of top restaurants.
What is the future of malls?
The future of malls is very bright. Nowadays, a growing number of people are shopping from malls and shopping complexes. People get more variety and convenience while they are in a mall.
Do you feel shops in malls generate more income than shops in the markets?
Indeed, shops in mall generate more income than shops in the market. It is due to additional foot fall in malls and other benefits that malls bring. Malls are fully air conditioned and there are other amenities in the same building, so more people will eventually visit malls than markets. More footfall means more sales.

Swimming pool
Have you ever visited a swimming pool?
Yes, I have been to a lot of swimming pools. The swimming pool I like the most is the one which is made in the sports complex of my city. The pool is indoors and is built according to the Olympics standards. A lot of people of all age groups come there to learn swimming.
Do you know swimming?
I am still learning the art of swimming. I took lessons last year but was not able to learn proper swimming in deep water. I can dive and float for a couple of seconds and that's it.
Do you feel swimming should be taught in schools?
I think swimming should be taught in schools because it is such an activity that everyone should know. I don't think that all the schools will be able to provide this facility, but they can aware kids about the benefits of swimming.

Is it a good idea to learn swimming at an early stage of life?
Anything that is learnt at an early stage of life is well learnt. Swimming is such an activity that can be learnt properly at young age. At this age, a child can learn and adopt anything easily.

What are the advantages of swimming?
There are numerous advantages of swimming. The first one is that it is a complete exercise as all the body parts are involved while swimming. Secondly, it can be a life saver in emergency.

Fruits

Which is your favourite fruit?
I like all fruits except papaya. My favourite are mango and banana. I also like watermelon in summers. Mango is sweet and delicious and is also known as the king of fruits whereas banana gives more minerals and nutrients than any other fruit.

What are the health benefits of eating fruits?
There are many health benefits of eating fruits. It clears up the digestive system thoroughly. Eating fruits also helps in preserving our skin. Fruits contains a lot of antioxidants that ensure good health for all our organs.

What type of fruits are there in your country?
There are all types of seasons in my country, hence we get all sorts of fruits. We have bananas, mango, apple, orange, watermelon, sun melon, musk melon, guava, kiwi, strawberry and so on.

At what time of the day do you eat fruits?
I mostly eat fruits in the evening after the dinner. This is the best time to eat fruits as it helps to digest the dinner because I generally take light dinner, so the fruits compliment it very well.

From where do you buy fruits?
I accompany my mother when she buys fruit. We buy fruits from Reliance mart. It is one of the biggest supermarkets in our area. Fruits available there are fresh and cheap.

Photography

Do you like taking pictures?
Yes, I like it very much. I have a decent camera in my smart phone so whenever there's an occasion or something special, I take out my phone and click photos and record videos.

Which camera do you use to take pictures?
Mostly, I take pictures from my mobile phone as it is quite handy and its always in my pocket. I also have a Sony digital camera in which I take pictures when I go for an excursion.

Do you feel we should click photos more often?
I think when we click pictures more often, we miss the real moments. We should click pictures once or twice in the event and rest of the times, we should enjoy the moment.

Speak about a special photo.
I have a special photo that hangs in the drawing room of our house in a grand frame. The photo was taken on my cousin's wedding and is of a big size. In that photograph there are all maternal family members of mine. All my cousins, my uncles, and aunts. I really love that photo.

Does photography require special skills?
No, I don't think there's any rocket science in clicking pictures. You just need to fit everything in the frame and click the button. Although one should be trained enough for professional photography.

Role model

Do you have a role model in life?

Yes, I have a role model and he's, my grandfather. He has achieved a lot of things in life. I have learnt a great deal of things from him. During his young days, he struggled a lot and eventually reached the heights of success.

Do you feel we should have role models for inspiration?
Yes, we should have role models in life. We can look up to them for inspiration. We should have role models in life who are our near and dear ones so that it gives us a chance to learn things from them.

What kind of role models do people choose?
People mostly look up to famous personalities and celebrities. Some people like to choose sportspersons as their role models. I think people generally look for successful people as their role models.

Do you feel actors can make good role models?
I don't think actors can be great role models as what they are on screen doesn't mean that they are the same off screen. We can't judge their real personalities so I think that one should not make actors as their role models based on their characters in movies.

What type of people can be good role models?
Scientists, politicians, teachers, spiritual leaders, and writers can be good role models. These people are the ones who reform societies and influence the thinking of people. They will make wonderful role models.

Women
What is the position of women today?
I think the position of women today is very strong. Women of today are independent and takes decisions on their own. In some societies the plight of women has not improved but in most places the change is visible.

Do you feel women are empowered enough in your society?
I feel in most of the developed countries and in countries where literacy rate is high, there has been a huge improvement in the position of women, and they are empowered enough to make their own place in society. In my country this is happening gradually.

Should women serve in police and army?
They should serve in police and the army as they are not inferior to anyone. In my country, women are already serving as women cops and commandos.

What should we do to empower women?
We should encourage girls from a young age about having their own choices so that they can take decisions on their own. The feeling of inferiority is induced in women from childhood. If we can stop it then we can empower women.

What do you think about women?
I think they are smarter than men. If you see the current trend in matriculation and 12th results, you will see more girls who top the rankings than boys. That's a clear sign that they are intelligent enough and we don't need to take decisions on their behalf.

History
Is it important to preserve history?
It's essential to preserve history as it reflects on our past and inception. If we preserve history, then only we will be able to make our children learn about the sacrifices and struggles that our ancestors made to bring us to a position where we are today.

Why do schools have history subject?
Schools have history subject because children need to learn about the important events and dates of the past. History has great value, and they can form interest in reading it if they learn it from childhood.

Do you like reading history?

I love reading history and historical events. I prefer reading about past scientists and events such as Mahabharata. This enhances our knowledge about past and gives us an insight into our culture.

Should history be made compulsory throughout the education?
Today's generation hardly know any facts from history. It's an old saying that we can't win present without knowing history. I think history should be taught throughout the educational years and it should be a compulsory subject.

Do you feel we should teach current history rather than the old one?
Yes, we should teach current history more than the older one. Both have equal importance, but I feel that kids will take more interest in learning the 21st century history than the ancient history.

Media
What is the role of media in shaping our society?
Media plays a big role in shaping our history. It has a huge impact on the lives of people from all walks of life. Everyone is hooked up to media every time for latest updates.

Do you feel media has become a part of our life?
It's a crucial part of our life these days. We are attached to media for the most part of our day. We rely on it for valuable information and entertainment.

Do you feel media is powerful?
Media is a powerful medium which can either bring all people on the same page or it can start wars on the difference of opinions. Media is the most powerful weapon in this era.

Should media interfere in the personal lives of celebrities?
I think it is a bad idea. Famous celebrities have their personal lives, and they have the right to enjoy it without anybody's interference. Sometimes, media takes it too far in the coverage of a story. That can be really irritating for celebrities.

Should there be a check on media?
No, I think media should be an independent body and there should not be any check on it by government or any organization. Media should be allowed to present the reality of the society without any restrictions.

Boats/ships
What is the purpose of boats and ships in your country?
Boats and ships are used to commute from one place to the other. It is also used to ship the cargo and goods. India is a country where extensive use of boats and ships is there.

Have you ever travelled on a boat or ship?
I have travelled once on a ship in Goa. It was a sun set tour of three hours in which the ship company picked and dropped us at the hotel and took us in the ocean to enjoy the sun set dinner. There was some entertainment with around 300 people on board.

Are there any famous ship ports in your country?
There are several important ship ports in India as our country has a long coastline. The most prominent ones are Mumbai, Chennai, Vishakhapatnam, Kolkata, and Cochin.

What's the difference between travelling in a ship and aero plane?
Travelling in ship is much slower than travelling in air, but the fare is cheaper in ships. One can find more luxuries and space in ships as opposed to an aero plane at affordable cost.

Do the people in your country often travel in boats and ships?
Yes, people in my county often travel in boats and ships as we are not a landlocked country, and we have a lot of rivers that flow from one city to the other. The voyage of boat is also cheaper, so many people use this as the transport method.

Online shopping
Do you feel future of online shopping is bright?
Certainly, today is the era of modern technology and internet has taken over many fields. People are inclining more and more towards online shopping due to its numerous benefits. I think online shopping has a healthy future.
What are the benefits of online shopping?
There are many advantages of buying things online. The biggest one is that you don't need to roam around markets and different places to buy a product. You can simply order it from any part of the world, and you will get it delivered at your doorstep.
Do you shop online?
Indeed, I like to buy a lot of things from the online shopping websites. There are certain products that are not easily available in the market. For that, I chose online shopping. The other reason I shop online is that it gives me more discounts than things that are available in the market.
Name some of the products that are sold commonly on online platforms.
There are thousands of products that are commonly sold online. Most common ones are clothes and shoes. I have seen a lot of people who buy such things from the online merchants. People also buy mobile phones and other electronic gadgets from online stores.
Do you feel online shopping is fraud?
No, I don't think this way. There are some websites that do some frauds but most of the renowned platforms are providing genuine products at unbeatable prices. There have been some reports of fraud by certain unregistered websites but majority of them are fine.

Tea / coffee
Do you like tea?
I love drinking tea on daily basis. I think it is a part of the Indian culture. It is also believed that tea is the second most consumed drink in the world after water. It is soothing and rejuvenating.
What are the benefits of having tea?
There are many benefits of consuming tea that have been scientifically proven. Tea contains a lot of antioxidants that provides energy and prevents ageing of organs. Also, it relaxes the mind after a hectic day.
Which drink is more popular in your country, tea, or coffee?
I think tea and coffee both are popular in my country, but I think tea is more common. Coffee is also consumed extensively but tea is more popular drink than any other beverage.
Which type of tea is famous in your country?
Our country is famous for its tea plantations. Assam tea is consumed all over the world. Most of the people in my country like oolong tea. This is a black tea which is often mixed with milk and sugar to make a traditional Indian tea. With growing health awareness, green tea is also becoming popular these days.
Do you like coffee?
I am a coffee and tea lover. I like consuming coffee a couple of times in a week. I like my coffee rich in flavor and with a lot of milk. I generally make latte as it's not that strong and is full of flavor.
Why do people drink tea or coffee?
People drink tea or coffee for several reasons. Tea rejuvenates the mind and provides antioxidants that controls ageing. On the other hand, coffee is a great laxative that helps in digestion. It also contains caffeine that helps to stay active.

Do you often invite people for tea or coffee?
Yes, I do. I like to invite my friends for tea generally in the evening. I think it is the best way to interact with your friends and you can have a great conversation over tea or coffee.

Do you like to have tea at home or cafe?
I prefer to make my tea at home. I also drink it outside when required but most of the times I like it at home. It's one of the easiest things to make. So, I prefer my tea at home.

Smile
Do you often smile?
Yes, I like to smile quite often. It is an activity that gives me energy and positive attitude. I think a smile on face is the greatest trait that a person can have.

Do you like to make people smile?
Yes, if I am given a chance, I like to make people smile. I am not a very talkative person who could make everyone smile, but I feel that bringing a smile on someone's face is a great act.

What are the benefits of smiling?
There are many benefits of smiling. The biggest one is that it keeps your mood lighter. It means that you are in a good mental space and can take better decisions. Apart from this, one looks good with a smile on face than a stoned face person.

Do you feel smiling enhances personality?
Yes, I completely believe in this. I reckon that a person looks different when he smiles. It brings energy within the person, and it also influences others. Thus, smile enhances personality.

On what occasions do you smile?
I mostly smile when I hear a joke or when I see a comedy program or movie. I also smile when someone does a foolish thing. Because I think reacting strongly to it can be bad, so I just smile off the situation.

Mathematics
Did you study mathematics at school?
I studied mathematics throughout most part of my schooling as it is a compulsory subject in Indian education system. I found it challenging and interesting at the same time.

Did you find it easy or difficult?
I found it to be easy in the early part of my schooling but when I grew up, it became quite a difficult subject for me. I used to score averagely in mathematics in high school.

What are the benefits of learning mathematics?
I think it is very useful for the development of the brain. That's why it has been made a compulsory subject in our education system. Moreover, it helps to develop the analytical and reasoning skills of a person.

Do you feel mathematics is a useless part of school curriculum?
Not at all, I think it is one of the most integral parts of the education. Without mathematics the study would be so boring and one dimensional. Moreover, it is helpful in most of the higher educational courses as well.

Did you ever fail in mathematics exam?
If I could remember properly then I think I failed once in my 9th grade class test. The reason I failed was that I could not get time to prepare for the exam as I was down with fever.

Garbage / rubbish
What is the reason behind increasing rubbish these days?

The main reason behind the ever-escalating problem of garbage is population and people's attitude towards hygiene. There has been a huge leap in the demand for the packaged food. This has led to the nuisance of rubbish.

How can we tackle this situation?
There are number ways through which we can tackle this situation. First, individuals should try to manage garbage at their own level rather than depending on the government. Secondly, they can keep separate bins for recyclable and non-recyclable waste so that the garbage can be sorted properly.

Do you feel people are responsible for creating more and more garbage?
Yes, I think people are the ones to be blamed for creating garbage everywhere. However, in some cases government must be blamed for poor management of the garbage.

Do you feel it is the sole responsibility of a government to take care of the garbage?
No, I think there should be collective efforts by administration and public to tackle this issue. This is one of the most dreadful problems these days that needs to be solved as quickly as possible.

Do you feel garbage should be recycled?
Indeed, garbage ought to be recycled in a way that we get the maximum return from that. In some countries, government even pays for the waste that you return to them which can be recycled.

Perfume

Do you wear perfume every day?
No, I don't usually wear perfume. I generally apply it when I go out for a dinner or for a special occasion. I have a decent collection of perfumes.

What type of perfumes do you like?
I like pungent smell. I think that a perfume should overpower all the odors that our body has. The perfume should also be long-lasting and impactful.

Do you feel wearing perfume has become a trend these days?
It certainly has become a trend these days and not many people use it as a requirement. I see people buying super expensive perfumes for no reason.

Are perfumes expensive in your country?
There are all types of perfumes that are available in my country. The range starts from as low as 100 rupees and goes up to as expensive as you want. It depends on brand to brand.

Do people of your country use perfume on regular basis?
I have seen majority of people using perfumes daily. I think it completely depends on the individuals. I have also seen some people who do not use perfumes at all.

Borrowing / sharing

Do you like sharing your things with others?
I certainly do. I have been taught by my parents from my childhood to share things with people who are needy. It gives me immense pleasure when I share things with others.

Is borrowing a good habit?
It can be both good and bad. I think borrowing something from a sibling or a good friend is fine but borrowing loans from bank and other stuff can be lethal sometimes.

Do you feel sharing is a quality that everyone should have?
Yes, I think that everyone should have this quality. The world would be a great place to live if everyone starts sharing. One should try to share things with the people who need them the most.

Have you ever borrowed something from others?
Yes, I have borrowed many things from my friends and siblings. They always give me the things that I need. I think sharing things with loved ones also enhances the relationships.

Have you shared any expensive thing with your friend?

Absolutely, once I lend my digital camera to my friend for a school trip.

Bottled water
What are the negative impacts on the environment of using bottled water?
There are many adverse effects of using bottled water on the environment. The major one is the plastic waste caused by it. It is estimated that the biggest cause of sea pollution in 2018 was from the plastic water bottles. This type of pollution has deadly impact on the environment and marine life in particular.

Do you feel bottled water is used extensively in your country?
Yes, there is no doubt that bottled water can be found in every corner of our country. Unavailability of clean drinking water in major cities has led to the increased production of bottled water.

Do you use bottled water regularly?
No, I generally drink from the government supply that arrives at our house. We have a water filter attached to the inlet pipe that filters the water we drink. If I am travelling outside the city, then I prefer drinking bottled water.

Is bottled water good for health?
If we consume bottled water in daily routine, then it is not good for health. First, it contains preservatives that keeps it good to drink for a long time. Moreover, it is mostly packed in plastic bottle, which is not the best material for packing edible products.

Do you feel bottled water should be banned?
No, I don't think that bottled water should be banned. Instead, government should provide clean drinking water in every city, town, and village of the country. The use of bottled water will naturally decrease.

Copyright
Do you feel copyrights should be abolished?
No, I don't agree with this. I feel the inventor, or the creator of a certain thing should keep his/her right of inventing that thing. The copyrights should always be awarded to the creator to keep him/her secure from infringement or piracy.

Why do you think copyright is necessary?
I think it is one of the most essential things in a writer's, scientist's, artist's, or a discoverer's life. It is important to give the credit of the work to the owner. Copyright is also important to avoid piracy of the work.

Do you know anyone who owns a copyright of something?
Yes, one of my uncles is a musician who has a copyright to his music album. He produces music and sells it to the film makers.

Do you feel copyright system in your country is secure?
Yes, there are strict rules and regulations regarding the copyright system in our country. Our system reserves the full right for the work of people and not allow anyone to copy it easily.

Do you think one day you will be able to have a copyright of something?
Perhaps I would be able to have a copyright of my own. I wish to write a book in future. So, I think that I will surely copyright that book.

Life experiences
Do you feel we can learn lessons from life experiences?
We can learn many things from life experiences. It's an old saying that experience is the best teacher. A person learns a lot from his/her experiences in life.

Have you learned anything from life experiences?
I have acquired a great deal of things from my life experiences. I have learned to be patient in life and believe that nothing comes easy. One must work hard in life to attain success.

Do you feel experience in life is the best teacher?
I believe experience in life is the best teacher. One should always learn from bad and good experiences of life.

Have you ever faced a bad experience in your life?
Yes, I have faced a bad experience in my life once. I was involved in an accident, and it took me some time to recover.

Do you feel life will be smooth if one has only good experiences?
I think there are ups and down in everyone's life. It is important to celebrate small achievements to keep life smooth. Life can be smooth with all sorts of experiences.

Retirement and old age

What sort of problems do people face at older age?
People face numerous problems at older age. They face health related issues. Some old, aged people also face loneliness as not all members in the family have time for them.

Have you ever thought about the day when you retire?
Not yet. I have not given it the slightest of the thought. I think I am young and there are many years to go before I retire.

Do you agree that the most difficult part of life is the old age?
It certainly is the most difficult part according to me. The reason is that the person is not at his/her full strength and there are many problems that come with old age. I think it is very difficult to be in that position.

Do you feel a person becomes more dependent in old age?
Yes, a person becomes lot dependent in old age just like kids. They need help in more tasks than in young age. I have seen my grandparents asking for help for smallest of tasks.

Do you think retirement age should be increased to 65 years for government services?
No, I don't think retirement age should be increased than the current limit. Ours is a huge nation and population is also high. If the retirement age bar is raised then youngsters will find difficulty in getting jobs.

Eating habits

Do you feel poor eating habits contributes to poor health?
Poor eating habits leads to many health issues. People can get chronic diseases and become fat. Poor eating habits also makes a person lazy.

Do you think eating habits needs to be in place to maintain good health?
Yes, most of the scientists claim that good health is associated with good diet. Having a controlled diet is important than doing exercise.

What are your eating habits?
I like heavy breakfast as it allows me to stay energetic for the whole day. After that I take decent lunch and light dinner.

What should we eat to stay healthy?
We should not eat oily food. Also, one needs to have fruits in daily routine. We should prefer homemade food over fast food to stay fit.

Do you feel one should eat nutritious diet?
Yes, one should always eat nutritious diet. There are many healthy options available to us. Taking nutritious diet has many advantages. It gives all the minerals and vitamins required for the smooth functioning of the body.

Universities

Are universities greedier these days?
Certainly, they are much greedier these days. Universities have become money minting machines. Most of the universities are not concerned about the wellbeing of the student.

Is it difficult for a poor kid to study at university?
It has become almost impossible for a poor kid to study at a university. The fee structures have shot up greatly and no scholarship programs are available for them.
Are universities losing importance in terms of educational quality?
As the number of new universities are growing, there has been deficiency in the quality of education they provide. I think very few universities are there that impart quality education.
Do you think universities concentrate more on theory rather than practical knowledge?
These days in our country the level of education has gone down because most of the universities are focused on theoretical knowledge. However, there are old universities that have not lost any importance because they still concentrate on practical studies.
Is college a better place to study than university?
I can't say that college is the better place to study than a university. Both type of institutions has its own merits. Although it is altogether a different environment to study in college as opposed to a university.

<u>Work and life balance</u>
How many hours do people generally work in your country?
People generally work for 8 – 10 hours in a day in my country. Some people work even longer than this. In most of the government sectors, the timings are fixed.
Do you think people these days are able to maintain a balance between work and personal life?
In most of the private companies, people are not able to make a balance between work and personal life. The companies put so much pressure on their employees and expect them to work long hours for the benefit of their company.
How many hours one should work in a day ideally?
Ideally, one should work for not more than 8 hours in a day. I think one needs to strike a balance between life and work. So, I believe that 8 hours work in a day is perfect.
Do you feel work is worship?
I don't feel that work is worship. Although work is crucial in life, but it should not be seen as worship. Work should be considered as work.
Was work life better in the past?
I can agree as well as disagree with this. There was not a lot of work pressure in the past which is a good thing. These days there are more perks in terms of salary, which is good too. So, it is a difficult question to answer.

<u>Island</u>
Have you ever been to an island?
Yes, I have been to an island named Sri Lanka. It is an island country located in the southern side of India. I went there last year with my family and had a great time there.
Why do you think that islands are different from inlands?
Islands are very different from inlands. One can enjoy beaches around the islands and the weather is also different there than other places.
Is there any special island in your country?
Yes, there is a very special island in our country. The name of the island is Andaman and Nicobar Islands. It is in the far east side of India, and it is one of the most beautiful parts of our country.
Speak about an island you wish to visit in future
If I am given a chance, then I would like to visit Maldives. It is one of the gorgeous island clusters in the world. It is situated in the southwest of India. The flight takes about three hours to reach there.
Is there any difference in weather in islands than mainland?

Yes, I have been to a couple of islands, and I have felt that the weather over there is more pleasant throughout the year. It might be different on some islands that I have not visited but I have generally heard that in most of the islands the weather remains pleasant all year round.

Make-up
Do you do make-up?
Yes, I do makeup. I feel that it makes my looks perfect. I feel more presentable and attractive when I apply make-up.
Do you feel make-up increases the confidence of a person?
Yes, it escalates the confidence of a person because one looks more attractive. Also, if there are any imperfections, it is concealed by make-up. Hence it increases the confidence of a person.

Do you use any expensive cosmetics?
I use inexpensive cosmetics in my daily routine, but I do have one concealer that is expensive. I feel cosmetics should be branded but it doesn't matter whether they are expensive or not.
Is there any person you know who does a lot of make-up?
Yes, one of my aunts does a lot of make-up. She puts on make-up all the time. She is very conscious of her looks, so she always does make-up.
Are there any side effects of applying cosmetics on face?
There are many side effects of applying excessive make up on the face. I think branded and herbal cosmetics are fine but local cosmetics can cause a great deal of problems.

Tiredness
Do you get tired?
Yes, I get tired when I work for long. I generally don't get tired in my daily routine but on some days I really get tired.
What do you do when you get tired?
I relax when I get tired. My best way to get rid of tiredness is by spending time at home. I relax by sleeping more and listening to my favourite songs.
Why do people get tired?
People get tired due to several reasons. The main factor is working over-time, but they also get tired when they travel more.
Is there any thing that makes you tired?
I think working more than my capacity makes me tired. I also get tired when I play sports on weekends.
Speak about a situation when you got tired.
I remember one day when I really got tired. I went to Dubai last year and had to walk in the world's largest mall for more than five hours. At that time, I really got tired.

Beach
Do you feel beaches are getting polluted day by day?
There is no doubt in this fact that beaches are getting polluted day by day. Although there have been some measures taken by government recently to control the littering on beaches but with no effects.
What are the disadvantages of living near a beach?
I think there is no such disadvantage of living near the beach but in case of a high tide, there can be flooding in the nearby areas.
Do you know anyone who lives near the beach?
Yes, one of my cousins lives in Goa. He lives by the beach where he owns a house and a small hotel.
Have you ever seen a beach area?

I have been to a couple of beach areas in the past. I have seen beaches in Goa as well as in Andaman and Nicobar Islands.

Do you like beaches?
I relish visiting the beach areas. I simply like to sit by the beach and enjoy the nature. I also love the sound of the waves.

Street markets
Have you bought something from street market?
Yes, I have bought many things from the local street markets. Once I bought a sling bag from a street market. It was very cheap and of good quality.

Is there any street market nearby your house?
There are street markets everywhere in India. This is how the society works here. There are temporary markets that are organized at certain locations near my house on selected days of the week.

What sort of things are generally sold in the street markets?
All sorts of things are sold in the street markets. Vendors sell dairy products, vegetables, fruits, spices, toys, and daily need products at the street markets.

Do you feel the quality of products in the street market is not good?
Sometimes the quality of products sold in these types of market is not up to the mark. However, some vendors sell quality things to their customers.

Do you feel street markets should be banned?
No street markets should not be banned as it is run by people who can't afford to pay the rent of shops or own shops for that matter. I think everyone has the right to sell things so the street markets should be allowed to run but should be managed by the government for smooth operation.

Visiting relative / friends
How often do you visit your relatives?
I visit my relatives regularly. I love my relatives, especially cousins. I have cordial relations with most of my relatives, so I often visit them.

Do you go to your friend's family functions?
Yes, if I am invited then I surely go to my friend's family functions. Recently I was invited to attend marriage of my friend's brother and I enjoyed the occasion very much.

Have any of your relatives invited you to his/her home recently?
Yes, my uncle and aunt recently invited me to a dinner. I went there with my parents and brother. We had a fun time together.

How often do your friends invite you to their homes?
My friends invite me regularly to their homes. Although I don't have lots of friends but the few friends that I have always invite me on weekends.

For what purpose do you visit your relatives and friends?
I visit their homes to meet them and play with them or simply for family gatherings. Recently I was invited to join a gathering at one of my friend's houses.

Places to play
Where did you play as a child?
I used to play in the park nearby my house. I also played in my friend's house a lot. I remember that I also played in our school ground in recess time.

Are there places in your hometown where kids can play?

There are countless public parks and a lake area where kids can enjoy themselves. There are few sports centers made by government in certain areas where kids can play.

Do you feel that places to play have changed over the years?
The play areas have changed drastically as compared to the past. In the past kids used to enjoy in the parks more than anywhere else. These days kids like to be indoors and play indoor or video games.

Where do most of the kids of today's era like to play?
Most of the kids in this era like to play in their homes on video games. They don't relish going out of their houses and play outdoor games / sports.

Sun

What is the importance of sun in our life?
Sun gives us light, and it also gives us life. If there was no sun, there would be no life possible on this planet. Plants grow due to sun light and sun is the most important aspect of this solar system.

Do you often bathe in sunlight?
Yes, I sit in the open and absorb sun light in winters. I feel warm and relaxed when I bathe in sunlight. I only do it in winters though.

Do you feel today's people have less access to sunlight?
With the growing number of skyscrapers and other infrastructure, sunlight is not reaching all places. People living in cities often complaint about having pain in joints which occurs due to the deficiency of Vitamin D which is absorbed from sunlight.

How do you feel when its sunny?
Sunny day is the best day for me. On some occasions I also like grey sky. But I love when the sun is out and is at its full glow. I feel energized and clear minded. If the day is not sunny, I can feel depressed.

Do you feel sun will ever die?
I don't know. Perhaps one day everything will end but I don't know about the sun. I have read somewhere that sun has a life expectancy and one day it may end.

Sunglasses

Do you wear sunglasses?
Yes, I love wearing sunglasses. It saves me from sun's glare. Sun can get very hot in summers, so sunglasses provide much cooler feeling to my eyes.

What kind of sunglasses do you wear?
Wayfarer and Aviators are my favourite kinds of glasses. I like to wear brown and blue colour glasses with black or golden frame.

For what purpose people wear sunglasses?
There are two main reasons for wearing sunglasses. The first one is that it protects our eyes from sun's glare and UV rays. The other reason is fashion, some people wear sunglasses to look better.

Do you prefer branded or local sunglasses?
I like Ray Ban and HRX brand the most. I think one should only wear branded sunglasses as local brand lenses can affect the eyes. Those glasses will not protect your eyes against ultraviolet rays.

Do you feel that wearing sunglasses has become more of a fashion than utility?
It certainly has become more of a fashion statement for some people. Although most of the individuals wear it for its intended purpose.

Cakes and desserts

On what occasions do people cut cakes?
People generally cut cakes on occasions such as wedding parties, birthday, and anniversary celebrations. It has now become a trend in some societies to cut cake to celebrate most of the occasions.

Is there a tradition of cutting cake in your country?

Yes, there is a widespread custom of cutting cake in weddings as well as birthday parties. People nowadays buy expensive and fancy cakes for their near and dear ones.

What is the significance of cutting cake?
Most people cut cake when they achieve something, or when they are happy. Sweets are generally consumed in celebrations. Cake is a sweet food so that's why people cut it to celebrate different occasions.

What sort of desserts do you like?
I like cakes, traditional sweets, ice cream and anything made from chocolate as I have a sweet tooth. I usually don't eat a lot of desserts, but I have them when I feel happy.

Are desserts good for health?
Yes, if one takes desserts in a controlled amount or occasionally, then deserts are not harmful. Although eating desserts on regular basis can have bad impact on body and health.

On what occasions do people eat desserts in your country?
People eat desserts on every occasion. In Indian society desserts are a part of the meal. People like to have them at the end of the meal on regular basis.

Do you make desserts?
Yes, I can make a couple of simple desserts. One of them is sweet curd. It is one of the simplest desserts to make and is very healthy to eat in summers. You just need to whisk some curd and then add some finely crushed sugar in it.

Numbers
Do you have a lucky number?
Yes, I do. I like number 7. I don't know the reason behind the liking, but this number looks better than others. If I choose something, I always look for a number 7 connection.
OR
No, I don't have a lucky number. I like all the numbers. I don't believe in superstitions much, so I feel I don't have a lucky number.

Are you superstitious about numbers?
No, I am not at all superstitious about numbers. I believe that all the numbers are same and there is no need to treat any number in a special way.

Do you remember any important number from your past?
Not really. I can't remember any important number from my past. I am not a believer of special numbers, so I can't recall any important number from my past.

Are you good at remembering phone numbers?
Yes, I remember many phone numbers of my family and friends. I learn numbers easily than any other type of text.

Breaks
Is it important to take short breaks during your job on daily basis?
It is vital to take short breaks from work on daily basis. I think little breaks can help maintain concentration and interest in the job.

Do you feel one should take a long break at least once a year?
Without a doubt. It is essential for everyone to get away from work for at least once a year. In my opinion, people should take a couple of weeks' off and go for a holiday with family.

Do you often take breaks from your study/work?
Yes, I take breaks from my study and work whenever I feel bored. I try to take short breaks every other month and a long one at least once a year.

What is the importance of taking breaks in life?
Taking break rejuvenates a person physically as well as mentally. It is essential to take breaks every now and then. Taking breaks allow you to break the monotony.

What should one do in breaks?
These days the life is too hectic. I personally feel that one should go to new places and explore the area and food. One can also go to mountains to feel peace and calm environment. People should also use their breaks in learning new things such as new languages or cuisines.

How do you spend your breaks?
I usually travel to a new place to spend my breaks. I like travelling so I pack my bags and go to faraway places for a week to enjoy the place. Sometimes I also utilize my breaks to learn some things that I don't know.

Wild animals

Which is your favourite wild animal?
My favourite wild animal is Giant Panda. It is an animal that is mostly found in China. It mostly eats bamboo shoots and leaves. It is a very peace-loving animal.

Do you feel wild animals are safe in forests?
Certainly, forests are the safest place for wild animals. Forest is the natural habitat of wild animals. Hence, they should be living there without interference from humans.

Do you feel government is taking enough steps to take care of the wild animals?
Yes, in some cases I have seen that government has taken active steps in making people aware about the species that are on the verge of extinction. Also, government has taken keen interest in the maintenance of the wildlife sanctuaries all over the country in the past few years.

What are the most common wild animals in your country?
Monkey, Leopard and Lion are the most common wildlife animals in my country.

Do you reckon wildlife is important for the survival of our planet?
Without a doubt, wildlife is crucial for the smooth running of our planet. Having a healthy wildlife ensures the proper balance in the life cycle of most of the species living on earth.

Do you believe some species of wild animals will extinct?
I am afraid to say yes. There are few species that face this danger, and we need to do something urgently to prevent this situation. One example is the white Bengal Tiger.

Scenery

Have you ever seen a wonderful scenery in your life?
I have seen many wonderful sceneries in my life. I live in the north part of my country, so mountains are never too far. There are numerous gorgeous spots which I have visited multiple times.

How do you feel when you see a beautiful scenery?
I feel humbled and refreshed. I always thank God when I see scenery. I also like to capture some photos of the scenery and relish them afterwards.

Is there a scenic spot in/near your hometown?
Yes, there is a lake in the east part of my hometown. The lake has lush green mountains on the back of it along with green areas all around. My hometown is surrounded by Shivalik Hills from one side, so we are never short of scenic spots in and around our hometown.

Do you often visit such places?
Yes, I like to spend some time in these places. I feel close to nature and, I feel peace at mind which I don't usually get in the city life. I visit these places a couple of times every month.

Have you ever drawn a scenery in your life?
I have drawn many sceneries in my life. I remember in school time when we were taught to make scenery on a drawing sheet. I must have drawn it hundreds of times.

Voice

What type of voice do you like?
I like loud and clear voice. I feel that anyone who has a clear and crisp voice can attract many people.

Can anyone change his/her voice?
Yes, there are many comedian and mimicry artists that change their voice to make people laugh. They can imitate famous actors and politicians.

Do you feel everyone should have same type of voice?
Not at all, I believe that beauty lies in diversity. If everyone will have the same voice, then it would become very difficult to recognize different people on phone. It will create a world of confusion.

Have you ever talked to a person who has an unusual voice?
Yes, one of my friends has a very unusual voice. I think he has some issue with his throat. His voice is very crumbly, and one can hardly understand him speak.
Is it important to raise voice against evils in society?
Yes, it is essential to raise voice against the evils in society. These days most people are busy in their life, and they hardly find time to give opinion in important matters. However, I feel that one should take out time and raise voice against evils and injustice.

Haircut
How often do you get your hair cut?
I get my hair cut every week. I like to see my hair in good shape, so I regularly visit a barber for my hair cut.
OR
I don't cut my hair, so I never go to barber for a haircut.
Do you like to have different haircuts every now and then?
No, I don't like to experiment with my looks. I try to stay the same. I get same haircut every time so that it doesn't affect my appearance.
OR
Yes, I like to do experiments with my haircut. I like to follow haircuts of celebrities and sportspersons. So, I change my haircut according to the trend.
From where do you get your hair cut?
I get my hair cut from a salon in my city. It is one of the oldest and best salons of my town.
Do you feel hair cutting is a special art?
Indeed, hair cutting is one of the most difficult arts around the world. It is extremely tricky to cut hair according to one's need. One must be trained and experienced to be a hair stylist.
Do you know anyone who is a hair stylist?
Yes, one of my school friends is a hair stylist and she is working with a leading salon. She's taken a 6-month training and has now become a certified hair stylist.
Which is your favorite type of hair cut?
I like plain haircut that balances my looks. I don't like fancy haircuts at all.

Plan
Do you often plan your day?
Yes, I always plan my day. I like to plan my day in a proper manner. I note down the things that I want to achieve in the day and review those things at the end of the day.
Do you plan before taking a holiday?
Absolutely I plan a lot of things before taking holidays. I search about the weather of that place and pack my clothes accordingly. I also browse the best hotels and landmarks before visiting the holiday destination.
Do you plan your weekends?
No, I usually don't plan my weekends. If I have some plan to go out with my friends and family members then I do plan for it.
Do you feel planning is important in life?
Planning is very important in life. One should always plan about the future and obstacles that can come in the way. Planning leads to success and better opportunities.
Have any of your planning failed in the past?
Yes, some of my plans didn't work in the past. I planned to learn guitar and bought one for the same reason. But due to busy schedule, I couldn't learn it.
Have you ever planned a surprise party for someone?

Yes, I have planned a surprise party for my brother a few years ago. I surprised him by arranging a party at our home. He was happy with this surprise and gave me a gift in return.

Spending time alone
Do you like spending some time alone?
Yes, I like spending time alone as it gives me peace and calm environment. I am a peace lover, so I regularly go to some places and spend some quality time alone.

What are the benefits of spending lone time?
In my case, the main benefit of spending lone time is that I can think about myself, and I can work on my future without any distractions.

How do you spend your time when you are alone?
I mostly listen to music or read books. Sometimes I also write about my life experiences and daily happenings.

Do you know someone who spends a lot of time alone?
Yes, one of my childhood friends like to spend some time alone every day. He goes to temple and sits there for 1 hour every day. He does it on daily basis and loves it very much.

Do you feel spending more time alone is good?
Sometimes spending more time alone can be dangerous. People can start to get depressed and can get frustrated.

Jeans
How many jeans do you buy in a year?
I buy three to four jeans in a year. I like Levis Brand.

How many pairs of jeans do you have?
I must be having around 7 or 8 pairs of jeans. I buy jeans every now and then. It is my favourite type of bottom wear.

What are the benefits of wearing jeans?
There are many benefits of wearing jeans. Number one, it doesn't get dirty easily and it is also quite durable. You don't need to wash jeans regularly. Moreover, it can pair up with any kind of shirt or top.

Do you feel jeans look very informal?
There are certain types of jeans that look quite informal. Some people wear jeans that are funky in colour and has threads hanging from all sides. On the contrary, there are jeans that look decent too. Despite that, jeans do look a bit informal.

Are jeans a good-looking piece of clothing?
Absolutely jeans are a good-looking attire. Nowadays it has become a widespread fashion. People all over the world prefer jeans over other stuff.

What colour of jeans do you like the most?
I mostly like all shades of blue and black when it comes to jeans.

Science
Is it necessary to learn science at school?
It is crucial to learn science at school because science is the basis of our life. We learn most of the practical things from science. Science gives us holistic knowledge of past, present and future.

Do you feel that science is a useful subject?
It is a useful subject. With science we can conquer most of our fears. With science we have reached the moon and came back safely. With science we have busted many myths of the past.

Is science the way forward?
Science is the way forward. We can use science as the binding factor between different countries, cultures, and societies. Science can be used to enlighten people about the nature and its principles.

Do you feel science is 100 % true?

I do believe that most of the scientific discoveries and theories are true. Although there can be some theories that can be regarded as false but most information on science till date has proven right.

Did you like science as a subject at school?

I liked science as a subject very much. Although my grades were not that great in science, but I liked the things that I learned from different science subjects.

Laughter

Do you often laugh?

Yes, I often laugh. I think it is good to laugh at small things as it keeps your mood joyous and helps you to stay away from stress.

What are the benefits of laughing?

There are proven benefits of laughing. Science says that blood flow through the body parts increases when we laugh. Also, some chemicals are released within our body that helps a person to remain calm and happy.

Do you watch laughter shows?

Yes, whenever I get a chance, I like watching laughter shows. There are many laughter shows that are telecasted on television. The best one is The Kapil Sharma Show.

Why do you think that laughter is important in life?

Laughter is like a therapy. It is crucial to have laughter in life. One should laugh whenever he/she gets a chance.

Do you like to make others laugh?

Yes, I like to make people laugh. If I see someone depressed, then I like to make them laugh by cracking a joke or making some fun out of the situation.

Water sports

Do you relish water sports?

Yes, I like water sports but the ones that are not dangerous. I like mild risky activities like riding a jet ski. It is a simple scooter kind of a vehicle that runs on water. This type of activity is generally held in sea areas.

What type of water sports you have participated?

I have only attempted jet ski a couple of times. I don't like other activities like para sailing and deep ocean diving. I have a fear of deep water and heights.

Are water sports good for fun?

Water sports are great for fun. Most of the people in my county doesn't live by the beach areas so they like to enjoy water sports and they consider that activity as fun.

Are water sports common in your county?

Yes, water sports are quite common in my country but only in coastal areas. Most of the people in my country live inland. There you hardly find water sports. But in coastal areas it is famous.

What type of water sport would you like to attempt in future?

If I get a chance to try any type of water sport, then it would be snorkeling. In this activity you don't go deep down the ocean. You float at the top and discover beautiful coral reefs in shallow waters.

PART – 3

Important Vocabulary for IELTS Speaking

1. Abandon – desert, forsake
2. Abbreviate – shorten, condense
3. Ability - skill, aptitude
4. Able – capable, skilled, talented
5. Above – overhead
6. Absolutely – unquestionably, undeniably
7. Abundance – enough resources, plenty
8. Abundant - ample, plentiful
9. Access – admittance, entree
10. Accolades – honours, awards, praises
11. Accomplish – achieve, complete, finish
12. Accumulate – amass, gather, collect, hoard
13. Accurate- correct, right
14. Achieve - accomplish, attain
15. Acquire – obtain, get, gain
16. Active - energetic, animated, lively
17. Adamant – firm, unyielding, inflexible
18. To add – augment, enhance
19. Adequate – sufficient, enough, ample
20. Adjourn – postpone, recess
21. Admire – respect, like, appreciate
22. Adore – love, admire
23. Adrenalin rush – a sudden surge of energy in a person
24. Adroit – expert, skilful
25. Adult – grown up
26. Advent – beginning, arrival, start
27. Adverse – hostile, opposing, contrary
28. Advocate - support, recommend
29. Affection – liking, fondness
30. Afraid – frightened, scared
31. After - following, next
32. Ageing – getting old, mature
33. Aggressive – violent, destructive, hostile
34. Aid – help, assist
35. Alarming – disturbing, upsetting
36. Alien – unknown, unfamiliar, strange
37. All walks of life – from all backgrounds or age groups
38. Allied – associated, related, connected
39. Allure – attract, appeal
40. Almighty – enormous, massive, huge (often used to represent God)
41. Alternatives – replacements, substitutes
42. Always – forever
43. Amass – accumulate, collect
44. Amateur – beginner, novice
45. Ambitious – aspiring, driven
46. Ambitious – determined, striving
47. Amenities – facilities, services
48. Ample – enough, plenty, sufficient
49. Amusement – laughter, enjoyment, delight
50. Analytical – logical, investigative, diagnostic
51. Ancestors – decedents, dynasties
52. Antagonize- provoke, annoy, irritate
53. Anxiety – nervousness, concerns, worry
54. Anxious – nervous, worried, concerned
55. Apolitical – unpolitical, a person who is not political
56. Apparels – attires, clothes
57. Apparent – deceptive, superficial
58. Appealing – attractive, interesting, tempting
59. Approve - accept, agree, favour, support
60. Aptly – appropriately, fittingly, suitably, rightly
61. Archipelago – a collection of small islands in an ocean
62. Aromatic – fragrant, perfumed
63. Array – collection, selection
64. Arrive – reach, come
65. Arrogant – haughty, egotistical
66. Artificial – fake, synthetic
67. Ascend – arise, rise
68. Ask – question, inquire
69. Aspect – feature, facet, characteristics
70. Assault – attack, beating
71. Association - connotation
72. Assortment – variety, collection, range, mixture
73. Assure – promise, guarantee, pledge
74. Astonish – surprise, amaze, astound
75. Atrocious – dreadful, terrible, brutal
76. Attire – clothing, dress, outfit
77. Authentic – true, reliable, dependable
78. Autobiographies – memoires, a self-written life journey
79. Average – ordinary, fair
80. Awe – wonder, admiration, respect
81. Awestruck – impressed, enthralled, overwhelmed
82. Awkward – clumsy, uncoordinated
83. Backdrop – at the back, background

84. Bamboozle – confuse, deceive
85. Ban – prohibit, forbid, outlaw
86. Bane – curse, misery
87. Banter – teasing, mockery, joking
88. Barely – just, hardly, scarcely
89. Barren – unproductive, infertile
90. Barricades – barriers, hurdles, blockades
91. Bashful – shy, timid, reserved
92. Bearable – manageable, tolerable, endurable
93. Beautiful – pretty, attractive, lovely
94. Before – prior, earlier
95. Beginning – start, initiate
96. Believe – trust, accept as true, have faith in
97. Below – under, lower, beneath
98. Beneficial – helpful, useful, advantageous
99. Best – finest, choice
100. Beverage – drink, hot drink, cold drink
101. Biographies – profiles, memoirs
102. Birth - beginning
103. Blend – combine, mix
104. Blueprint – plan, drawing, design, proposal
105. Bond – promise, pledge, oath
106. Boon – benefit, advantage, bonus
107. Boredom – dullness, monotony
108. Bottom – base, foundation
109. Brave – courageous, bold, heroic
110. Break – discontinue, disruption
111. Breakdown- failure, collapse
112. Breath-taking- magnificent, spectacular
113. Brief - short, concise
114. Briefly- fleetingly, momentarily
115. Brittle- fragile, breakable
116. Broad – wide, expansive
117. Browse- look, glance
118. Bulk - wholesale, loose
119. Bump - collision, smash
120. Bustling - lively, busy
121. Busy – active, occupied, working
122. Buy – purchase
123. Buzz - crowd, chaos
124. Bygone – past, previous
125. Cakewalk – easy or very easy
126. Calm – quiet, tranquil, still
127. Candid – straight forward, frank
128. Capture – apprehend, seize, arrest
129. Care – concern, protection
130. Careful – cautious, watchful
131. Catapulted – threw, hurled
132. Cease – stop, discontinue
133. Certain – positive, sure, definite
134. Chaos – disorder, confusion
135. Charity – aid, contribution
136. Charming – delightful, appealing, enchanting
137. Cherish – appreciate, relish
138. Chilly (cold) – cool, nippy
139. Chores – errands, task
140. Chronologically – historical, sequential
141. Chubby – plump, pudgy
142. Circulation – flow, movement
143. Cited – quoted, mentioned
144. Clarify - explain, simplify
145. Close - near, nearby, adjacent
146. Close quarters – from a close perspective
147. Coarse – stiff, rough
148. Coastal – seaside, beach
149. Coastline – shoreline, seashore
150. Cognitive – reasoning, intellectual
151. Colonized – populated, settled
152. Colossal – enormous, immense, mammoth
153. Combine – blend, unite, join
154. Comical - amusing, funny, humorous
155. Commemorate – honour, memorialize
156. Commendable – admirable, worthy, praiseworthy
157. Commercialization - development
158. Commit – pledge, promise
159. Commute – travel, shuttle
160. Compact – compressed, condensed
161. Competent – capable, able, knowledgeable
162. Complete – conclude, finish
163. Complex - complicated, intricate
164. Complimentary – free, courtesy
165. Comprehend – understand, grasp
166. Compress – crush, condense, squeeze
167. Comprise – include, encompass
168. Conceal – hide, cover
169. Concession - discount
170. Concrete – real, tangible, solid
171. Concur- agree, cooperate
172. Condemn – censure, denounce
173. Condense – compress, concentrate
174. Confess – admit, acknowledge

175. Confine – contain, enclose, restrain, restrict
176. Conflict - oppose, differ, clash
177. Conform – comply, submit
178. Confuse - complicate, muddle, jumble
179. Congested – overcrowded, stuffed
180. Connect – join, link, attach
181. Conscientious – careful, meticulous, reliable
182. Conscious – aware, mindful, cognizant
183. Consecutive – successive, continuous
184. Consequences – penalties, punishments
185. Conservation – preservation, maintenance
186. Conservative – traditional, conventional
187. Considerable – substantial, significance
188. Considerate – thoughtful, kind, understanding
189. Consoled – comforted, supported
190. Constantly – continuously, repeatedly
191. Constellations – gatherings, group
192. Contaminate – pollute, defile, infect
193. Contented – satisfied, pleased
194. Continue – persist, persevere
195. Convalesce – recuperate, recover, heal, improve
196. Convenience – suitability, ease
197. Convenient – suitable, fitting
198. Conventional – customary, traditional
199. Converse – opposite, contrary
200. Conviction – belief, opinion, faith
201. Coral reefs – underwater ecosystem
202. Correct - accurate, right, proper
203. Courage – bravery, valour
204. Courteous – polite, civil
205. Courtyard – yard, garden
206. Cover - conceal, hide
207. Cosy – comfortable, snug, homey
208. Cram – fill up, pack
209. Cramming – packing, stuffing
210. Cramps – pains, contractions, spasms
211. Cranky – crabby, irritable
212. Crazy – insane, daft, mad, silly
213. Creek – narrow river, stream, bay
214. Cremate – burn, incinerate
215. Criticism – disapproval, condemnation
216. Cruel – mean , heartless, ruthless
217. Crunch – critical situation, crisis
218. Cry- sob, weep

219. Cuisines – foods, cookeries
220. Curb – control, limit
221. Cure – treatment, therapy
222. Curious – interested, inquisitive
223. Customs – duties, taxes
224. Dally – loiter, linger
225. Damage – hurt, spoil, harm
226. Dangerous – unsafe, hazardous, perilous
227. Dark – dismal, black, miserable
228. Daring – bold, audacious, brave
229. Darling – wonderful, gorgeous, lovely, adorable
230. Daunting – intimidating, scary
231. Dawn – daybreak, sunrise
232. Dead – lifeless, deceased
233. Decay – falloff, decline
234. Dedicated – devoted, keen
235. Deduct – subtract, remove
236. Deed – action, act
237. Defend – protect, shield
238. Defy – resist, challenge, rebel
239. Delicate – fragile, dainty
240. Delicious – tasty, palatable
241. Demolish – destroy, wreck
242. Denounce – blame, condemn, criticize
243. Dense – thick, heavy, compressed
244. Depart - leave, proceed, advance
245. Departed – dead, deceased, late
246. Dependent – reliant on, in need of
247. Deposit - credit, payment
248. Depress – reduce, dampen, lower
249. Designation – title, name, description
250. Desolate – deserted, isolated
251. Desperate – anxious, worried
252. Desperately – badly, urgently
253. Despise – hate, scorn , loathe
254. Destitute- poor, penniless
255. Destroy – ruin, wreck, devastate
256. Detach – separate, unfasten ,remove
257. Deter – discourage, daunt
258. Deteriorate – worsen, decline
259. Determined – strong minded, resolute
260. Detrimental – harmful, damaging, unfavourable
261. Devote – dedicate, offer, give
262. Die – expire, perish
263. Different – distinct, unlike, dissimilar
264. Difficult – hard, challenging

265. Dilemma – difficulty, problem
266. Dilute – weaken, thin
267. Diminish - curtail, lessen, weaken
268. Diminishing – lessening, fading, waning
269. Dirty – soiled, messy, muddy
270. Disagree – differ, dispute
271. Disaster – tragedy, adversity, ruin
272. Disintegrating – crumbling, decomposing, decaying
273. Dispute – debate, oppose, argument
274. Distinctive – different, distinguishing
275. Distracted – unfocussed, side-tracked
276. Diverse – different, distinct, varied, assorted
277. Diversions – changes, deviations, alteration
278. Diversity – variety, range
279. Divide – separate, split
280. Docile – tame, gentle, passive
281. Dormant – sleeping, inactive, latent
282. Doubt – mistrust, hesitation, uncertainty
283. Drab – dull, lifeless
284. Drastic – severe, extreme, radical
285. Dreadful – terrible, unpleasant
286. Drowsiness – sleepiness, lethargy, tiredness
287. Dry – arid, parched
288. Dubious – doubtful, uncertain, questionable
289. Dull- cloudy, gloomy
290. Dumb – stupid
291. Dumping – removal, discarding
292. Duplex – double storied house with inner staircase to   access the upper floor
293. Durable – long lasting, hard wearing
294. Dwarf – short
295. Dwell – reside, live
296. Dynamic – lively, active
297. Dynasty – reign, family, rule
298. Eagerly – keenly, excitedly, enthusiastically
299. Early - premature, beforetime
300. Earthen – clay, mud
301. Easy – simple, laidback, informal
302. Eccentric – peculiar, unusual, strange, odd
303. Echoes – repeats, resonances, reverberations
304. Ecstasy – joy, rapture, elation

305. Efficient – effective, well-organized
306. Elated – overjoyed, delighted
307. Elevate – raise, lift
308. Embarrass – shame, humiliate
309. Embedded – fixed, rooted, entrenched
310. Eminent – famous, renowned
311. Emissions – releases, discharges
312. Emphasized – highlighted, stressed
313. Empower – authorize, allow
314. Empty – drain, unload
315. Encourage – promote, support
316. Endurable – manageable, tolerable
317. Enemy – opponent, foe
318. Engage – involve, occupy
319. Enhance – improve, augment
320. Enjoy – like, appreciate
321. Enlarge – expand, magnify
322. Enormous – vast, immense, colossal
323. Enough- sufficient, ample, plenty
324. Enrol – register, join
325. Ensure – safeguard, guarantee
326. Enthusiasm – eagerness, interest
327. Enticing – tempting, alluring
328. Entirely – wholly, completely, solely
329. Equivalent – equal, comparable
330. Eradicate – eliminate, destroy
331. Erudite – very knowledgeable
332. Escalate – intensify, heighten
333. Essential – vital, important
334. Establish – found, start
335. Eternal – everlasting, unending, perpetual
336. Ethics – morals, beliefs
337. Etiquettes – manners, protocols
338. Euphoric – overjoyed, elated
339. Eventually – finally, ultimately
340. Evident – obvious, clear
341. Evil – bad, wrong, wicked
342. Evolution – development, growth
343. Evolved – changed, advanced
344. Exaggerated – overstated, inflated
345. Except – excluding, apart from
346. Exceptional - remarkable, outstanding, excellent
347. Excess – extra, additional, surplus
348. Excite – stimulate, enthuse, animate
349. Excitement – enthusiasm, eagerness
350. Excursion – trip, outing
351. Execute – perform, implement

352. Exhaust – consume, drain
353. Exhilarated – overjoyed, ecstatic, elated
354. Exile – outcast, refugee
355. Existence – presence, survival
356. Expect – suppose, assume
357. Expedition – excursion, trip
358. Expenditure – spending, outflow
359. Explicit – exact, clear, obvious
360. Explore – travel, discover
361. Exposure – contact, experience
362. Exquisite - delightful, charming, attractive
363. Extensive - widespread
364. Extensively – widely, broadly
365. Exterior – outside, outer
366. Extraordinary – unusual, unexpected
367. Extravagant – extreme, excessive, luxurious
368. Exuberant – excited, energetic
369. Fabulous – marvellous, amazing, wonderful
370. Façade - front
371. Face – confront, meet
372. Facet - aspect
373. Fair - honest, impartial, reasonable
374. Fake – imitation, counterfeit, artificial
375. False – incorrect, untrue
376. Fancy – elaborate, decorative, extravagant
377. Fantastic – incredible, outrageous
378. Fascinate – captivate, attract
379. Fast – rapid, quick, swift
380. Fat – chubby, plump, stout, obese, heavy
381. Fatal – deadly, mortal, killing
382. Fatigue – tire, exhaust
383. Fauna – wildlife, animals, creatures
384. Feasible – possible, attainable, practical
385. Features - characteristics
386. Feeble – weak, frail
387. Fellow – associated, related
388. Feminine – female, womanly
389. Ferocious – fierce, savage, brutal
390. Fertile – fruitful, productive
391. Few – scarce, insufficient, rare
392. Fiction – fantasy, untruth, myth
393. Fill – seal, stop, plug, block
394. Firm – stable, fixed, steady, strong
395. Fix – mend, repair

396. Flashy – showy, gaudy
397. Flaunt – exhibit, display
398. Flaw – deflect, fault, blemish
399. Flawless – perfect, faultless
400. Flimsy – frail, fragile, delicate
401. Flippant – impudent, sassy
402. Flock – group, herd
403. Flora – vegetation, plants, flowers
404. Fluffy – cottony, furry
405. Fluid – liquid, watery, runny
406. Foe – enemy, adversary, opponent
407. Follow – succeed, trail
408. Foodie – a person who likes food
409. Forbid – ban, prohibit
410. Forgive – pardon, excuse, absolve
411. Former – previous, earlier
412. Forthcoming – approaching, upcoming
413. Fortunate – lucky, privileged
414. Fraction – part, portion, segment
415. Fragile – delicate, brittle
416. Frank – candid, straightforward, blunt
417. Frenzy – fury, rage, anger, turmoil
418. Frequency – occurrence, rate, regularity
419. Frequently – often, regularly, normally, commonly
420. Fresh – unused, new
421. Friend – comrade, buddy, pal
422. Frigid – freezing, frosty, chilly, cold
423. Trivial - unimportant, silly
424. Front – fore, face
425. Frustrated – irritated, unsatisfied
426. Fulfilment – completion, execution
427. Full – packed, stuffed
428. Furious – angry, enraged, infuriated
429. Future – coming, tomorrow
430. Gadgets – devices, appliances
431. Gain – acquire, obtain, receive
432. Gallant – chivalrous, courteous, polite
433. Gather – collect, accumulate, compile
434. Gaudy – showy, garish, flashy, bright
435. Gaunt – scrawny, skinny, thin, lean
436. Generous – giving, selfless, big hearted
437. Genuine – real, authentic, sincere
438. Genre – type, kind, sort, category
439. Gentle – tender, mild
440. Genuine – honest, sincere
441. Gesture – sign, signal, hand movements
442. Gigantic – immense, colossal, enormous
443. Give – donate, present, offer

444. Glad – happy, pleasant, delighted
445. Glittering – sparkling, dazzling
446. Gloomy – dark, dismal, depressing, dull
447. Glorious – splendid, magnificent, superb
448. Good – nice, fine, well behaved
449. Gorgeous – ravishing, dazzling, stunning
450. Gratitude- thankfulness, appreciation
451. Great – outstanding, remarkable
452. Grievance – complaint, protest
453. Groceries – foodstuffs
454. Guilty – shamefaced, embarrassed
455. Gust – breeze, strong winds
456. Gymnasium – fitness centre
457. Habitat – home, territory
458. Handful – a few
459. Handy – useful, convenient, skilful
460. Hard – firm, solid, difficult
461. Hardcore – committed, uncompromising
462. Harmony – agreement, accord, concord
463. Harsh – strict, severe, punitive
464. Haste – speed, swiftness
465. Hate – loathe, detest, dislike
466. Heatstroke – issues arising from extremely hot environment
467. Hectic – frantic, chaotic
468. Help – aid , assist
469. Heritage – inheritance, legacy
470. Hesitant – uncertain, cautious
471. High – elevated, lofty, tall
472. Highlands – hilltops, uplands
473. Hire – rent, lease
474. Hit the sack – go to sleep, go to bed
475. Hoist – lift, elevator
476. Hold – grasp, grip, retain
477. Holistic – overall, rounded
478. Honest – truthful, sincere, frank
479. Horizon – skyline, limit
480. Hospitable – welcoming, cordial, friendliness
481. Hostile – unfriendly, aggressive
482. Huge – vast, immense, great
483. Humble – modest, unpretentious, polite
484. Humid – moist, sticky
485. Humiliate – embarrass, disgrace, dishonour
486. Humorous – funny, entertaining
487. Humungous – huge, great
488. Hygiene – cleanliness, sanitation
489. Hymns – songs, chants
490. Iconic – major, famous
491. Ideology – philosophy, thought
492. Idle – indolent, free
493. Idol – star, favourite
494. Illiterate – uneducated, unschooled
495. Imitation – fake, mock
496. Immaculate – spotless, pure
497. Immature - childish, inexperienced
498. Immense – huge, vast, enormous
499. Immune – resistant, exempt
500. Impact – effect, influence
501. Impartial – neutral, unbiased, fair
502. Impatient – eager, anxious, intolerant
503. Impeccable – perfect, flawless
504. Obligatory – compulsory, crucial, mandatory
505. Imperfect – marred, defective, faulty
506. Imperial – grand, majestic
507. Impetuous – impulsive, rash, reckless
508. Important – significant, meaningful
509. Impose – execute, enforce
510. Impression - imprint
511. Imprisoned – confined, captive
512. Inaugurate – initiate, install
513. Incentives – motivations, enticements
514. Inclined – tending, persuaded
515. Incredible - unbelievable
516. Inculcate – teach, instruct, coach, train
517. Incurred – experienced, suffered
518. Indeed – certainly, really
519. Independent – self-reliant, autonomous
520. Indigenous – native, original
521. Indispensable – essential, crucial, vital
522. Induce – encourage, persuade
523. Industrious – hardworking, diligent
524. Inevitable – unavoidable, predictable
525. Inferior – lesser, substandard
526. Inflation – rise, increase
527. Infrastructure - structure
528. Infuriate – enrage, agitate, provoke
529. Ingenious- clever, creative, original
530. Ingredients – elements, components
531. Inhale – gasp, huff
532. Inherit – receive, succeed to
533. Injurious – harmful, damaging
534. Innate – inborn, characteristic
535. Innocent – gutless, blameless
536. Insane – crazy, deranged, mad

537. Inscribed – adorned, emblazoned
538. Insecurity – uncertainty, diffident
539. Insights – visions, understanding
540. Insomnia – sleeplessness, restlessness
541. Inspect – examine, check
542. Inspire – motivate, encourage
543. Instance – example, illustration
544. Instant – on the spot, immediate
545. Instrumental – contributory, helpful
546. Insufficient – inadequate, deficient
547. Integral – essential, vital
548. Integration – combination, incorporation
549. Intelligent – bright, sensible, rational
550. Intent – determined, committed
551. Intentionally – purposely, deliberately
552. Interaction – contact, communication
553. Interesting – provocation, engrossing
554. Interfere – hinder, inhibit
555. Intermittent – sporadic, periodic
556. Internal - inner, inside
557. Intimidate – threaten, frighten
558. Intolerant – bigoted, prejudiced
559. Intriguing – fascinating, enthralling
560. Introvert – shy, reserved
561. Invade – attack, occupy
562. Invent – discover, create
563. Irrelevant – inappropriate, unrelated
564. Irritate- annoy, agitate, provoke
565. Join – connect, unite, link
566. Jolly – merry, joyful
567. Joyous – jolly, festive
568. Jubilant – overjoyed, delighted, elated
569. Keep - save, protect, guard
570. Kind – considerate, tender, thoughtful
571. Kitchenette – kitchen, pantry
572. Knack – ability, skill
573. Lament – mourn, grieve
574. Landlocked – surrounded by land, blocked in
575. Landmark – milestone
576. Lane – path, track
577. Large – big, massive, huge
578. Last – final, end
579. Laxative – cleansing, emptying
580. Leaps and bounds – by multiple times
581. Least – fewest, minimum, smallest
582. Legible – readable, understandable, comprehensible
583. Lenient – soft, merciful, easy
584. Lentils – curry food
585. Lethal – deadly, fatal
586. Lethargic – lazy, sluggish
587. Liabilities – obligations, charges
588. Likewise – similarly, equally
589. Listless - lethargic, indolent
590. Literally – actually, factually
591. Littering – throwing waste
592. Logical – sensible, sane, rational
593. Long – lengthy, extended, extensive
594. Long-lasting – lifelong, enduring
595. Loose – slack, limp, movable
596. Loyal – faithful, trustworthy
597. Loyalty – faithfulness, trustworthiness
598. Lure – attract, seduce, entice
599. Luxurious – extravagant, elegant
600. Magnificent – wonderful, brilliant
601. Magnify – expand, enlarge, exaggerate
602. Majestic – royal, grand
603. Mandatory – compulsory, obligatory
604. Manoeuvre – manipulate, handle, move, movement
605. Manifesto – policy, strategy
606. Manned – operated, staffed
607. Manuscripts – documents, copies
608. Marine – sea, aquatic
609. Martyr – sufferer for a cause, sacrifice, victim
610. Marvellous – amazing, wonderful
611. Marvels – aces, prodigies
612. Masculine – male, manly
613. Massive – huge, enormous
614. Maximum - greatest, uppermost, highest
615. Meagre – scanty, sparse, poor
616. Mean - unkind, malicious, nasty
617. Medicinal – remedial, therapeutic
618. Mediocre – fair, moderate, average, ordinary
619. Melodious – musical, harmonious
620. Menace – threat, danger
621. Mend – repair, fix
622. Merchandise – produce, stock
623. Merchants – wholesalers, dealers
624. Mere – simple, sheer
625. Merrymaking – celebration, partying
626. Mesmerized – fascinated, awestruck
627. Metabolism – digestion, absorption
628. Migrant – drifting, travelling, transient
629. Militant – combative, radical, aggressive

630. Minimal – slight, negligible
631. Minor – lesser, inferior, secondary
632. Minutest – smallest, miniature, tiniest
633. Miraculous – unbelievable, astounding, incredible
634. Mirth – humour, fun, laughter
635. Miscellaneous – various, mixed
636. Mischievous – naughty, impish, playful
637. Misfortune – hardship, catastrophe, mishap
638. Mist – fog, vapor
639. Mobile - moveable, changeable
640. Moderate – reasonable, medium, modest
641. Momentous – important, crucial, historic, significant
642. Momentum – thrust, energy
643. Monotonous – boring, tedious, repetitive
644. Monotony – dullness, boredom
645. Monument – memorial, shrine
646. Moral – ethical, virtuous, righteous
647. Morose – gloomy, sullen, moody, dark
648. Mourn – grieve, lament, bemoan
649. Myriad – many, innumerable
650. Mysterious – elusive, occult, secret
651. Myth – legend, saga
652. Mythology – tradition, folklore
653. Naughty - bad, disobedient, wrong
654. Neat – clean, orderly, tidy
655. Negligent – careless, neglectful
656. Negligent – careless, inattentive
657. Nervous – ruffled, anxious, worried
658. New – unused, fresh, modern
659. Nice – pleasing, desirable, fine
660. Noble – decent, moral
661. Nonchalant – casual, calm, relaxed
662. Normal – ordinary, typical, usual
663. Noteworthy – significant, notable
664. Nuisance – annoyance, pain, irritation
665. Numerous – several, abundant, considerable
666. Obesity - overweightness
667. Obey – mind, heed, comply
668. Oblivious – unconscious, preoccupied, unaware
669. Obnoxious – offensive, hateful
670. Observe – examine, study, scrutinize
671. Obsolete – extinct, dated, outdated
672. Obstinate – stubborn, fixed, adamant
673. Occasionally – rarely, irregularly
674. Odd – peculiar, weird, strange
675. Offend – insult, affront, upset
676. Offspring – children, decedents
677. Often – frequently, repeatedly
678. Ominous – threatening, menacing
679. Opaque – cloudy, muddy, dense, milky
680. Open – begin, unfold, originate
681. Opponent – enemy, rival, foe
682. Optimistic – hopeful, confident, positive
683. Optimum – best, finest
684. Optional – voluntary, elective
685. Ordinary – usual, average, normal
686. Outrageous – shameful, shocking, disgraceful
687. Outstanding – unpaid, remaining
688. Overly – excessively, exceedingly
689. Overtaken – passed, outdone
690. Painstaking – meticulous, careful, scrupulous
691. Palatable – edible, pleasant, tasty
692. Panic – terror, fear
693. Parallel – equivalent, similar
694. Partial – incomplete, limited
695. Passive – inert, submissive, inactive
696. Past - former, previous, preceding
697. Patience – tolerance, endurance
698. Patience – tolerance, perseverance
699. Patrol – tour, watch, round
700. Peculiar - weird, bizarre, strange, odd
701. Pedestrians – walkers, amblers
702. Penal – severe, strict, punitive, punishing
703. Perception – insight, awareness, observation
704. Perfect – flawless, accurate
705. Permanent – enduring, lasting
706. Perpetual – eternal, endless, continuous, everlasting
707. Persistent – determined, tenacious
708. Persuade – convince, influence, encourage
709. Pessimistic – negative, doubtful, cynical
710. Phenomenal – extraordinary, remarkable
711. Pinnacle – highpoint, peak
712. Plausible – believable, reasonable, logical
713. Pleasure – desire, wish

714. Plentiful – ample, enough, abundant
715. Pliable – supple, flexible, bendable
716. Plight – dilemma, difficulty
717. Plume – trail, cloud, spiral
718. Polite – gracious, refined, courteous
719. Ponder – think about, consider
720. Poor – destitute, needy, impoverished
721. Portion – part, segment, piece
722. Posh – noble, superior
723. Possible – conceivable, feasible, plausible
724. Posture – position, stance, attitude
725. Potential – probable, possible, latent
726. Potholes – holes, dips
727. Precarious – dangerous, uncertain, shaky
728. Precedent – example, model
729. Precious – cherished, valuable, prized, costly
730. Predators – killers, hunters
731. Predict – forecast, foresee
732. Preference – fondness, favourite
733. Prejudiced – biased, opinionated, influenced
734. Premature - early, hasty
735. Premeditated – planned, intended, calculated
736. Premises – buildings, locations
737. Preserve – uphold, guard, save, reserve
738. Pretty – lovely, beautiful, attractive
739. Prevail – overcome, conquer, succeed, triumph
740. Prevalent – customary, widespread, dominant
741. Prevent – thwart, prohibit, hinder
742. Prior – previous, former
743. Priority – importance, significance
744. Probable – likely, apt, possible
745. Proficient – skilled, adept, competent
746. Profit – gain, earnings, benefit
747. Prohibit – forbid, bar, restrict
748. Prominent – eminent, famous
749. Promote – endorse, sponsor
750. Prompt – quick, rapid, swift, speedy
751. Prone – disposed to, inclined to
752. Prosperous – thriving, successful, flourishing
753. Protest – objection, complaint
754. Proud – honoured, gratified, pleased, satisfied
755. Publish – print, put out
756. Push – shove, thrust
757. Qualified – competent, fit, capable
758. Question – query, inquiry, request
759. Quiet - silent, hushed, tranquil
760. Quit – cease, stop, withdraw
761. Racket – noise, commotion, disturbance
762. Radiant – luminous, shinning, glowing
763. Raise – hoist, elevate
764. Random – accidental, chance
765. Rapidly – quickly, swiftly
766. Rare – occasional, infrequent, sporadic
767. Ratify – approve, confirm, endorse
768. Rational- coherent, balanced, sensible
769. Ravage – devastate, ruin, damage
770. Raze – destroy, demolish, level, flatten
771. Recite – perform, rehearse, narrate
772. Reckless – irresponsible, thoughtless
773. Reckon – calculate, count, estimate
774. Reconciliation – settlement, understanding
775. Recreational – amusement, pleasure, leisure
776. Reduce – lessen, decrease, diminish
777. Refrain - restrict
778. Refute – contradict, dispute
779. Regular – routine, customary, steady
780. Regulate – control, oversee, handle
781. Regulated – planned, controlled
782. Rejuvenate – revive, refresh
783. Releasing – to leave, freeing
784. Relentless - persistent, merciless
785. Relevant – pertinent, suitable, stable
786. Reliable – trustworthy, steadfast, dependable
787. Relieve – dismiss, discharge
788. Relish – enjoy, delight
789. Reluctant – unwilling, hesitant
790. Rely – depend upon, count on
791. Remarkable – extraordinary, amazing
792. Remedy – medication, therapy
793. Remote – secluded, isolated, distant
794. Renowned – famous, well-known
795. Repulsive – revolting, offensive
796. Reputable – decent, trustworthy, honest
797. Rescue – save, release, liberation
798. Resist – oppose, withstand, defy

799. Respiratory – breathing
800. Restrict – limit, confine
801. Retaliate – avenge, revenge, reciprocate
802. Reveal – show, disclose, divulge
803. Revenge – retaliation, vengeance
804. Revere – admire, respect, worship
805. Revive – come around, recover
806. Ridiculous – nonsensical, foolish, preposterous
807. Rigorous – hard, difficult
808. Risky – hazardous, perilous, chancy
809. Rituals – rites, ceremonies
810. Roam – travel, wander
811. Rowdy - disorderly, loud, noisy
812. Rude – impolite, discourteous
813. Rushed – hurried, quick
814. Sachet – packet, pouch
815. Sacred – holy, blessed
816. Sad – unhappy, dejected, gloomy
817. Same – identical, alike, equivalent
818. Sanctuary – national preserve, national park
819. Savage – violent, barbarous, vicious
820. Save – preserve, conserve, keep
821. Savour – taste, smell, aroma
822. Scarce - uncommon, rare, unusual
823. Scarcity – shortage, insufficiency
824. Scary – terrifying, frightening
825. Scenario – situation, set up
826. Scorching – roasting, sweltering
827. Scrawny – skinny, gaunt, bony
828. Scrupulous- reliable, ethical, dependable
829. Sculptures – statues, figures
830. Sedatives - tranquillizers
831. Segments – sections, parts
832. Segregated – separated, isolated
833. Seize- apprehend, grab, snatch
834. Seldom – rarely, occasionally
835. Separate- divide, segregate, partition
836. Serene – calm, peaceful
837. Several – numerous, some
838. Severity – cruelty, strictness
839. Shatter – smash, destroy
840. Shrewd – clever, cunning, crafty
841. Shy – bashful, timid, reserved
842. Sick - ill, ailing
843. Significance - importance
844. Sinful – bad, evil, wicked
845. Sitcom – series of TV programs
846. Skip – hop, or to leave a step
847. Skyrocketed – shoot up, rise steeply
848. Skyscrapers – high rise buildings, towers
849. Slim – lean, thin
850. Sluggish – listless, lethargic, inactive
851. Small – little, insignificant, trivial
852. Smooth – flat, even, level
853. Snatch - fetch
854. Snorkelling – swimming, diving
855. Sociable – friendly, cordial, gregarious
856. Soothing – comforting, calming
857. Sore – tending, painful
858. Sorrow – woe, anguish, grief
859. Souvenir – memento, reminder
860. Spacious – airy, large, roomy
861. Span – distance, length
862. Special - exceptional, notable, particular
863. Species – classes, types
864. Spontaneous – impulsive, unprompted, natural
865. Sporty – athletic, active, fit
866. Stable – steady, unchanging, settled
867. Stationary- fixed, immobile, firm, motionless
868. Steer – manoeuvre, to move
869. Stiff – rigid, firm
870. Stimulate – rouse, kindle, inspire
871. Stone face – no reaction at all
872. Stop – halt, cease, rest
873. Stray – lost, wandering, homeless
874. Strenuous – active, energetic, laborious
875. Stress buster – something that gets rid of stress
876. Strict – stringent, severe, stern
877. Striking – outstanding, prominent
878. Strive – struggle, try
879. Stroll – wander, promenade
880. Strong – powerful, mighty, potent
881. Stupid - unintelligent, dense, foolish
882. Subscriptions – contributions, payments
883. Subsequent – following, succeeding, consequent
884. Subsidiary – minor, secondary
885. Substantial – considerable, significant
886. Subtle – delicate, understate, refined
887. Successful – thriving, enough, adequate
888. Succulent – moist, tender

889. Sufficient – ample, enough, adequate
890. Superb – magnificent, exquisite, excellent
891. Superstitions – delusions, fantasies
892. Supplements – additions, complements
893. Suppress – overpower, conquer
894. Surplus - excess, additional, extra
895. Survive – last, endure
896. Suspect – doubtful, suspicious
897. Sustainable – bearable, maintainable
898. Swift - fast, speedy, hasty
899. Synthetic – man–made, artificial, fake
900. Tall – high, lofty, elevated
901. Tangible – concrete, definite
902. Tariff – rate, price, charge
903. Taut - rigid, stiff
904. Temperate – moderate, mild, pleasant
905. Tender – loving, caring, affectionate
906. Terrace – walkway, porch
907. Terrain – land, territory
908. Terrible - dreadful, horrible, vile
909. Thaw – melt, defrost
910. Thick and thin – happiness and sorrows
911. Thrifty - economical, frugal, prudent
912. Thrive – flourish, prosper
913. Timid – nervous, fearful
914. Traits – personalities, qualities
915. Tranquil – calm, serene
916. Transition – change, conversion, evolution
917. Tremendous – marvelous, great, wonderful
918. Trigger – start, activate
919. Trivial – small, minor
920. Turbulent – stormy, raging
921. Turf – lawn, grass
922. Turmoil – chaos, disorder, confusion
923. Twigs – branches, brushwood
924. Typhoon – storm, cyclone
925. Unanimous – common, undisputed, agreed
926. Unbiased - impartial, unprejudiced, neutral
927. Underneath – under, below
928. Undoubtedly – certainly, unquestionably
929. Uninterrupted – continuous, non-stop
930. Unpredictable – random, erratic, impulsive
931. Unwrap – open, undo
932. Upset – distressed, disappointed, dismayed
933. Urgent - crucial, important, imperative
934. Utilize – use, employ, exploit
935. Vacant – unoccupied, empty
936. Vague - unclear, obscure, indistinct
937. Valiant – courageous, brave, heroic
938. Vanish – disappear, die out
939. Verdict – decision, judgement
940. Versatile – multipurpose, handy, adaptable
941. Version – form, type
942. Viable – practical, feasible
943. Vibes – feelings, vibrations
944. Vibrant – lively, exciting
945. Vibrate- shake, quiver, tremble
946. Vicious - malicious, spiteful, ferocious
947. Victim – prey, target
948. Vigil – watch, wake
949. Vigilance – watchfulness, observance
950. Vital – important
951. Vividly – brightly, vibrantly, intensely
952. Vouch – promise, vow, swear
953. Voyage – journey, trip
954. Vulgar - offensive, uncouth, coarse
955. Wardrobe – clothing, attire
956. Wealth - riches, prosperity, assets
957. Weary – tired, fatigued, lethargic
958. Weird – strange, odd
959. Wholehearted – passionate, sincere
960. Wicked – good, great, terrific, cool
961. Wild – rough, barren, remote
962. Win - triumph, succeed, prevail
963. Window shopping – shopping without intent of buying
964. Wisdom – understanding, insight, knowledge
965. Wise – knowing, scholarly, smart, intelligent
966. Witness – observer, bystander
967. Wonderful - marvellous, incredible, splendid
968. Woods – forests, woodlands
969. Worn - used, impaired, old
970. Wreckage – debris, remains
971. Wrong - incorrect, untrue, mistaken
972. Yester years – past years, recent years
973. Yield - produce, bear, provide
974. Zenith - peak, pinnacle, top

PART – 4
8 BAND Tips for IELTS Speaking Test

IELTS SPEAKING TEST FORMAT

Don't be nervous at all before your IELTS Speaking Test as these Tips and Book will surely help you score your desired BAND.

These are 10 Tips formulated by Ex-examiners and Bestselling Author for you to gain confidence before your Speaking Test.

The face-to-face Speaking test is made up of three parts for both paper-based and computer-delivered IELTS. Here's how the three parts of your speaking test are:

Part 1
In Part 1, you will have a 4-to-5-minute conversation with an IELTS examiner about yourself. Topics might include, **work, family, home life, Personal interests, and so on. (Refer this book for more topics)**

Part 2
You will be given a topic in part 2 of the Speaking Test. You will have one minute to take notes on the topic, and you will be given a pencil and paper to prepare your response, you will then speak on the topic for **two minutes** (maximum).

Part 3
In Part 3, you will have a conversation with the IELTS examiner around the topic given in part 2, discussing it in more detail. Part 3 should take approximately 4 - 5 minutes to complete.

TIP 1: Don't memorize answers

Don't memorise answers, especially in Part 1. Memorised language doesn't give the examiner an accurate measure of your English-language skills. The examiner will be able to tell if you have memorised your answers and this may influence your final band score.

Read this book only for ideas and try to formulate your own answers by practicing them. Just be natural with the answers and don't use too much memorised phrases and vocab words.

TIP 2: Don't use big and unfamiliar words

You may want to amaze the examiner with complex words in your Speaking test. But to be safe, prevent using words you are not familiar with. There is a higher chance of making mistakes by either mispronouncing words or using them in the wrong context. Mistakes can affect your final band score.
Use a range of vocabulary that you know which is relevant to the topic being discussed.

TIP 3: Use a range of grammatical structures

When IELTS examiners assess your speaking skills, they mark you against the following assessment criteria:
Fluency and coherence
Lexical resource
Grammatical range and accuracy

Pronunciation

Try and use a range of grammatical structures using complex and simple sentences to express what you want to say. Know your own errors and practice speaking to friends in English or record yourself to see if you can spot errors. If you hear an error, make sure to correct yourself. You are assessed on your ability to use different grammatical structures accurately, so it's important to practise speaking about the past, the present and the future using correct tenses.

TIP 4: Don't worry about your accent

With a face-to-face Speaking test, the IELTS examiner understands a wide range of accents so will be able to understand what you say, unlike an AI machine. If you can communicate well, then there is nothing to worry about. But you need to be aware of sounds that you have difficulty with and make sure to use stress and intonation as English is a stress-timed language. Practice with friends and they will tell you if they can't understand what you are saying.

TIP 5: Pause to think

There is no harm in taking a brief pause to think about what to say. We all do it to process questions. You can use phrases to give you time to think during the Speaking test - phrases such as:

That's an interesting question
I have never thought about that, but...
Let me see
That's a good point
That's a difficult question, but I'll try and answer it
Well, some people say that is the case, however I think...
Let me think about that for a minute

TIP 6: Avoid using fillers

Speak confidently and avoid using filler words. We generally use fillers when we don't know what to say, however, this shows the examiner that you can't access the appropriate language or ideas so it's important to avoid them and to use the phrases discussed in **TIP 5**.

Avoid the following fillers:
Like
You know
Umm...
Ahh...
Ehh...
Well
Yeah...

TIP 7: Extend your answers

Try and answer the examiner's questions in full. Extend your answers and don't wait for the examiner to prompt you with a question. When your answers are short, this shows the examiner that you cannot talk in detail about a topic. If the examiner says 'Why?', they are prompting you to give a reason for your answer and to extend more fully.
So, you must include the justification clearly in your answers.
Like, if the question is: Which is you favourite colour?
Your answer should not be like this: My favourite colour is Blue.

Your answer must be: My favourite colour is blue because it is very soothing to my eyes. Clothes made of this colour also suits my personality.

TIP 8: Smiling helps pronunciation

Smiling can help calm your nerves which in turn helps your pronunciation. Make sure to enunciate clearly, opening your mouth wide enough so that sounds come out clearly. When we smile, our mouth is bigger, and the tone of our voice is more friendly. Using clear enunciation and tone will show the examiner that you can use a range of pronunciation features.

TIP 9: Don't speak in a monotone

Sometimes when we speak, we produce a flat sound, a monotone, with little variation. This makes it more difficult to express what you say and makes it more difficult for the listener to identify what parts of your message are important. Putting emphasis on certain words and pausing at sections in your speech can make your conversation with the IELTS examiner more engaging. When we emphasise certain words, it makes it easier to compare and contrast ideas by stressing key words. It also increases the flow of conversation, so remember:

Don't speak in a monotone
Vary the stress and intonation to add emphasis
Use your hands to gesture and help the rhythm of the conversation

When the examiner asks you about your hobbies, you must have a happy sounding tone as hobbies are something that everyone like to do. On the contrary, if the examiner asks you about any sad moment in your life, then the answer must sound sad as well. Doing this will not only make your conversation with the examiner more engaging, but also improve your tone, expressions of English Speaking.

TIP 10 - Practice common IELTS topics

Part 2 of the IELTS Speaking test requires you to speak on a given topic for about 2 minutes. Practice common IELTS topics with friends, family, or colleagues to improve and to learn vocabulary associated with each topic.

Common topics you can practice for the Speaking test include:

Tourism and travel
Education
Transport
Environment
Family life
Sport and recreation
Crime and punishment
The internet
Advertising and retail

*Try reading all the Cue card topics from this book before taking your final test as you will have abundance of ideas on how to speak on different topics.

Manufactured by Amazon.ca
Bolton, ON